Personal Construct
Theory

Personal Construct Theory

Concepts and Applications

J. R. Adams-Webber

Brock University
Ontario

JOHN WILEY & SONS

Chichester · New York · Brisbane · Toronto

Library of Congress Cataloging in Publication Data:

Adams-Webber, J. R.
  Personal construct theory.

  Bibliography: p.
  Includes indexes.
  1. Personality. 2. Psychometrics.
3. Kelly, George Alexander, 1905–1967. I. Title.
BF698.A327   155.2   78–8638

ISBN 0 471 99669 6

Photosetting by Thomson Press (India) Limited, New Delhi,
and printed in Great Britain at The Pitman Press, Bath

To
G. A. K.

Acknowledgements

The author is especially indebted to Don Bannister for his encouragement, enthusiasm and many useful suggestions. Discussions with John Benjafield, Larry Cochran, Steve Duck, Brian Hayden, Brian Little and Dan Lordahl were also extremely helpful. I would like to thank my Publishers, John Wiley and Sons, for all their advice and assistance. Much of the work on this volume was completed while I was on leave from Brock University in the UK supported by a Canada Council Leave Fellowship and a grant from Brock. I am grateful to the following for permission to reproduce copyright material: Academic Press, American Psychological Association, Cambridge University Press, Penguin Books, The Journal Press, and the University of Nebraska Press; also to Mrs Gladys J. Kelly and W. W. Norton & Co. for permission to quote extensively from George A. Kelly, *The Psychology of Personal Constructs* (1955). Finally, I would like to express my appreciation to Cameron Adams-Webber, Thomasin Adams-Webber, and Larry Cochran for their help in preparing illustrations.

Contents

Preface

The standard format used to report scientific investigations—a theoretical introduction, a description of measurement operations, a quantitative summary of the results, and finally, a discussion of the general significance of the work for the field of enquiry—provides a metaphor for the way in which research in the psychology of personal constructs has developed.

At the outset, Kelly constructed an original theory in the context of which a wide range of psychological problems could be reconceptualized. His theory provided the basis for the formulation of many novel hypotheses by Kelly and others (Chapter 1). Kelly also devised a sophisticated set of measurement operations which relate logically to central constructs in his theory (Chapter 2). At an early stage in the evolution of this model, however, there emerged a tendency to rush on into the discussion phase before completing the experimentation and systematic assessment needed to write a 'results section'. It was perhaps the lack of results which, for a long period of time, retarded the development of interest in personal construct theory, especially in North America, where results are always of paramount importance.

Fortunately, during the last two decades this gap has been partly filled through a rapidly expanding programme of research informed by the principles of this theory. The early initiative was assumed primarily by British and European psychologists; however, an increasing number of North American psychologists are becoming actively involved in this enterprise. At first, a few highly innovative investigators 'kept things going' in personal construct research until others gradually began to show interest. Bonarius (1965) has furnished us with an excellent summary of these beginnings. Most of the research discussed in Chapters 3 to 7 grew out of this early work, which focused upon a somewhat narrow, but clearly defined, set of related problems. On the other hand, the studies considered in Chapter 8 reflect the recent extension of the principles of the theory in several new directions, some of which may emerge as major lines of enquiry as the psychology of personal constructs continues to evolve.

In general, research in personal construct theory, of which this volume attempts a representative rather than an exhaustive review, has served as the basis for the gradual expansion of the range of convenience of the theory in terms of both the variety of phenomena which it can subsume and its formal unity as a system of constructs for interpreting and predicting events.

Brock University, 1977   JACK ADAMS-WEBBER

1

Behaviour from the Standpoint of a Psychologist

But every *datum* is a behavioural datum; physical reality is not a datum but a constructum. (Koffka, 1935)

Kelly (1969) claims that the basic tenets of his psychology of personal constructs can be derived logically from a single philosophical assumption, which he refers to as the principle of 'constructive alternativism'. This principle asserts that reality does not directly reveal itself to us, but rather it is subject to as many alternative ways of construing it as we ourselves can invent. Hence the *variety* of human experience. In our efforts to anticipate our experience each of us develops a coherent system of constructions and attempts to impose them upon the events with which he is confronted. This personal construct system provides the *unity* in the experience of each individual.

In Kelly's (1970, p. 1) own words:

Whatever nature may be, or howsoever the quest for truth will turn out in the end, the events we face today are subject to as great a variety of constructions as our wits will enable us to construe. This is not to say that at some infinite point in time human vision will not behold reality out to the utmost reaches of existence. But it does remind us that all our present perceptions are open to question and reconsideration, and it does broadly suggest that even the most obvious occurrences of everyday life might appear utterly transformed if we were inventive enough to construe them differently.

Kelly contends that, although a given event is open to several different interpretations, in the long run some ways of construing it will probably prove more useful than others for anticipating its recurrences. He suggests also that most, if not all, of our current interpretations of events are subject to continual revision and ultimate replacement by more useful ones.

Since events do not carry their own meanings 'engraved on their backs', it must be the constructions which we impose on them which endow them with whatever significance they may have in relation to our own activities. Thus, Kelly's constructive alternativism has clear implications for how human actions can be

1

linked with other kinds of events in our attempts to predict behaviour. Since at least as far back as Dewey's (1896) critical analysis of the reflex arc concept in psychology, many 'cognitive' theorists have recognized that, although the *nominal stimulus* can often be identified as a 'physical' event (i.e. adequately described by a physicist), the *functional stimulus* (i.e. what needs to be explained by a psychologist) is constituted by the anticipatory processes of the organism itself.

Dewey emphasized the anticipatory nature of behaviour and the person's use of hypotheses in thinking. The psychology of personal constructs follows Dewey in this respect. (Kelly, 1955, p. 129)

As Heidbrieder (1933) points out, Dewey's analysis led Watson (1919) to the conclusion that the scientific investigation of sensation and perception was impossible because the conscious experience of the organism is not directly accessible to observation by others. This dogma provided the philosophical groundwork for the development of a radical 'behaviourism' which, in its most extreme form, attempts to explain all behaviour—even 'verbal behaviour' (Skinner, 1957)—in terms of external events consisting of present inputs to the organism and the organism's responses as related to the past history of inputs. Deese (1969) notes, however, that psychology is concerned not only with overt behaviour as such, but also with experience, including our many conscious acts of interpretation and anticipation. As Bannister (1966) concisely puts it, Man is not simply 'a ping-pong ball with a memory'.

Other cognitive theorists besides Kelly have emphasized the constructive nature of even the most elementary perceptual processes. For example, Bartlett (1932) argues that all perception and memory involve both the registration of sensory patterns and the construction of these sensory data into something having significance which goes beyond their immediate sensory character. He refers specifically to the process of connecting a given stimulus pattern with some preformed setting, or schema, as an 'effort after meaning'. He also suggests that, although a stimulus array may possess 'reactive significance' at the level of neurophysiological analysis, as soon as the reacting person becomes aware of the material with which his reactions deal, there is 'meaning'. More recently, Neisser (1967) contends that stimuli do not simply impose their impressions on a passive receptor. For instance, we are able to 'see' an object only after an elaborate process of construction, which typically makes use of both the available stimulus information and 'traces' of previous acts of construction. It follows that the whole conception of structured cognitive processes is fundamentally different from that of a simple response sequence (cf. Neisser, 1976).

'MAN-AS-SCIENTIST'

In formulating his psychology of personal constructs, Kelly (1955) explicitly rejects simplistic forms of behaviourism on the grounds that 'one does not learn certain things from the nature of the stimuli which play upon him (but) only what his cognitive framework permits him to see in the stimuli' (p. 75). This suggests that the appropriate model of human nature for psychology is not Skinner's 'organism', but rather Skinner himself, that is, the scientist who interprets and predicts events. Kelly (1969, p. 136) submits that 'it is not that Man is what Skinner makes of him, but rather what Skinner can do Man can do—and more'. Not only the professional scientist, but everyman, in his 'scientist-like-aspect', tries to make sense out of his experience and anticipate events. Thus, Kelly eschews the distinction between the behavioural scientist and the 'subject' of his enquiry at the very outset. He suspects that they need not be seen as different orders of being, but rather they can be viewed as sharing the same human nature. In fact, Kelly argues that it is their human character which makes scientists what they are. The basic problem is one of how we can characterize human nature so as to account for the development of science:

But science itself is a form of human behaviour, and a pretty important one at that. Why then, should we feel compelled to use one set of parameters when we describe *man-the-scientist* and another set when we describe *man-the-laboratory-subject*. (Kelly, 1969, p. 97)

In short, Kelly's model of human nature is the incipient scientist with his capacity to represent and anticipate events. His notion of 'man-as-scientist' is not intended to apply only to that particular class of people who engage in formal SCIENCE. It is an abstraction based on a fundamental aspect of all human experience. Kelly also does not claim that men are *nothing but* scientists. He is well aware that they assume many other guises. He does suggest, however, that the paradigm of Man's scientific activity can be used to shed light on all of his psychological processes. It was Kelly's conviction that science, when it is viewed in the perspective of human history, has turned out to be our most successful enterprise to date. Thus, it is in a pragmatic vein that he proposes that an understanding of 'scientific behaviour' might hold the most promise for the full realization of human potentials in the future.

Originally, the central focus of personal construct theory was psychotherapy. As we shall see in Chapter 6, forms of psychological 'treatment' derived from this theory, for example, 'fixed role therapy', are conceived as programmes of experimentation in which the client is the principal investigator and the psychologist more or less fulfils the role of 'research supervisor'. That is, the principal function of the 'therapist' from the standpoint of personal construct theory is to assist his client in formulating theories, deriving and testing hypotheses, evaluating the results of his own experiments and revising his hypotheses in the light of the data. Kelly (1955) points out many striking parallels between his own experiences in psychotherapy and thesis supervision.

Thus, within the framework of Kelly's model of human nature, each individual must be understood in terms of his own efforts to anticipate his experience. This model is explicated in terms of a single 'fundamental postulate', which asserts that 'a person's processes are psychologically channelised by the ways in which

4

he anticipates events', and eleven 'corollaries' which are used to elaborate the implications of this postulate. These corollaries will not be presented in this discussion in the same order in which Kelly originally derived them. They have been rearranged here in an attempt to reveal as clearly as possible Kelly's emphasis on the development of individual conceptual structures and the central importance of interpersonal communication and understanding in this process.

SAME AND DIFFERENT

Kelly's 'construction corollary' states that 'A person anticipates events by construing their replications'. This proposition does not imply that the 'same' events ever actually repeat themselves, but rather that we can often detect certain recurrent themes in our own experience. The important point is that two or more events can be construed in a similar way. Kelly (1969, p. 100) furnishes the following illustration of this principle:

Suppose a child distinguishes between two objects, say a ball and a cube. On the following day, let us say that he distinguishes between another ball and another cube. Why are his two performances similar? One thing we can say is that because the pairs of objects were physically similar on the successive days the child's responses were similar. This explanation is based on the assumption that the child is under the control of the objects and therefore similar pairs of objects must always elicit similar responses . . . suppose we make use of the principle of constructive alternativism and seek other kinds of explanation. Suppose we turn our attention to the child, rather than to the objects, and ask how it is that he was able to do with them what he did. Suppose we say that it is not enough that the objects be similar; what more is required is that the child have some capability that enables him to respond as if they were similar. The psychological point I want to emphasize is that he construed the objects similarly, in spite of the fact that the occasions were different and the particular concrete objects were different.

Kelly assumes that the essential *psychological* feature in this example is neither the ball nor the cube nor the set of circumstances. We are not looking for 'stimuli'. Personal construct theory focuses directly upon the child's own way of organizing his responses to balls and cubes regardless of the changing circumstances. The basic unit of analysis is a construction which the child did not discover in the objects, but which he himself imposed on them. As Bartlett (1958) puts it, 'all our perceptions are inferential constructs'.

Bartlett (1932) argues that the perception of similarity depends on underlying organizing tendencies which lead to the grouping together of items which possess a surprising welter of diverse sensory characteristics. Whenever two events which are separated by an interval of time (as in the example above) are perceived as the 'same', according to Bartlett, some information must be retained during the interval. More specifically, the perceptual system must somehow store information about its own prior acts of construction. Bartlett (1932, p. 193) hypothesizes that 'In all cases recognizing is rendered possible by the carrying over of orientation, or attitude, from the original presentation to the re-presentation'. It follows that in constructive processes the stimuli are not simply copied or stored as 'templets' which are subsequently aroused in recall and recognition (cf. Neisser, 1967). Bartlett proposes that there is a gradual building up of cognitive structures which are non-specific but organized representations of a great number of individual acts of construction.

Kelly (1955) goes considerably beyond this hypothesis of Bartlett's with his notion that the same act of construction which establishes some basis of perceived similarity between events also serves to differentiate them from still other events. He suggests that a construct is fundamentally an integrating and differentiating operation whereby at least two events are regarded as similar to one another and, at the same time, different from at least one other event.

It must be understood that the personal construct abstracts similarity and difference simultaneously. One cannot be abstracted without implying the other. For a person to treat two incidents as different is to imply that one of them appears to be like another he knows. Conversely, for a person to treat two incidents as similar is to imply that he contrasts both with at least one other incident he knows. We intend this to be considered as an essential feature of the personal construct by means of which we hope to understand the psychology of human behaviour. (Kelly, 1969, pp. 102–103)

BINARY DISTINCTIONS

Kelly's 'dichotomy corollary' asserts that 'A person's construction system is composed of a finite number of dichotomous constructs'. Each of these constructs essentially consists of a single bipolar distinction, e.g. *friendly-aloof*. It is intended by the person who uses it to refer to one aspect of a specific domain of events. The construct is meaningful in so far as it provides the basis of perceived similarities and differences among the events to which it is applied. One pole of the construct represents the basis of perceived similarity between at least two events, and the other pole denotes the basis of their contrast with at least one other event. A person's construct cannot be understood fully without encompassing both its poles, since the contrast is just as necessary as the similarity in defining its meaning. Kelly regards this dichotomous nature of personal constructs as an essential feature of all thinking (see Chapter 7).

In more formal terms, given a set of three elements—A, B, and C—the minimum context of any construct, A and B might be viewed as similar to one another in the same respect in which C contrasts with both. For example, Alice and Betty may be seen as 'friendly' and Carol as 'aloof'. If the same person could be regarded by a single individual as simultaneously friendly and aloof in the same respect, then this construction of events would have no definite meaning for him. What it is that is dichotomous in nature is the form of the distinction which the person makes when he employs one of his personal constructs to anticipate events. As Kelly (1970, p. 13) explains,

A construct is the basic contrast between two groups. When it is imposed it serves both to distinguish between its elements and to group them. Thus the construct refers to the nature of the distinction one attempts to make between events, not to the array in which events appear to stand when he gets through applying the distinction between each of them and all the others.

If we assume that all constructions entail binary distinctions, then whenever one person interprets the speech and actions of another, for example, Charlie seems to be a friendly guy', he is not only categorizing that person's behaviour in a certain way, 'friendly', but also contrasting it directly with behaviour which is different, say 'aloof'. There may be many other forms of behaviour which he interprets as neither 'friendly' nor 'aloof'. That is, the distinction does not seem to be especially applicable to them. In Kelly's terms, such behaviours fall outside the 'range of convenience' of the individual's construction of *friendly-aloof*.

RANGE, FOCUS, AND CONTEXT

The 'range corollary' stipulates that 'Each construct is convenient for the anticipation of a finite range of events only'. That is, each construct is assumed to have a limited range of convenience which comprises all those things to which the individual would find its application useful. In addition, each construct is assumed to have a particular 'focus of convenience', which is defined as that sector of its range of convenience wherein it is maximally useful. Moreover, neither a construct's range of convenience, nor its focus of convenience is identical to its 'context', that is, all those things to which it is ordinarily applied. The context is usually more extensive than the focus of convenience and more circumscribed than the range of convenience.

For example, consider an individual's possible usage of his construction of *masculine-feminine*. The range of convenience of this distinction could include French nouns, types of master key and certain items on the *MMPI*, as well as a variety of interesting biological and socio-cultural differences between women and men. The context of his construct might consist mainly of the routine appearance, dress, activities and speech of his circle of personal acquaintances. Its focus of convenience could be limited to his unique relationship with one woman.

CONCEPTUAL ORGANIZATION

Although each construct has its own particular range and focus of convenience, as well as context, it is usually deployed together with other constructs in interpreting and predicting events. As Mischel (1964) points out, a construct seldom stands alone in our experience. According to the 'organization corollary', 'Each person characteristically evolves for his own convenience in anticipating events a construction system embracing ordinal relationships between constructs'. Shotter (1970, p. 243) suggests that 'the system so produced is best described as a system of *compartments*, where the compartments are distinguished from one another in terms of binary distinctions, i.e. *constructs*, and where each compartment may be identified by the relation that it bears to all others in the system'. Each of these 'compartments' can be viewed as a 'logical possibility' for anticipating a given event within the explicit framework of a person's construct system. The individual arranges these compartments so that in following a line of inference he can move from one to another in some orderly fashion. In fact, as we shall see in Chapter 4, a necessary condition for organized thought and action is some degree of 'linkage' between constructs.

Within the context of a personal construction system, every construct by virtue of its relationship with other constructs, will imply a set of predictions about each of the events to which it is applied. Whenever a person interprets an event, essentially he construes people or objects in terms of one or more of his constructs; and then, by reviewing his personal network of related constructs (theory), he can derive predictions (hypotheses) about the people or objects thus construed. For example, if a person's constructions of *kind, generous,* and *polite* are all closely interrelated within his 'implicit theory of personality', he will tend to expect generous and polite behaviour on the part of anyone whom he construes as kind. Furthermore, the more constructs which an individual can bring to bear on a particular event in his attempts to anticipate it, the more clear and distinct its meaning will be within the framework of his construct system. Kelly (1965, p. 4) submits that:

An event seen only in terms of its placement on one dimension is scarcely more than a mere datum. And about all you can do with a datum is just let it sit on its own continuum. But as the event finds its place in terms of many dimensions of consideration it develops psychological character and uniqueness.

For example, Shotter (1970) notes that a system which consists of only eight constructs, each involving a single binary distinction, can encompass the entire sound system of a language with about forty distinct phonemes with approximately 50 per cent redundancy (cf. Jakobson, Fant, and Halle 1952).

THE ELABORATIVE CHOICE

The structure of an individual's system of interrelated constructs is assumed to be hierarchical in nature. Thus, whenever he makes a choice as to how he will act in a given situation, the specific implications of each alternative course of action will be defined in terms of the hierarchical organization of his constructs. Kelly's 'choice corollary' states that 'A person chooses for himself that alternative in a dichotomized construct through which he anticipates the greater possibility for the elaboration of his system'. He views people as constantly experimenting with their own behaviour. Their experiments are seen as based on hypotheses, not always explicitly formulated ones, which are derived from the relationships between constructs within their own personal systems. The 'independent variable' in their experiments is always their own behaviour. Their hypotheses involve choices between using the contrasting poles of one or more of their personal constructs in regulating their behaviour and evaluating the outcome.

Kelly argues that the choice will always be made in favour of that alternative which seems, at least at the moment, to enhance the individual's capacity to anticipate events.

He suggests that in some instances the choice will be made in favour of the alternative which seems to pull one's constructions together into the most consistent pattern. That is, the choice might represent an opportunity to consolidate further the organization of one's system, minimizing inconsistencies. On another occasion, an individual might choose that alternative which seems to provide the greater scope for extending the range of convenience of his personal construct system into new areas of possible experience. Whatever the direction of his choice, the person evaluates the outcome of his experiment in terms of its implications throughout his own network of hierarchically related constructs.

Let us consider a relatively simple hypothetical example of an elaborative choice offered by Bannister and Fransella (1971). Suppose an individual's construct *polite-impolite* is subsumed under his construct *kind-unkind*. He might typically behave in a way which he considers to be polite in order to be perceived as kind. This course of action would be consistent with the relationship between these two constructs within his system, and therefore serves to consolidate further its existing 'logical' structure. On the other hand, he may find himself in a situation in which it occurs to him that it might be kinder in the long run to be impolite to someone whom he finds especially boring. Thus, he might experiment with the hypothesis that under certain circumstances it makes good sense to be impolite in order to be kind, thereby extending the range of convenience of his system to encompass a novel experience. On the other hand, within the current framework of his system, it would not make sense for him to be unkind to someone for the sake of politeness.

LOGICAL RELATIONS

Bannister and Fransella (1971, p. 23) further explicate the meaning of the organization corollary in the following terms:

The term 'system' in the phrase 'a personal construct system' directly implies that a person's constructs are interrelated and in the (organizational) corollary Kelly is stressing that the relationship is often one of inclusion or subsuming. For some people the construct *traditional jazz* versus *modern jazz* may be subsumed as a subordinate implication of the construct *good jazz* versus *bad jazz*, and both poles might be subsumed under the music end of the construct *music* versus *noise*. This hierarchical quality of construct systems is what makes our world a manageable place.

We can conceptualize these relationships between personal constructs in terms of Boolean set theory, upon which the traditional logic of propositions is based (cf. Adams-Webber, 1970a). Given the assumption that each construct defines a set of events in terms of one of their perceived common aspects, we can determine the relationship between the set defined by any construct and the set defined by any other construct within a specific domain of events. In comparing the extensions of any two constructs we can encounter any one of five possible cases:

(1) construct A defines a subset of the set defined by construct B; (2) construct B defines a subset of the set defined by construct A; (3) there is a relation of one-to-one correspondence between these two sets; (4) they are mutually exclusive; and (5) there is at least one element which is a member of both sets, but neither set is a subset of the other. Each of these relationships can be represented by a simple Venn diagram, for example the diagram in Figure 1 represents Case 2 above.

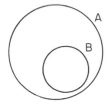

Figure 1.   Case 2. (Figure by
Thomasin Adams-Webber, 1978)

The main advantage of describing the relationships between constructs in terms of set theory is that they can be readily translated into logical propositions of the form 'if A, then B' according to the principle that all members of a subset of a given set are also members of that set. For example, the proposition 'if B, then A' can be inferred from the information given in Figure 1. As Deese (1969) notes, Venn diagrams are useful for revealing the 'parallel between the more general psychological process and the logical one'. This approach to representing relationships between personal constructs provides the theoretical rationale for Hinkle's (1965) 'implication grid' technique, which will be discussed in Chapters 3 and 6.

Another approach to representing relations between constructs has been developed by Bannister (1965a). Suppose we ask someone to nominate forty individuals personally known to himself, and to categorize each of them in turn as either *moral* or *immoral*. Let us then ask him to categorize them all once more as either *honest* or *dishonest*. If we were to observe that eighteen of twenty people adjudged by him to be 'moral' were also designated as 'honest', and all but three of those he said were 'immoral' were also referred to as 'dishonest', then we would probably be safe in inferring that there was a positive relationship between these two constructs in his own system. We could always fall back on a χ^2 test in estimating the probability that our inferrence was in error. In short, the degree of statistical association between the two distributions of judgements when both constructs are applied to the same set of figures is presumed to reflect the extent to which these two constructs are psychologically related for the particular individual who is doing the sorting. This basic assumption underlies the rationale of various forms of repertory grid technique used so extensively in personal construct assessment and research. Repertory grid methodology is the topic of the next chapter.

DIFFERENTIATION OF STRUCTURE

It is necessary for us to take into account not only the nature of the relationships between pairs of constructs, but also that of relationships between different subsystems of constructs within the same personal construct system. As we have seen, the principle of 'constructive alternativism' implies that events do not inherently belong to any particular set of constructions, but rather the same events can be interpreted within the context of alternative systems or subsystems, although not necessarily with the same degree of predictive efficiency. In each situation, the most 'useful' mode of construction must also be evaluated in terms of the total functioning of the construct system as an operational whole.

For example, Bannister (1969) has applied the logic of constructive alternativism in an analysis of the so-called 'mind-body' problem. He points out that if we accept the premise that the same events are subject to alternative constructions, then it is illogical to label certain events as either 'psychological' or 'physiological' in nature. The same events can be interpreted in terms of both psychological and physiological systems of constructs (cf. Rotter, 1954). This does not mean, of course, that one kind of interpretation will prove just as useful as any other for predicting those events. Alternative constructions of the same events need to be compared and evaluated in terms of their relative predictive efficiency. Thus, the important issue is not whether a given event is 'really' psychological or physiological in origin, but rather which kind of constructs provide the most effective basis for prediction and control.

From the standpoint of individual cognitive development, constructive alternativism implies that a person's construct system can become progressively differentiated in terms of a number of independently organized subsystems, each of which is relatively specialized with respect to its range and focus of convenience.

Specifically, the 'fragmentation corollary' (see Chapters 3 and 4) asserts that 'A person may successively employ a variety of construction subsystems which are inferentially incompatible with each other'. It follows that an individual's successive constructions of events are not necessarily derivable from one another. Kelly (1955) himself also assumed that the degree of systematization of a set of interrelated constructs can be enhanced by limiting the domain of events within which it is customarily employed, that is its context, because it can then be developed into a highly integrated network for processing information without undue concern about the inconsistencies which certain 'peripheral' events could reveal. It would seem to follow that differentiation into separately functioning subsystems can increase the deployability and scope of the entire construct system as an operational whole. Also, as we shall see in the next section, a further implication of the fragmentation corollary is that 'superordinate' constructions can be used to resolve apparent inconsistencies at lower levels of abstraction.

When viewed strictly in terms of its own internal organization, the 'rules' for processing information within each subsystem will be a direct expression of the specific relationships between constructs which define its 'logical' structure. On the other hand, the function of a given subsystem within an individual's personal construct system regarded as a whole can be seen, in Piaget's (1969, p. 165) words, as 'the role played by a substructure (or functioning sector) in relation to the functioning of the total structure'. In general, the differentiation of the operations of a cognitive system into sets of subprocesses, each of which can function without direct reference to the other subprocesses, by permitting the 'parallel processing' of information input in addition to its sequential processing, can considerably lower the overall demands on the system (Neisser, 1967; Ashby, 1968). Thus, the more differentiated the structure of an individual's personal construct system, the greater the variety of events which can be meaningfully discriminated within its framework at any one time.

AN EVOLUTIONARY PERSPECTIVE

Kelly (1955, p. 77) contends that 'If we are to see a person's psychological processes operating within a system which he constructs, we need also to account for the evolution of the system itself in a similarly lawful manner'. Adams-Webber (1970a) suggests that the normal course of development of an individual's personal construct system involves the progressive differentiation of its structure into independently organized subsystems and the increasing integration of the operations of these subsystems within the system as a whole. This hypothesis contains explicit parallels with the developmental models of both Piaget and Werner. For example, Werner's (1957) 'orthogenetic principle' states that all cognitive development proceeds from states of relative globality and undifferentiated structures toward states of increasing differentiation and hierarchical integration of concepts. Crockett (1965) elaborates some of the implications of Werner's principle within the specific framework of personal construct theory. Piaget (1960) argues that psychological structures evolve through a process of differentiation and reintegration of operational 'schemata' at increasingly higher levels of abstraction. Biggs (1969, p. 289) notes, 'The emphasis of Piaget upon growth with age of increasingly abstract structures is another way of saying that the growing child becomes adept at handling more and more environmental information with increasing economy of means'. There is a striking similarity between this assumption and Kelly's (1965, p. 5) own 'minimax principle':

One way to be aware of greater variety is to conjure up more constructs. But the number of constructs does not increase in direct ratio to the number of events to be distinguished. So what we have is a minimax problem; how to discriminate meaningfully the greatest variety of events with the least number of constructs. Since constructs are not only hard to come by, but are difficult to keep in mind once you get them, it becomes psychologically strategic to devise a system which will do the most with the least . . . Moreover, the minimax solution must vary within certain human limits from person to person.

Adams-Webber (1970a) points out that this principle relates to two major lines of research within the framework of personal construct theory. The first of these is concerned with the differentiation and integration of constructs and subsystems of constructs in individual cognitive development. This area of research is dealt with in Chapter 3. The second focus of enquiry is the progressive disintegration of conceptual structures in the genesis of clinical thought disorder, which is the topic of Chapter 4. In the course of this discussion it will become increasingly clear that both of these strands of investigation, by logical extension, must eventually converge upon a single set of principles governing all progressive variation within an individual's personal construct system.

First, an individual's system can become so fragmented in structure that, although he may have available a large repertory of constructs, there will be insufficient relationship between them for him to relate one aspect of his experience to another. As a consequence, his system can no longer function as an operational whole. The second limiting case would be the opposite logical extreme. A construct system could become so tightly organized that the implications of all possible constructions of events will converge ultimately upon the contrasting poles of the most superordinate construct in the system. Every line of reasoning which the person pursues, every argument he devises, will 'boil down' to one fundamental distinction, such as *godly-ungodly*. Thus, as Schroder, Driver, and Streufert (1967, p. 14) point out,

The number of dimensions taken alone has no necessary relationship to the level of information processing; but given complex combinatory rules, the potential for generating new attributes of information is higher, and the degree to which one stimulus can be discriminated from another is increased as the number of perceived dimensions increases.

Therefore, it cannot be differentiation alone which reflects the level of development of an individual's personal construct system. Rather, it must be the progressive differentiation and reintegration of conceptual structures at increasingly higher levels of abstraction which gradually enhances the efficiency of the system. Schroder *et al.* (1967) suggest that, at the most complex levels of organization 'abstractness (that is, lack of fixity) becomes a formal rule of the system' (p. 21). This process is, in Piaget's (1969, p. 164) words, one of 'development or evolution, in the sense of the gradual production of organized forms with qualitative transformations taking place in the course of the various stages of their development'. Bartlett (1932) characterizes this form of evolution as the building up of cognitive structures which are non-specific but organized representations of a great number of individual acts of construction. In short, developmental change in a personal construct system involves the gradual evolution of the system as a whole; not simply the accumulation of new elements and connections between them. Kelly (1955, p. 79) himself makes this point quite clear:

Progressive variation must itself take place within a system . . . one's personal constructs can only be changed within subsystems of constructs and subsystems within more comprehensive systems.

PERMEABILITY AND CHANGE

Kelly assumes that systematic changes in conceptual structures can occur only within the range of convenience of 'permeable superordinate constructs'. Under the terms of the 'modulation corollary' (see Chapter 4): 'The variation in a person's construct system is limited by the permeability of the constructs within whose range of convenience the variants lie'. According to Kelly, a construct is permeable if it is so constituted that 'new experience and new events can be discriminantly added to those which it already embraces'. In short, a permeable construct will admit to its context elements which are not yet included in it. Kelly (1955, p. 81) suggests that 'it is under the regency of such constructs that the more subordinate aspects of one's construction system can be systematically varied without making his whole psychological house fall down'. Thus, the modulation corollary implies that the more permeable the superordinate constructs within a person's system, the greater the amount of systematic change that can take place within the substructures which those constructs subsume.

At this point, Kelly's model of development is again closely parallel to that of Piaget. Piaget (1960) submits that cognitive development proceeds continually towards an 'ideal stage' of functional differentiation between schemata and their logical integration at sufficiently high levels of abstraction such that the introduction of novelty does not create any disequilibrium. A newly assimilated experience will no longer alter mental structures which refer to it, nor the relation of mental structures to each other, because at the highest level of abstraction thought is 'reversible' and a compensatory thought is available with which to restore the equilibrium. More precisely, Piaget (1960) asserts that his principle of reversibility 'implies an equilibrium such that the structure of operational wholes is conserved while they assimilate new elements'.

Kelly's fragmentation corollary explicitly permits the differentiation of an individual's construct system into independently organized subsystems; however, the extent of this differentiation is limited by the degree of permeability of his most superordinate constructs. As Kelly (1955, p. 87) puts it.

The fragmentation corollary follows as an explicit statement of the kind of inconsistency which the modulation corollary implicitly tolerates. The modulation corollary tolerates inconsistency between subsystems. More specifically, it tolerates the successive use of subsystems which do not add up.

In general, when an individual's superordinate constructs are relatively permeable, they can provide a thread of consistency throughout his system as a whole. They do so by permitting him to abstract features of similarity and difference across the various substructures which they subsume. Thus, sub-systems which are functionally differentiated at lower levels of abstraction can be reintegrated at higher levels when they are scanned for recurring regularities and abstractly cross-referenced within the context of superordinate constructs. This principle of organization is clearly illustrated by the 'maps' of the topological structure of personal construct systems derived from repertory grid data by Makhlouf-Norris, Jones, and Norris (1970), discussed in Chapter 3.

On the other hand, it is only within the range of convenience of the most permeable aspects of superordinate structure that overall consistency must be maintained. In order to incorporate new components of structure systematically, it is essential that the person be able continually to readjust his superordinate constructs so as to minimize inconsistencies and incompatibilities at the highest level of abstraction. If the development of a construct system is modulated by means of relatively permeable superordinate constructs, then the progressive differentiation of substructures will allow the continual extension of the range of convenience of the system as a whole, and an increasing variety of events can be discriminated within its framework.

This means that the modulation corollary also bears directly on the choice corollary. The latter implies that the individual always chooses for himself that alternative construction which seems, at least for the moment, to put him in a better position to anticipate future events. Kelly points out that his choice may be either 'extensive' or 'definitive'. That is, he may choose that alternative which provides a basis for extending the range of convenience of his system into new areas of experience (an extensive choice), or he may choose that alternative which would pull his constructions together into a more consistent overall pattern (a definitive choice). The modulation corollary implies that the extensive choice requires relatively permeable superordinate constructs. Thus, within the context of personal construct theory, it is only within the range of convenience of relatively permeable superordinate constructs that an individual's experience can lead to the gradual evolution of new conceptual structures to accommodate novel events without prejudice to the integrity of the system as a functioning whole. In short, permeability of superordinate constructions is a necessary condition of individual cognitive development. This argument will be elaborated further in Chapters 3 and 4 in the light of the results of relevant experiments.

STRUCTURE AND EXPERIENCE

According to the 'experience corollary', A person's construction system varies as he successively construes the replication of events'. Adams-Webber (1970a) argues that new structure emerges within an individual's personal construct system to accommodate events which are ambiguous within the context of current structure. That is, events can precipitate change in an individual's construct system when he encounters a person or object whose behaviour does not 'fit' the specific pattern of construct relationships which define the existing structure of his system. Bannister and Mair (1968, p. 212) suggest that 'such an unpredictable figure might be seen as *kind* and *hypocritical* and *stupid* and *successful* by a subject who lived in a world where he expected kind people to be sincere and stupid people to fail'. It is such sequences of events which are outside the range of convenience of one's construct system which tend to initiate the elaboration of new constructs and relationships between constructs. This notion is similar to Piaget's concept of a 'need-to-function'.

According to Piaget (1960) a 'need-to-function' arises from the temporary instability of schematic organization following an attempt to assimilate a novel element into a schema prior to a fully adequate accommodation of the structure of that schema to the nature of the element. A 'novel' person or object might be said to create a need-to-function in Piaget's sense of the term to the extent to which it emerges as the focus of constructions which are inconsistent with respect to the specific network of relationships between constructs within an individual's construction system. When a particular element does not 'fit' the pattern of construct relationships within one subsystem, an individual can employ the strategy of trying to assimilate it more consistently to another subsystem. The more differentiated the current structure of his system in terms of independently organized subsystems, the more likely that he will be able to 'fit' a given element into one of them more or less consistently. If, on the other hand, an element remains a focus of ambiguity within the context of all existing structure, it may be necessary to develop new substructure in order to accommodate it adequately. This, of course, would involve further differentiation of the system and require reintegration of both new and pre-existing substructures at higher levels of abstraction.

Learning, which is typically dealt with as a special kind of psychological process, as distinct from cognition, development, motivation, etc., is regarded by Kelly (1955) as 'synonymous with any and all psychological processes'. On the other hand, he departs from traditional 'learning theory' in his assumption that what is 'learned' is not determined directly by the nature of the stimuli which the environment happens to present and relations of contiguity and contingency between stimuli; but rather it depends upon the specific anticipations, and by implication, the idiosyncratic conceptual framework of the individual. This emphasis is dictated by Kelly's intention to use what we know about scientific enquiry to throw light on all psychological processes. More precisely, he invites us to examine the implications of the assumption that a person's behaviour can be understood as the 'independent variable' in a sequence of experiments carried out to test his own hypothetical constructions of events. In Kelly's (1955, p. 72) own words,

The constructions one places on events are working hypotheses which are about to be put to the test of experience. As one's anticipations are successively revised in the light of the unfolding sequence of events, a construction system undergoes a progressive evolution.

Each individual is presumed to use the hypotheses which he derives from his own system of interrelated constructs both to anticipate events and to assess the accuracy of his forecasts *post hoc*. When his experience confirms his anticipations, he enjoys 'validation' of his constructions. When his experience does not confirm his expectations, his constructions are 'invalidated'. Thus, it is assumed that he is continually evaluating his constructions on the basis of their predictive efficiency.

Since he assess 'feedback' from the environment in terms of the same system of constructs from which he derived his original anticipations, it is difficult to see how a person's anticipations can ever be invalidated by events. As Mischel (1964) points out, all of his prophecies have every opportunity to be 'self-fulfilling'. For example, Mischel (pp. 180–181) poses the hypothetical case of an individual who construes his boss as 'dominating', and then insults the boss in order to show that he himself cannot be dominated. However, if you construe your boss as dominating and then insult him, this is likely to make him behave in a dominating way toward you; for instance, he might fire you.

Warren (1964) offers an exceptionally clear analysis of this problem from the standpoint of Kelly's principle of constructive alternativism. Firstly, Warren notes, this issue is hardly peculiar to personal construct theory:

Taking a more general view, I consider the point Mischel raises here to be a basic problem for all psychological theories which attempt to take 'perception' seriously. It is a matter of the veridicality of perception or construction and how this is checked by the perceiver. It crops up under headings like 'The Selectivity of Perception' or the 'Transformation of Information Input'. All theories using the concepts of 'hypotheses' or 'expectation' run into this issue sooner or later. (p. 11)

This would apply also to 'cognitive' or 'expectancy' theories of social learning (e.g. Rotter, 1954; Rotter, Chance, and Phares, 1972; Bandura, 1969; Mischel, 1968), as well as to theories of thinking, perception, and cognitive development (cf. Neisser, 1976).

Secondly, Warren points out that Kelly employs internal consistency as a criterion of validity:

Kelly goes the whole hog, with complete internal consistency. He makes the business of validation of constructs also a matter of construing, either at a different level of construing from the original construction or by employing different but systematically related constructs . . . construct theory attains consistency on this particular issue by positing as criterion for a person's assessment of the outcome of his anticipations the internal consistency of the constructions within the person's construction system. Thus, there is no recourse to the awkward notion of 'reality', which doesn't make much sense within construct theory anyway, and truth becomes a matter of coherence within a system rather than of correspondence with reality. (p. 11)

Thus, although the evaluation of hypotheses derived from one's system of personal constructs must be carried out wholly within that same system, an individual usually assesses the outcome of his anticipations at a different level of abstraction than that at which he originally derives them. For instance, the bigot who expects his daughter to marry someone of the same race bases his prediction of the skin colour of the prospective bridegroom on a different level of construction than that at which he may eventually perceive it at his daughter's wedding. His anticipations may derive from his belief that his daughter shares his own convictions concerning inter-racial marriage, whereas the outcome is 'seen' in terms of the subordinate construct *white-not white*.

Mischel (1964, p. 304), himself concedes the crucial point that, although an individual may initially view his boss as dominating, he may not be able to continue to construe the boss' behaviour as dominating because to do so would not be entirely consistent with, that is, would not 'fit into' the 'interweaving of construed likenesses and differences' which articulate the structure of his own personal construct system. In short, how does the individual know, from the point of view of construct theory, that all his experience is not his own dream? The answer is that he cannot know this for certain, but he does know that the long dream of his waking life is far more coherent in structure than the shorter dreams which punctuate it from time to time.

INTERPERSONAL RELATIONS

The 'individuality corollary' states that persons differ from each other in their constructions of events'. Kelly (1970) explains that this proposition implies not only that people tend to impose different constructions on the same events, but also that it is unlikely that any two people put their constructs together in terms of the same set of 'logical' relationships. If we assume with Kelly that each individual relies on an unique system of personal constructs to interpret his environment and regulates his own behaviour according to these interpretations, then it follows that specific information about the content and structure of an individual's construct system should provide others with some basis for understanding his psychological processes and predicting his behaviour. In the next chapter we shall see that much of the research which has been carried out within the framework of this theory is concerned with the development of 'repertory grid' methods for assessing individual differences in cognitive structure. However, unless an individual is so unfortunate as to have only professional psychologists as his associates, he is likely to find that the people with whom he interacts everyday employ a variety of informal techniques for making inferences about the personal construction systems of others and anticipating their actions. He is also likely to find that some people have acquired far more skill than others in 'construing the construction processes' of persons on the basis of what they say and do.

Thus, from the standpoint of Kelly's model of interpersonal communication and understanding, discussed in Chapter 5, 'social cognition' is not simply a matter of characterizing the behaviour of others in terms of one's own personal constructs. It also involves making inferences about their construct systems. Specifically, the 'sociality corollary' asserts that 'to the extent that one person construes the construction processes of another, he may play a role in a social process involving the other'. In this context, the term *role* is defined explicitly as 'a course of activity which is played out in the light of one's construction of one or more other persons' construct systems' (Kelly, 1955, p. 117). This novel definition of role underlies the rationale of several innovative approaches to psychotherapy derived from personal construct theory, which are discussed in Chapter 6. It clearly implies that individual social development involves the gradual acquisition of increasing skill in making inferences about the personal construct systems of other people in social situations (Adams-Webber, 1968, Adams-Webber, Schwenker, and Barbeau, 1972).

Salmon (1970) points out that there is a close parallel between Kelly's elaboration of the implications of his sociality corollary and Cameron's 'role theory' in that both of these approaches emphasize understanding the points of view of other persons. For instance, Cameron (1947, p. 167) contends that 'the less practiced a person is in sharing the perspectives of others the less opportunity he will have of finding out how different from himself other ordinary people can be'. There are obviously many other characteristics of people, apart from the particular personal constructs they employ and the ways in which they relate them to one another, which can be useful in distinguishing between them and making differential predictions about their behaviour. On the other hand, an individual who is skilled in detecting differences between persons in the ways in which they interpret and predict behaviour—his, their own, that of others—is likely to make a variety of distinctions among his associates on this basis. This seems especially important in light of the evidence, discussed in Chapter 8, that as children mature they use an increasing number of 'psychological' constructs and fewer 'appearance', 'behaviour' and 'social role' constructs to structure their impressions of their social environments.

Thus, within the explicit framework of Kelly's model of interpersonal relations, 'sociality' is fundamentally a question of the extent to which one individual can accurately infer the personal axes of reference of another person as a basis for effective communication and understanding. It seems obvious that making inferences about the psychological processes of another person will be easier when they are similar to our own in structure and content. Kelly's 'commonality corollary' stipulates that 'to the extent that one person employs a construction of experience which is similar to that employed by another, his processes are psychologically similar to those of the other person'. Bannister and Mair (1968, p. 23) explain that,

Kelly indicates here that two 'similar' people need not have experienced the 'same' events, or even 'similar' events, nor need the ways in which they have tested out their constructions of these events have been the same or similar. What has to be similar, in order for their processes to be psychologically akin, is their constructions of experience.

Duck (1977, p. 392) notes that when the sociality and commonality corollaries are considered in relation to each other, they imply that 'the more similar one's constructs are to those of another person the easier it will be to grasp the other person's psychological processes and play a role in social behaviour with him'. The individuality corollary is also an implicit assumption in this argument, since without the individuality corollary, the sociality and commonality corollaries would be unnecessary. In developing this model of interpersonal relations, Kelly emphasizes the *interaction* between different construct systems. Research dealing with sociality and commonality between strangers, acquaintances, friends, couples, and therapists and clients is reviewed in Chapter 5, together with experimental techniques for enhancing communication and mutual understanding between individuals.

RECAPITULATION AND PROSPECT

We have seen that the formal structure of personal construct theory consists of one fundamental postulate and eleven related corollaries. Kelly (1969) argues that all twelve of these propositions can be derived logically from his principle of constructive alternativism, which is the philosophical basis of his model of 'man-as-scientist' employing his own behaviour to test his constructions of events. Although this theory evolved out of Kelly's personal experiences with clients in psychotherapy, it was not originally intended to serve any specific area of investigation within the field of psychology, such as personality, psycho-pathology, cognition, development, etc. Rather it was initially formulated as a general theory of all psychological processes. Nonetheless, research in personal construct theory has explored its range of convenience further in some directions than in others.

The principal focus of enquiry since the inception of this theory has been the systematic assessment of individual differences in cognitive structure by means of the 'repertory grid' technique, which is the topic of Chapter 2. The next four chapters are concerned with the analysis of the structure and content of personal construct systems: their development (Chapter 3), their disintegration (Chapter 4), their revision and reorganization (Chapter 6), and their central role in interpersonal relations (Chapter 5). Chapter 7 deals with the structural properties of individual constructs and processes of assimilation and contrast. Some new directions which have recently emerged in personal construct theory research, including perception of the environment, the evaluation of professional training and dimensions of aesthetic experience, are discussed in Chapter 8.

2

Evaluating Idiographic Contexts of Meaning

REPERTORY GRID THEORY AND TECHNIQUE

Repertory grid methodology has played an integral role in the development of personal construct theory. Much of the research discussed in subsequent chapters is based on some form of repertory grid measurement. This technique is also used widely in the assessment of individuals in clinical settings. Many investigators and clinicians have employed forms of grid test in research and assessment which have no logical relation to the principles of personal construct theory, and which consequently remain outside its range of convenience. In this chapter we shall be concerned only with those aspects of repertory grid technique which have a direct bearing on this theory. More specifically, we shall consider briefly the essential structure and underlying theoretical assumptions of repertory grid methodology as a frame of reference for our review of research involving various types of grid indices in the following chapters. More comprehensive discussions of the general rationale and uses of repertory grids have been provided by Bannister and Mair (1968) and Fransella and Bannister (1977).

Repertory grid technique is basically a method of quantifying and statistically analysing relationships between the categories used by a subject in performing a complex sorting task. Bannister and Mair (1968, p. 136) define a repertory grid as 'any form of sorting task which allows for the assessment of relationships between constructs and which yields these primary data in matrix form'. It differs from conventional sorting tests (e.g. Vygotsky, 1962) in that persons are substituted for the usual objects and the relationships between categories are evaluated rather than the accuracy of the sorting.

Kelly's (1955) original *Role Construct Repertory Test*, from which all forms of repertory grid derive, is designed to elicit a representative sample of those constructs upon which an individual customarily relies to interpret and predict the behaviour of significant people in his life, and to assess the way in which he relates these constructs to one another. As Allport (1958) notes, this technique is essentially 'idiographic' in approach since 'it leads to the discovery of the unique pattern of relationships among several constructs of a given person'. For example, the principal difference between Kelly's test and Osgood, Suci, and Tannenbaum's (1957) *Semantic Differential* is that in the latter the same standard list of dimensions is supplied to all subjects alike, while in the former a set of constructs is elicited individually from each subject. This 'idiographic' emphasis of Kelly's test derives directly from his individuality corollary, which asserts that 'Persons differ from each other in their constructions of events'.

In the *Role Construct Repertory Test* each subject is first shown a standard list of brief 'role titles' such as *Your Father, Your Boss, The Person with Whom You Feel Least Comfortable, A Person You have Met Recently Whom You Would Like To Get To Know Better*, and asked to nominate for each of them 'that individual personally known to you who seems to fit it best'. The name of each person ('figure') nominated by the subject is recorded on a separate card, together with the corresponding role title (the same person can be nominated only once). Next, a triad of these figures is presented to the subject and he is asked to 'think of some important way in which two of these three persons are similar to one another and different from the third'. Whatever the subject states to be the basis of perceived similarity and contrast is recorded verbatim as a single bi-polar construct, for example *reserved-outgoing*. A series of such triads, preselected so that all figures are used an approximately equal number of times, is used to elicit twenty or thirty bi-polar constructs from each subject. This procedure will be referred to from here on as Kelly's 'method of triads'.

The elicitation of constructs from each subject individually directly reflects the emphasis within personal construct theory on the idiosyncratic nature of each person's system of cognitive dimensions for interpreting his social environment. Kelly assumes that the constructs which are elicited from a person by means of his method of triads constitute a representative sample of those dimensions which he uses to construe his own behaviour and that of other important people in his life. This assumption is consistent with evidence that when this procedure is used to elicit constructs from the same subjects on different occasions, many constructs are repeated.

In a preliminary study, Hunt (1951) found that both hospitalized, psychiatric patients and normal college students repeated approximately 70 per cent of their constructs when the same triad procedure was readministered to them one week later with a second set of figures. First, he elicited from each of nine psychiatric patients the names of forty personal acquaintances, using Kelly's (1955) original list of role titles. One week later, he used forty triads composed of only the twenty odd-numbered figures to elicit forty constructs individually from each of the same patients. At the end of another week, he repeated the same procedure using only the twenty even-numbered figures. Any construct that was elicited on the second occasion was considered to be the 'same' as one elicited on the first occasion if, and only if, (a) both constructs were judged to be similar by the patient himself, (b) he could apply both constructs to the same figures in identical ways, and (c) he answered affirmatively to the question 'Is a person who is——(Construct A) almost always——(Construct B)?', and its logical converse. Using these fairly stringent criteria of construct similarity, the estimated percentage of constructs repeated by each patient ranged from 59 to 75 per cent, with a grand mean of 69 per cent. Hunt repeated this experiment with a sample of 30 normal university students, and obtained almost identical results.

Hunt also found that the number of constructs which could be elicited from each subject was, on average, quite limited. Not many new constructs appeared after between twenty and thirty triads had been presented, and very few novel constructs emerged following the fortieth triad. Bieri and Blacker (1956) also found that individual subjects tend to be highly consistent over a period of a fortnight with respect to the number of different constructs which can be elicited from each of them by the presentation of twenty triads made up from the same list of figures ($r = 0.82$). As we shall see in the next chapter, the number of constructs elicited from an individual has been used as one index of the degree of 'differentiation' of his personal construct system (cf. Crockett, 1965).

In a subsequent study of the tendency of subjects to repeat the same constructs on different occasions, Fjeld and Landfield (1961) administered the *Role Construct Repertory Test* twice, the second time after an interval of a fortnight, to three groups each composed of twenty undergraduates. They judged the degree of equivalence between constructs on the basis of an elaborate set of criteria which have been summarized by Landfield, Stern and Fjeld (1961). When the same figures were used to elicit constructs on both occasions (Group I), subjects exhibited a high level of agreement between the two sets of constructs which they employed on both administrations of the test ($r = 0.78$). When subjects were given the same list of role titles on the second occasion, but asked to nominate different figures (Group II), there was again a high degree of agreement between the two samples of constructs elicited from them ($r = 0.79$). Finally, when subjects were simply provided with a blank form of the test on the second occasion and instructed to readminister it to themselves (Group III), the results were about the same as in the other two conditions ($r = 0.80$).

Bannister and Mair (1968, p. 158) plausibly conclude on the basis of the evidence summarized above that 'grids are delving into a limited repertoire of constructs which the subject has available, and there is no fear of being confronted with the everlasting pages of an infinite personal directory'. Bonarius (1965) also points out that these studies lend support to Kelly's (1955) assumption that mostly 'pre-existing' constructs are elicited by his method of triads, since it seems highly unlikely that constructs which are newly formed on the occasion of the initial administration of the test would reappear with such consistency on subsequent occasions. In addition, the evidence suggests that the constructs which are elicited by this procedure are relatively 'permeable', that is, 'open to the addition of new figures beyond those upon which they have explicitly been formed' (Bonarius, 1965, p. 5), since subjects are able to apply the same constructs to different figures when they are retested.

ELICITED VERSUS SUPPLIED CONSTRUCTS

There is also considerable evidence that the constructs which are elicited from subjects individually are more personally meaningful to these subjects than are constructs supplied to them from other sources. This is an important issue since many forms of repertory grid test currently used in both research and clinical assessment (e.g. Bannister and Fransella's (1967) *Grid Test of Schizophrenic Thought Disorder*, discussed in Chapter 4) rely on supplying all subjects with the same standard list of adjectives rather than individually eliciting a sample of each subject's own personal constructs, as in Kelly's original repertory grid procedure. The main advantage of supplying constructs to subjects is that it permits a higher degree of standardization in administration as a basis for 'nomothetic' comparisons between different populations, for example schizophrenics and normals. It does, however, represent a major departure from Kelly's own emphasis on the personal nature of each individual's construction processes. Bannister and Mair (1968, p. 67) indeed complain that 'the procedure of supplying adjective labels has become more widely favoured than can be theoretically or experimentally justified'.

The importance of this problem is underlined by the results of a recent experiment by Oswalt (1974). He used a 'free formulation procedure' (cf. Bonarius, 1970a) to elicit approximately 3800 words used to describe personal acquaintances from four female and four male American university students. He found that of the total number of *different* words used by his subjects to characterize persons, only ninety-five (26 per cent) were used more than once. Oswalt presented his subjects with lists of those words which they had used previously more than once to characterize a particular acquaintance and asked them to identify the person in question. They were able to do so with 85 per cent accuracy. He argues (p. 283) on the basis of this finding that 'a subject has very specific words that he uses to describe certain people'. This seems consistent with the results of Hunt (1951) and Fjeld and Landfield (1961) reviewed above. Oswalt (p. 283) also found that 'there is only a small amount (median 12 per cent) of overlap between seven standard investigator determined word lists and the 95 salient words (those used more than once by his own subjects)'. It is interesting to note that the highest degree of overlap was found for the list of ten constructs used in Bieri's (1966) modification of the repertory grid test (62 per cent), which is discussed in Chapter 3.

Research which directly compares elicited and provided constructs in repertory grid testing has been reviewed previously by Adams-Webber (1970b), Bonarius (1970a) and Landfield (1968). Fortunately, the majority of investigators working on this problem have employed more or less the same operational definition of the term *personal construct*, that is, a bi-polar dimension elicited from an individual by presenting him with names of three persons he knows and asking him to indicate how two of them are alike and different from the third. This fact allows a much closer comparison between the results of different experiments than is possible in most areas of research in personal construct theory. Some alternative methods of eliciting constructs from subjects are discussed by Bannister and Mair (1968), Bonarius (1970a) and Epting, Suchman, and Nickeson (1971).

In general, most of the available evidence seems to support Bonarius' (1965, p. 26) earlier conclusion that 'the research has shown convincingly that the individual prefers to express himself and to describe others by using his own personal constructs'. For example, when subjects are given the choice of describing their personal acquaintances in terms either of constructs elicited from themselves (subjects) or of constructs elicited from peers, they significantly prefer to use their own (Fager, 1954). In addition, subjects consistently rank the constructs elicited from themselves as more useful in describing a particular acquaintance than constructs elicited from the 'target' (Bonarius, 1965).

Landfield (1965) asked clients at the beginning of psychotherapy to rank-order a set of bi-polar dimensions in terms of their 'felt usefulness in describing others'. These dimensions included both personal constructs elicited from the clients themselves and personal constructs elicited from their respective therapists. He reports that 'the five top-chosen constructs were more likely to be those of the client, and the bottom five those of the therapist' (Landfield, 1971, p. 49). In a related experiment Isaacson (1966) requested subjects to rank-order a list of dimensions which included a random assortment of personal constructs elicited from themselves, *Semantic Differential* dimensions and *Manifest Anxiety Scale* items on the basis of their 'personal usefulness in understanding others'. He found that thirty-nine of fifty subjects ranked their own personal constructs higher than either set of supplied dimensions.

It is clear in the light of the results of these experiments that people tend to regard the constructs elicited from themselves by means of repertory grid technique as more personally useful than other sorts of dimensions for characterizing themselves and others. One limitation of the studies considered so far, however, is that they rely exclusively on the subject's own judgement concerning the relative meaningfulness of elicited and provided constructs. A working assumption of many users of repertory grid tests (e.g. Bieri, 1966) is that, although persons may prefer to use a particular set of constructs to interpret their social environment, most people are practised in communicating their personal judgements to others in terms of a fairly wide range of common adjectives. Thus, they can be expected to make about the same discriminations among people, within limits, whether they employ constructs elicited from themselves or supplied lists of adjectives. As Bannister and Mair (1968, p. 67) put it, it can be assumed that 'they would all share *some* common understanding of these terms, and that such commonalities would provide a fair basis for comparisons of *structural* features of construing' (cf. Bannister, 1962a). Even Kelly (1969) himself points out that, regardless of the words he uses, each person does his own construing.

On the other hand, there is also considerable evidence that subjects judge both themselves and others more extremely on elicited constructs than on supplied ones, which is consistent with the finding that they rate the former as more personally meaningful than the latter. Cromwell and Caldwell (1962) found specifically that subjects' ratings of six old acquaintances and six new ones on 11-point scales based on their own elicited constructs fell more towards the extremes of the scales than did ratings of the same persons on scales based on constructs elicited from another subject. They also observed a marginal tendency for the old acquaintances to receive more extreme ratings than the new ones.

A further test of the same hypothesis was carried out by Isaacson (1966). He asked subjects to rate a list of ten of their personal acquaintances on a 7-point scale on the basis of thirty dimensions. These dimensions included ten *Manifest Anxiety Scale* items, ten *Semantic Differential* dimensions and ten personal constructs previously elicited from themselves. As predicted, ratings based on elicited constructs were found to be significantly more extreme than those based on either type of supplied dimension. Landfield (1965) also reports that the self-ratings of clients in psychotherapy were more extreme in terms of constructs elicited from themselves than in terms of constructs elicited from their own therapists (see Chapter 6).

All of the studies involving direct comparisons between elicited and supplied constructs in terms of extremity of judgement that we have considered so far employed American undergraduates as subjects. Similar experiments, however, have produced comparable results with British, Canadian, Dutch, and Finnish subjects. For example, Bender (1968a) asked a sample of British university students to rate themselves and ten of their personal acquaintances on 11-point scales on the basis of twenty-four different dimensions. This set of dimensions included six constructs elicited from the subjects themselves, six constructs elicited from their best friends, six constructs elicited from their wives or fiancées, and six constructs elicited from 'just an acquaintance'. The degree of rating extremity was observed to decrease significantly across these four types of constructs with the most extreme ratings appearing on the subjects' own constructs, the next most extreme on their best friends' constructs, then their spouses' constructs, and finally those of the casual acquaintances. Bonarius (1966, 1967a, 1970a) also presents experimental evidence that Dutch university students rate persons more extremely on their own elicited constructs than on those elicited from other persons or supplied from another source, for example *Semantic Differential* dimensions.

Nevertheless, a different result was obtained by Warr and Coffman (1970). In this study a sample of British subjects rated the same list of persons on 7-point scales based on twelve elicited constructs and twelve supplied ones. Each of the three major *Semantic Differential* components of connotative meaning—evaluation, activity, and potency (Osgood *et al.*, 1957)—was represented by four of the supplied constructs. Warr and Coffman report that the mean rating extremity scores for elicited and supplied constructs were 'almost identical'. They note that their own results are not consistent with previous findings and suggest that, although the earlier studies probably reflect important differences between elicited and provided dimensions in terms of 'personal relevance', it does not necessarily follow that provided constructs must always fall short of elicited ones in this respect. They argue on the basis of their own data that it is possible through careful selection to obtain a set of supplied constructs which do not differ significantly from a subject's own elicited constructs in terms of personal meaningfulness. This study serves to underline the importance of making the rationale for the selection of a particular set of supplied constructs as clear and explicit as possible. As Bannister and Mair (1968, p. 202) point out 'the experimenter must consciously guard against the temptation to supply constructs which are a naïve equivalent of the psychological dimensions in terms of which he is framing the experiment'.

Bender (1974) attempts to explain away Warr and Coffman's (1970) 'anomalous finding' on the grounds that their particular method of eliciting constructs from their subjects was, in at least one important respect, different from that employed in most of the previous studies. Specifically, Warr and Coffman used Kelly's (1955) 'sequential procedure' in which only one figure is replaced from each triad presentation to the next one. Bender suggests that this method tends to elicit constructs which are relatively unimportant to the subject because 'the first construction of an element is likely to be the most important . . . if one does not remove the element from the next trial, the subject is faced with an element whose most important attribute he has already stated' (p. 329). This seems to be a plausible hypothesis; however, it has not yet been demonstrated that subjects rate people less extremely on constructs elicited from them by the sequential method than on constructs elicited by alternative methods used in other experiments (cf. Kelly, 1955, p. 225).

There is also evidence that personal meaningfulness and rating extremity are related in terms of the specific set of constructs which Warr and Coffman supplied to their subjects. Adams-Webber and Benjafield (1973) asked thirty Canadian undergraduates individually to rank-order these twelve constructs on the basis of their perceived 'usefulness for describing people'. These subjects also rated themselves and eleven of their personal associates on 7-point scales based on the same twelve dimensions. It was found that the more highly a particular subject ranked a given dimension, the more extremely he rated himself and others on it. Thus, even within the context of a set of dimensions which have been carefully counterbalanced in terms of evaluation, activity, and potency, idiosyncratic preferences for using particular constructs to describe people relate significantly to extremity of judgement. This result is consistent with Meertens's (1967) earlier finding that there is a significant correlation ($r = 0.42$, 84 df) between the degree of individual preference for particular constructs in terms of their 'felt usefulness' and rating extremity.

The results of Adams-Webber and Benjafield (1973) are also consistent with evidence reported by Mitsos (1961) that idiosyncratic construct preferences interact with the three major components of connotative meaning in determining *Semantic Differential* structure. Mitsos provided each of his subjects with twenty-one *Semantic Differential* dimensions, seven of which loaded highly on evaluation, seven on activity, and seven on potency. The subject was asked to select the three dimensions from each of these three groups of seven which were in his own judgement 'the most personally meaningful in thinking about people'. The subjects then used Osgood *et al.*'s (1957) standard procedure to rate seven different concepts on all twenty-one dimensions (e.g. politician, communist, foreman, etc.). Mitsos found that the nine scales chosen by each subject were significantly more saturated with 'meaning' than the full set of twenty-one, and the three scales chosen least often were significantly less saturated than the entire set (cf. Bonarius, 1970a; Landfield, 1971).

MEANING AND CONTEXT

Bonarius (1970a) argues that the meaning of any construct in use must depend at least in part on its context, that is, the specific domain of experience within which it is ordinarily applied by an individual.

Take, for instance, the contrast *progressive-conservative*. It is probably a meaningful contrast for a politician, but more so when he is talking about political programmes than about his wife. The politician's daughter who is studying medicine finds the word *progressive* more meaningful to characterize a disease, whereas his son in applied mathematics thinks predominantly of the conservative statistical test. (Bonarius, 1970a, p. 21)

Bonarius (1968) suggests specifically that the constructs which are elicited by means of Kelly's (1955) repertory grid procedures are especially useful to the individual in characterizing himself, members of his family and his closest associates. It is assumed that these are the figures who constitute the original context of a majority of his constructs. Bonarius refers to these specific figures as an individual's 'personal others' to distinguish them from more superficial acquaintances, to whom he refers as 'extraneous others'. He hypothesizes that the latter tend to be outside the focus of convenience of most of the constructs elicited from a person, and predicts on the basis of this hypothesis that differences between elicited and supplied constructs with respect to rating extremity will be greater for 'personal others' than for 'extraneous others'.

In order to test this prediction, Bonarius asked 125 male students attending a Dutch university each to write down what they felt to be the 'two most important dimensions for describing people'. He refers to this method of eliciting personal constructs from subjects as the *Free Formation Procedure* to distinguish it from Kelly's own method of triads. Then the names of five close associates were elicited from each subject—*mother, father, brother, or sister, boy or girl friend,* and *a former close friend.* These figures were designated as 'personal others'. Each subject then nominated five 'extraneous others'—an *influential teacher, successful person, physician* or *pastor, happy person,* and *disliked teacher.* All of these role titles are derived from Kelly's (1955) original list. Finally, each subject rated all ten of these figures on the basis of four different bi-polar constructs including the two previously elicited from himself and two standard, supplied dimensions—*objective-emotional* and *dependent-self-confident.* Bonarius found a significant interaction between the type of construct used and the kind of figure judged in terms of rating extremity. As he predicted, the observed difference in rating extremity in favour of elicited constructs was greater when 'personal others' were judged than when 'extraneous others' were judged.

These results are interpreted by Bonárius (1970a, p. 32) as evidence that the constructs elicited from an individual are 'primarily meaningful if applied to the kind of people from whom the person originally derived them'. His findings were replicated by M. Bonarius (1968) with twenty-two women attending a Finnish university, Van Os (1968) with a group of fourteen-year-old high-school students (five girls and five boys) and a group of college-educated adults (five women and five men) in the Netherlands, and Wissema (1968) with thirty female and thirty male, first-year psychology students at a Dutch university. No significant differences between men and women with respect to rating extremity were observed in the last two experiments, although they have appeared in other studies (e.g. Hamilton, 1968; Warr, 1971). There were also no significant interactions involving sex observed in any of these studies.

Bonarius (1970a) himself conducted a further experiment to explore the nature of the interaction between constructs and their contexts in determining the degree of 'personal meaningfulness' of a particular set of judgements. Eighty students in an Introductory Psychology course at a Dutch university were divided randomly into forty separate pairs. They individually wrote down two constructs which they regarded as 'personally meaningful when describing and comparing paintings'. Then, each subject was asked to select from a set of ten paintings (slides) the one which he found to be the 'most moving'. Finally, every subject rated both the painting which he, himself, had chosen and the one selected by his partner on 7-point scales based on four constructs: the two constructs previously elicited from himself and the two constructs elicited from his partner. Bonarius reports that subjects rated their own paintings more extremely on their own personal constructs than on their partners' constructs; however, their ratings of the paintings chosen by their partners were no more extreme on one set of constructs than on the other. This is an important experiment because it shows that the hypothesis that 'personal meaning' is determined by the interaction between construct and context applies also to judgements outside the sphere of characterizing oneself and one's associates on interpersonal constructs.

MEANING AND IMPLICATION

Lemon and Warren (1974) question the assumption that rating extremity directly reflects personal meaningfulness. They point out that the meaningfulness of a construct can also be viewed in terms of its 'implicative potential', that is, the number of inferences which can be made from that particular construct to other related constructs. They also suggest that, if the informational content of a given construct is organized in terms of an underlying bi-polar structure, as Kelly himself assumes, then rating extremity may indirectly reflect 'meaningfulness'. That is, it is possible that in order 'to permit stronger or wider inferences from it, a construct must generate clear-cut, that is, extreme ratings itself' (p. 123).

Lemon (1975) presents some 'real world' evidence that a particular elicited construct may have more 'meaning', in terms of its range of implications, in one specific context of experience than in another. He argues that the extent to which a construct relates to other constructs can serve as an index of its 'meaningfulness' in the sense that the more constructs which relate to a given construct within an individual's cognitive system, the more specific implications that construct will have for him. Lemon carried out an experiment in which twenty-eight Tanzanian secondary-school pupils rated both a group of their own classmates and a list of nations in terms of a set of constructs some of which had been elicited in English and some of which had been elicited in Swahili. He reasoned that if a particular language is customarily used in a specific domain of experience, then constructs elicited in that language, employing elements from the relevant domain, will tend to be related to one another through their association in everyday usage. His own subjects were observed to speak mostly Swahili in interacting socially with their peers outside school and English in the classroom while studying geography. Lemon found, as he had predicted on the basis of his 'interaction hypothesis', that there was a higher degree of statistical association among sets of ratings based on different constructs when these subjects rated nations in terms of constructs elicited in English and their classmates in terms of constructs elicited in Swahili than when they rated either classmates on 'English constructs' or nations on 'Swahili constructs'.

There is also some direct evidence that elicited constructs carry more implications for subjects than do supplied ones, at least in the sphere of interpersonal judgement. Delia, Gonyea, and Crockett (1970) found that subjects are able to form more highly differentiated impressions of an individual's personality when information about him is presented to them in terms of their own elicited constructs than when it is based on 'normative' constructs. They assumed that information which is expressed in terms of a person's own elicited constructs can be assimilated into the structure of his construct system more quickly and more completely than information expressed in terms of supplied dimensions which have less immediate relevance in terms of his personal constructions. Therefore, individuals can be expected to draw a wider range of inferences from the former type of information than from the latter kind.

Delia et al. assigned a sample of American undergraduates randomly to each of four experimental conditions. In the first condition, information about a hypothetical figure—'John'—some of it positive in valence and some of it negative, was presented to subjects entirely in terms of their own previously elicited constructs. In the second condition, negative information about John was presented in terms of elicited constructs and positive information about him was presented in terms of 'normative' constructs, for example he is 'confident', 'punctual', etc. In the third condition, positive information was presented in terms of elicited constructs, and negative information in terms of 'normative' constructs. In the fourth condition, all information about John was presented in terms of the 'normative' constructs. Each subject then wrote a characterization of John's personality on the basis of the information provided. These sketches were scored in terms of their degree of 'differentiation', operationally defined as the total number of different constructs applied to John (Crockett, 1965), and the overall valence—positive or negative—of the impression.

It was found that subjects produced the most differentiated descriptions of John's personality when all the information about him was based on their own elicited constructs, and the least differentiated descriptions when it was based entirely on 'normative' constructs. Moreover, the predominant valence of the whole character sketch tended to be negative when only the negative information was presented in terms of elicited constructs, and positive when only the positive information was presented in terms of elicited constructs. These results strongly suggest that elicited constructs are more 'meaningful' than supplied ones in terms of their 'implicative potential' (Lemon and Warren, 1974; Lemon, 1975). That is, individuals seem to draw a wider range of inferences from information which is encoded in terms of their own personal constructs than information encoded in terms of other dimensions. This lends further support to Kelly's basic assumption that the constructs elicited from an individual are integral parts of a network of relationships; and consequently, information presented in terms of a subject's own elicited constructs should have more specific implications within the explicit framework of his personal construct system as a whole than information given in terms of dimensions which do not form parts of his system.

Lemon and Warren (1974) hypothesize also that 'salient' (elicited) constructs are more 'self-relevant' than non-salient ones in the sense that they are judged by individuals to be more important in their own self-characterizations. There is some evidence that people do, in fact, differentiate between themselves and others to a greater extent on the basis of their own elicited constructs than on the basis of supplied ones. Adams-Webber and Benjafield (1976) asked thirty Canadian undergraduates to categorize themselves and six of their personal acquaintances—three with positive valences (e.g. 'the warmest person you know') and three with negative valences ('the weakest person you know')—on the basis of twenty-four constructs. Twelve of these constructs were the same as those used by Warr and Coffman (1970), which were found not to fall short of elicited constructs in terms of rating extremity. These constructs were interspersed randomly with twelve constructs elicited individually from each subject. It was found that subjects differentiated themselves from both 'positive' and 'negative' other figures to a significantly greater extent in terms of their own elicited personal constructs than in terms of Warr and Coffman's set of supplied constructs. In a subsequent study, Benjafield, Jordan, and Pomeroy (1976) also found that members of the same encounter group differentiated between themselves and other members more on the basis of elicited constructs than on the basis of the Warr and Coffman dimensions. The results of these two studies seem consistent with Lemon and Warren's (1974) own finding that a group of British women rated their own elicited constructs as more important in characterizing themselves than lists of supplied constructs.

In an earlier study by Morse (1965), thirty-six American undergraduates attempted to predict the self-characterizations of three new acquaintances following a brief conversation with each of them separately. These subjects predicted significantly fewer differences between themselves and their 'targets' when they used the latters' elicited constructs than when they used their own. This finding was later replicated by Adams-Webber (1968). In general, it is not difficult to interpret the consistent finding that individuals differentiate between themselves and others to a greater extent on the basis of their own elicited constructs than on the basis of provided ones within the context of personal construct theory. Kelly (1955) assumes that the constructs elicited from a particular person constitute a representative sample of an unique system of cognitive dimensions which he customarily uses to organize information about his social environment. Thus, we can expect that he will gradually become aware of a variety of specific differences between himself and those around him in the context of these personal constructs as he acquires interpersonal experience. (cf. Mair, 1977).

On the other hand, the term *personal construct* does not refer only to the verbal labels which an individual assigns to people in formulating and communicating his impressions of them, but also to the underlying cognitive structures used in processing this information. In interpersonal communication each of us must rely on his own interpretations of the language used by others. Chapter 7 reviews some recent research which deals with the complex problem of how normal adults can employ the same words to describe people and understand them to have common 'lexical' meanings, while at the same time using them to represent and communicate idiosyncratic 'personal meanings'.

In the research considered so far in the present chapter it has been demonstrated convincingly that individuals exhibit consistent preferences for using particular words to describe themselves and others, judge people more extremely in their own terms, and draw more inferences from information presented in their own language.

ASSESSING INDIVIDUAL CONCEPTUAL STRUCTURES

Kelly was interested in assessing the structural properties as well as the content of each individual's personal construct system. Therefore, he developed a 'grid' format for measuring relations between constructs. In his original repertory grid test, immediately after each construct is elicited on the basis of three figures selected from the 'role title' list, the subject is asked to sort all the remaining figures into two piles according to which pole of his construct seems to him to describe them more adequately. All the cards containing the names of the figures are shuffled thoroughly before each one of these sorting sequences and no limits are imposed with respect to the number of figures which can be allotted to either pole of the construct on a given sort. On each sorting trial, all figures which the subject allots to one pole of his construct can be given a score of 1, and those which he allots to the opposite pole can be scored 0, so that the results of each sort can be recorded individually as a single n-digit, binary number, where n is the number of figures being sorted on every construct. The data elicited in this way from each subject can be entered into a simple two-dimensional table, or 'grid', in which there is a separate row for each construct and a separate column for every figure.

Fransella and Bannister (1977, p. 1) offer the following highly simplified example of how the psychological relationship between two different constructs can be inferred from the degree of statistical association between them in this type of grid matrix. Suppose that a subject first sorts a list of 100 acquaintances on the basis of the construct *warm-eyed* versus *cold-eyed*, and then sorts them again on the basis of the construct *mean* versus *generous*. Let us say that, of the thirty people whom he perceives as having cold eyes, only two are regarded as generous. On the other hand, fifty-one of the persons whom he sees as having warm eyes are, from his point of view, generous. On the basis of these data, we can infer that there is a significant correlation between these two constructs, which presumably reflects the relationship between them within his personal construct system (i.e., r phi $= 0.61$; $p < .001$).

Slater (1969) concisely summarizes the essential mathematical properties of this 'repertory grid matrix' as follows: (a) all the variation recorded therein is due to the interactions between a set of constructs and a group of figures; (b) the dispersion of the constructs in the figure space is defined in terms of columns; (c) the dispersion of figures in the construct space is defined in terms of rows; and (d) the total variation can be broken down into a limited number of independent components which can be ordered from largest to smallest.

The same basic grid format can be used to organize and statistically analyse the data from many different complex sorting tasks. As a consequence, a wide variety of tests and questionnaires are labelled as 'repertory grids' which are only remotely related to Kelly's original instrument (cf. Fransella and Bannister, 1977). Also, during the last two decades there has been a remarkable proliferation of novel statistical procedures for analyzing 'repertory grid' data. One result of this has been the appearance of 'new' operational definitions for many traditional concepts in psychology, for example *identification* (Jones, 1961); *thought-disorder* (Bannister and Fransella, 1966); *transference* (Sechrest, 1962); *differentiation* (Bieri, 1955); *obsessional thinking* (Makhlouf-Norris, *et al.*, 1970). As the statistical methods used in deriving such indices become progressively more complex, their interpretation can become increasingly difficult.

At an early stage in the development of repertory grid technique, Cronbach (1956) pointed out that, although this methodology is extremely flexible and can be applied to a broad range of measurement problems, 'the complexity of the data has lured Kelly's students into analyses so involved as to obscure errors in reasoning'. His warning has gone mostly unheeded as individual investigators have continued to devise highly specialized modifications of Kelly's grid technique to meet the limited requirements of their own research without paying much attention to how very similar procedures have been used by other experimenters to measure different variables. At present, there is considerable confusion surrounding the meaning of many repertory-grid-based measures currently used in both research and clinical assessment. We shall encounter several examples of this confusion in our attempts to compare and integrate the results of different experiments in the chapters which follow.

Bonarius (1965, p. 18) suggests that many of the logical problems, as well as technical deficiencies in repertory grid analysis, could have been prevented 'by careful study of the reliability and validity of the measures used'. At this point in the rapidly accelerating evolution of new forms of grid method it still may not be too late to identify some of the major sources of confusion and try to eliminate them. Such an attempt must focus primarily upon questions concerning the reliability and validity of grid tests in current use by both clinicians and experimenters.

In discussing the issue of reliability in relation to grid methods in general, Bannister and Mair (1968, p. 156) note that the welter of diverse forms it has assumed in the hands of various investigators necessitates the conclusion that 'since there is no such thing as *the* grid, there can be no such thing as *the* reliability of *the* grid'. It would seem to follow that it is entirely the responsibility of the individual investigator who develops a grid test to demonstrate the reliability of his own measurements. Unfortunately, many have failed to do so. On the other hand, there do seem to be some aspects of the issue of reliability which are common to most forms of grid test.

Slater (1972) points out that there are several basic questions which can be raised concerning the reliability of any form of repertory grid test. The first of these is the problem of whether subjects exhibit consistency over time in the way in which they apply the same constructs to the same figures. This aspect of grid reliability is referred to as 'element consistency' (e.g. Fransella, 1970). The problem of element consistency has been studied principally in relation to constructs which have been elicited directly from subjects themselves and figures who are personally known to them.

One advantage of the matrix format of the repertory grid is that it permits us to analyse the relationships between constructs independently of the content of the verbal labels used by the subjects themselves. Any two constructs can be directly compared simply in terms of their respective patterns of application to the same set of figures. Thus, the conclusion that the 'same' construct appears in each of two grids elicited successively from the same subject should rest in part on evidence that it is applied in a nearly identical way to the same figures on both occasions. Slater (1972, p. 48) points out that

The definition of 'consistency' may become clearer if methods for measuring it are compared with ones, long established, for measuring reliability. Let us consider the relationships involved when two grids A and B record an informant's evaluations of the same elements on two occasions. The data then can be treated as test-retest results for the same grid. If the evaluations tend to be the same for a construct in A as for the one aligned with it in B, its test-retest reliability will be high; if the evaluations differ markedly, it will be low. Accumulating evidence for all the constructs will provide a measure of the reliability of the grid as a whole.

For example, Pedersen (1958) randomly selected five constructs from the repertory grid protocols of thirty-eight subjects, and asked them to reapply these constructs to the same set of figures on a second administration of the test two weeks later. A comparison of the two row patterns of each construct across both grids yielded a median phi coefficient of 0.72 ($p < .005$), which indicates a fairly satisfactory level of element consistency. Subsequently, Fjeld and Landfield (1961) asked twenty subjects to use the same list of figures and the same set of constructs on two grid tests administered to them a fortnight apart. Their subjects exhibited a high degree of consistency in the way in which they categorized figures on each construct as evidenced by the fact that 83 per cent of their judgements were the same on both occasions.

A second aspect of the reliability of any repertory grid test, as Slater (1972) notes, is the problem of whether specific patterns of relationships among constructs are consistent over time. This facet of reliability can be evaluated independently of the question of whether the same constructs are applied to the same figures in a similar way from one occasion to another. Slater points out that the correlation between any two constructs can remain approximately the same although the categorization of particular figures on each construct is changed, provided that they have changed in terms of both constructs in a consistent way. For example, the constructs *friendly* and *outgoing* may be observed to be closely related in the same person's grid protocol on two separate administrations, whereas he may have categorized several figures as both friendly and outgoing on the second occasion whom he categorized previously as unfriendly and reserved.

In general, the term *relationship consistency* is used to refer to consistency in the pattern of relationships between constructs to distinguish it from element consistency (cf. Fransella, 1970). The research of Fransella and Joyston-Bechal (1971) indicates the importance of differentiating between these two forms of consistency in repertory grid data. They show empirically that shifts in patterns of construct relationships ('meaning') are not always accompanied by corresponding changes in the categorization of particular figures on these constructs; and conversely, people sometimes revise their specific impressions of their associates without altering the pattern of relationships between their constructs (i.e. the logical structure of their conceptual systems; cf. Bannister, 1962a).

Further evaluations of relationships consistency in repertory grids have been carried out by Bannister (1960, 1962a, b) and Bannister and Fransella (1966). They conducted a series of experiments concerned with the immediate test-retest consistency of the pattern of construct relationships in different forms of repertory grid. For example, Bannister (1960) asked twenty British adults to nominate thirty-six personal acquaintances, and to categorize eighteen of them (randomly selected) successively on the basis of ten bi-polar constructs. These subjects were instructed to allot only nine of these figures to each pole of a construct. Bannister refers to this particular modification of Kelly's original procedure as 'split-half technique' (which will be considered further in Chapter 7). The degree of statistical association between each construct and every other was assessed in terms of a matching score, which is more or less equivalent to a phi coefficient. Each subject was then asked to categorize the second set of eighteen figures on the basis of the same ten constructs, and the relationships between constructs were reassessed. Bannister reports a Pearson r of 0.60 between the forty-five matching scores from the first grid and the forty-five from the second.

In his second study on the same problem, Bannister (1962a) asked thirty normal adults to categorize a set of twenty photographs of strangers (again using 'split-half' procedure) on the basis of nine constructs twice in immediate succession. As in his previous experiment, Bannister determined the degree of match between each construct and every other separately for each grid protocol, and then calculated a Pearson r between the matching scores for the same constructs across both grids elicited from the same subjects. The observed value of r, which was 0.71, was significantly higher than that found in the first experiment (t (48 df) = 2.22, $p < .05$). This increase in reliability may have resulted from the fact that in the second experiment the same elements were used in both trials.

In a third experiment concerned with relationship consistency (Bannister and Fransella, 1966), thirty normal adults rank-ordered eight photographs of strangers (four women, four men) successively on the basis of six different adjectives. Immediately upon completing this task, each subject repeated it. Spearman rank-order correlations were calculated between all possible pairs of constructs, and the resulting fifteen correlations were themselves rank-ordered from the largest positive one to the largest negative one separately for each grid protocol. Bannister and Fransella report a correlation of 0.80 between these two sets of rankings. The results of these three studies considered together indicate that repertory grid technique provides a consistent measure of the pattern of relationships between subjects' constructs, although they tell us little about the stability of such patterns over time. Mair (1964, p. 58) notes that, 'when we consider that all of these assessments were immediate retests, the stability scores obtained . . . are not very high'. He concludes, as did Cronbach (1956) earlier, that 'one of the big problems regarding the study of stability of grid scores is the number of ways in which grids can be varied' (p. 59).

Slater (1972) has developed a method for directly comparing grids elicited from the same subject which he calls the 'coefficient of convergence'. He first calculates and lists the correlations and angular distances between constructs in each grid independently, and then he determines the differences between these angular distances across grids. His coefficient of convergence (C) is calculated as the intra-class correlation between the two sets of angular distances for the same constructs across grids. Slater (p. 46) points out that 'In cases where Bannister's formulae can be applied, very little difference is likely to be found between C and the consistency score calculated in his 1966 method (see Bannister and Fransella, above or between 100 C and the score calculated by his 1962 method'. For example, Garside and Van der Spuy (1968) compared two sets of repertory grids elicited from forty-six schoolchildren. They report a C of 0.49, while Bannister's 'consistency of relationship' score was 0.44. Given that both methods provide more or less comparable information, it seems mostly a matter of convenience, for example the availability of computer programs, which technique an investigator employs to evaluate the reliability of his grid measurements. The important consideration is that he should recognize his responsibility for assessing the reliability of whatever grid indices he uses (cf. Gathercole, Bromley, and Ashcroft, 1970).

CONSTRUCT AND FIGURE INTERACTIONS

Different investigators have applied various forms of 'factor' or cluster analysis to repertory grid data. A high degree of mathematical sophistication is not required in order to grasp the basic logic of this mode of analysis. In general, it is used to answer the question 'on which constructs have the figures been judged in a similar fashion?'. Constructs on which the same figures have been grouped, rated, or ranked in a similar way are found to be closely related to one another and to form a factor (cf. Pervin, 1975). Thus, constructs within the same 'factor' or cluster are highly related to each other, and not to constructs within other clusters.

A method of 'non-parametric factor analysis' which can be applied to all data elicited from an individual subject by means of the original binary grid technique is described by Kelly (1955). Kelly (1969) points out that the main limitation of conventional factor analysis applied to repertory grid data (e.g. Levy, 1956) is that the factors must be based entirely on either constructs or figures, and not both at the same time. His own 'non-parametric' approach not only discloses patterns of relationships between constructs, but also identifies the particular figures with respect to which each pattern is specifically manifested. Thus, its chief advantage is that it relates both constructs and figures to the same basic factors, taking into account the interaction between them. Thus it fulfils Hope's (1969) requirement that a 'complete analysis' of any repertory grid matrix should reveal 'a reciprocity between variables (constructs) and entities (figures)' (p. 1069), i.e. the structure of construct-figure interactions should be clearly indicated.

In Kelly's (1955) original technique, each row in the grid is viewed as giving the co-ordinates of a point in an n-dimensional hyperspace, where n is the number of figures (columns). The analysis is essentially a 'hyper-space vector analysis' (Kelly, 1969) in which the hypothetical row which gives the position of the first 'factor' point locates the centre of the most concentrated group of points within the system as a whole. A fiducial level of statistical significance (e.g. $p < .05$) can be used to specify how far from the hypothetical factor point that a point described by any given row (construct) on the grid can lie and still be considered within the cluster whose centre is defined by the factor point itself (J. V. Kelly, 1964). Jaspars (1963) found that this first factor point is usually a fairly good approximation of the 'first centroid factor', that is, that point which best describes the position of all points which locate constructs actually represented by rows in the original grid.

The content of the first factor extracted from the repertory grid protocols of individual subjects by means of Kelly's method of non-parametric factor analysis seems to be quite consistent. For example, Pedersen (1958) reports an average test-retest correlation of 0.83 for the loadings of specific constructs on the first factor for a sample of thirty-eight subjects retested after a two-week interval. On the other hand, the 'explanatory power' of this factor appears to be less reliable. The explanatory power of a factor is defined by Kelly (1955) as the sum total of all matches between the hypothetical row which locates the factor point itself and all rows (constructs) which load 'significantly' on that factor. Pedersen (1958) found a two-week test-retest correlation of 0.48 (36 df, $p < .01$) for the explanatory power of the first factor.

More recently, Ryle (1975) hypothesizes that those constructs which account for a relatively high percentage of the total variation in a grid will prove more resistant to change over time than will those constructs which account for relatively little overall variance. To test this hypothesis, Ryle administered a repertory grid test to nineteen British adults on two occasions between one year and twenty months apart. The two grids completed by each subject were first compared in terms of element consistency, that is, the extent to which the same figures were rated in the same way on the same constructs in both grids. This analysis permitted the identification of the three most stable and the three least stable constructs out of a total of sixteen. These two sets of constructs were then compared with respect to the percentage of the total variation in the first grid for which they had accounted. It was found that for fourteen of nineteen subjects the 'stable' constructs accounted for a greater proportion of the variation than the 'unstable' ones, which is consistent with Ryle's hypothesis.

Ryle's results suggest that constructs which have relatively high loadings on Kelly's first factor point may be more stable over time with respect to how specific figures are rated on them than those constructs with relatively low loadings on the first factor point. We noted in the previous section that the way in which particular elements are rated in terms of a set of constructs can vary while the pattern of relationship between those constructs remains the same (cf. Slater, 1972). Thus, a lower degree of 'element consistency' in terms of those constructs which have relatively small loadings on the first factor might account for the fact that, while the specific 'content' of this factor in terms of construct relationships is fairly high, its 'explanatory power' is considerably lower.

Bonarius (1965) points out that the explanatory power of the first factor typically accounts for more than half of the total variation in the grid; whereas factors other than the first are derived from a much smaller portion of the grid, and consequently, 'represent samples which are themselves inconsistent because of the small number of rows contained' (p. 10). It is also the case that once the first factor has been extracted, subsequent factors, by definition, must be based on constructs which account for progressively less of the total variation in the matrix as a whole, and therefore, according to Ryle's hypothesis, should be less consistent in their structure over time. Thus, it is not surprising that the total number of factors extracted from a grid is not a consistent index of its structure ($r = 0.19$; Pedersen, 1958).

The results of Kelly's non-parametric factor analysis are not limited to the projection of constructs (rows) on to 'horizontal' factors and/or the projection of figures (columns) on to 'vertical' factors. Adams-Webber (1968) developed a method of also analysing the interaction between constructs and figures within the context of the factors derived by Kelly's method. All constructs (rows) which are significantly related to a given factor point can be 'mapped' on a blank, binary grid form and scanned with the hypothetical row which gives the location of the factor point itself. Every inconsistency between this hypothetical row and the row representing any specific construct can be located with respect to a particular figure (column). Thus, we can enumerate all the 'inconsistencies' falling within the extension of each figure with respect to the structure of any factor. In most grids elicited from people, in constrast to computer simulations (cf. Bavelas, Chan, and Guthrie, 1976; Benjafield and Green, 1978), inconsistencies with respect to a given factor pattern tend not to be evenly distributed across the figures, but rather they tend to pile up disproportionately in the columns representing a few figures.

An 'ambiguity ratio' can be derived for any figure in terms of any factor simply by dividing the sum of all the inconsistencies associated with that figure within the context of the factor pattern by the sum of all the corresponding consistencies. Thus, an ambiguity ratio of one would indicate that the figure is perfectly equivocal with respect to the axis of reference represented by the factor point. Although ambiguity ratios greater than one are logically possible, we have not actually observed any in grids elicited from live subjects. Not surprisingly, figures which have relatively large ambiguity ratios in terms of the first factor point extracted from a grid tend to have relatively low ambiguity ratios with respect to one of the subsequent factors (cf. Bannister and Mair, 1968, p. 211). Thus it is easily determined for most of the figures in the grid which factor best explains the way in which the subject makes sense of their behaviour in terms of some 'consistent theme'.

An experiment by Adams-Webber (1970c) demonstrated that the arbitrary segregation of construct relations ('structure') and figure relations ('content') in the analysis of repertory grid data is unwarranted in the light of the fact that there tend to be relatively high correlations between most 'horizontal' and 'vertical' indices derived from the same grids. For example, the average match between rows (reflected) was found to correlate 0.99 with the average match between columns (reflected). These correlations reveal that there is considerable interaction between figures and constructs in repertory grid data. This conclusion also receives direct support from the experiments of Kapp (1970) and Bavelas *et al.* (1976, p. 34), who found that 'scoring systems which differed only in whether they were vertically or horizontally applied correlated highly, especially when the grid was disproportionately full of incidents or voids'. The phenomenon of 'lopsidedness' in the distribution of grid data alluded to here is a chronic problem in the analysis of repertory grid data, which will be discussed further in Chapter 7.

As an alternative to Kelly's original non-parametric factor analysis, Slater

(1964, 1965, 1967, 1972) has applied principal component analysis to repertory grid data. In his approach, the entire grid matrix is first 'centered for constructs' by expressing all entries in terms of their deviations from their respective row (construct) means. Then, the original grid matrix is replaced by a two-dimensional table of deviation scores (D) in which there is still a row for every construct and a column for every figure. Differences between the construct variances can be eliminated by normalizing each row, that is, each deviation score is divided by the square root of its respective row sum of squares. Finally, the total sum of squared deviations around the construct means is broken down into separate amounts due to variation in orthogonal axes (components) from largest to smallest. These components can be viewed as a set of hypothetical reference axes to which both constructs and figures can be related directly.

Each component is defined completely by a *latent root*, a *construct vector* and an *element vector*. The latent root gives the portion of the total sum of squares attributable to the component. Thus, the sum of the latent roots of all the components extracted from the matrix will equal the total variation of scores around the construct means. The construct vector consists of a set of loadings, one for each construct, which gives the amount which the component contributes to the total sum of squares for that particular construct. Similarly, the element vector gives the corresponding loadings for each figure with respect to the same component. Thus, the total sum of squares for each vector is equal to the associated latent root for the same component. An example of a complete principal component analysis carried out on a sample repertory grid is presented by Hope (1966).

Slater (1964) has also developed a 'spherical co-ordinate' model for the geometric representation of constructs and figures in relationship to one another. In general, each construct can be viewed as a line and each figure as a point in a hyperspace which has as many dimensions as there are components with non-zero latent roots. His specific approach to 'mapping' this space is to represent the first three components by a set of orthogonal diameters of a hypersphere (which can be plotted on a geographer's globe): (1) the diameter emerging at 0° longitude, and 0° latitude represents the first component; (2) the North-South polar axis represents the third component; and (3) the second component is represented by the only remaining axis which describes right angles with the other two. As Hope (1969) points out, the space which is being mapped is not primarily a construct space or a figure space, but a 'component space' articulated by construct-figure interactions.

In this model each construct can be represented as a diameter of the hypersphere, the direction of which is defined in terms of the angles which it describes with the three major axes of reference. It can be located in the component space by plotting either of the two points at which it meets the surface of the hypersphere. For example, a construct which is wholly accounted for by the first component would emerge on to the surface at 0°, 0°. Hope (1966) provides a brief outline of the specific method used to derive these polar co-ordinates for each construct on the grid. The general pattern of construct points on the surface of a globe will serve to summarize the dimensional structure of the system as a whole. As Hope (1969) points out, if the central point of each of several clusters of closely related constructs is taken as the end-point of a 'component-diameter', then the orthogonality of the components can be determined by inspection without recourse to rotating the matrix on the basis of arbitrary assumptions.

The space through which constructs pass on their way to the surface is called the 'figure space', that is, each figure can be viewed as a hypothetical point within the interior of the hypersphere. The theoretical line which joins this point to the centre of the sphere, the centre of gravity of all points within the system, has a length which is given by the square root of the variance of the corresponding column in D. This line is more like a 'radius' than a diameter of the hypersphere in that it can only reach the surface at one point. Moreover, since the columns in D do not ordinarily have the same variance, the lines will probably terminate at a variety of distances from the centre rather than all lying on a common surface. Nevertheless, Hope (1966) has shown that the polar co-ordinates of each figure can be calculated just as easily as those of each construct. On the other hand, since they will seldom be found to lie on a common surface, 'a literal mapping of the entity (figure) vectors is impracticable' (Hope, 1969, p. 1072).

Thus, within the context of Slater's model, figures can be viewed as points dispersed in n dimensions around a hypothetical central point. Although the model as a whole is multi-dimensional, the distance between any two figures cannot be other than one-dimensional. Thus, this distance is independent of the dimensionality of the space. The distance (d) between any randomly selected pair of figures can be calculated from the entries in the original repertory grid matrix on the basis of the following formula (Hope, 1969, p. 1075):

$$d = (SS_1 + SS_2 - 2SP)^{\frac{1}{2}}$$

where SS_1 is the sum of squares for Figure 1, SS_2 is the sum of squares for Figure 2, and SP is the sum of their products.

The average distance between the *self* and other figures seems to be highly reliable in repertory grid data. Sperlinger (1976) reports an eight-month, test-retest correlation of 0.95 for this index with a sample of eighteen British adults. Jones (1954), who named this particular measure the *identification score*, found a two-week, test-retest reliability of 0.86 for a large sample of American undergraduates. Pedersen (1958) has shown that the separate components of this composite index are also, for the most part, quite stable. He reports the following two-week, test-retest correlations for the average distance between the *self* and the subject's parents, siblings, and closest associates (Bonarius's, 1968, 'personal others'): *Mother*, 0.82; *Father*, 0.41; *Brother*, 0.71; *Sister*, 0.75; *Spouse*, 0.59; *Ex-Flame*, 0.83; *Pal*, 0.74; *Ex-Pal*, 0.72 (Figures 2 to 9 in Kelly's, 1955, original list of 'role titles'). Pedersen's sample consisted of thirty-eight American undergraduates. In general, the evidence indicates that the 'identification score' is probably the most reliable of any structural index which can be derived from the repertory grid.

Adams-Webber (1970c) found that identification accounted for more than half of the variance in several other indices of repertory grid structure, including the degree of correlation between constructs ($r = 0.74$), the explanatory power of the first construct factor ($r = 0.79$), the number of significant ($p < .05$) correlations between constructs ($r = 0.72$), and the average distance between figures ($r = 0.75$). With 28 df all of the observed correlations are highly significant ($p < .005$). Moreover, the correlation between each of these measures and the identification score is higher than its own test-retest correlation (Adams-Webber, 1970c; Bavelas *et al.*, 1976). In addition, each of these structural measures was found to correlate between 0.40 and 0.51 (28 df) with the extent to which subjects characterized a new acquaintance as similar to themselves on the same set of constructs several weeks following grid testing (Adams-Webber, 1968; 1970c). This evidence is consistent with Lemon and Warren's (1974, p. 119) hypothesis that 'judgments of others automatically involve a kind of self-comparison process'.

Traditionally, there has been far more concern with the question of which particular figures in the grid are construed as similar to the *self—mother, spouse, therapist, ideal-self*—than with the broader, and possibly more important, issue of what proportion of figures in general are allotted to the same categories as the *self* across a given set of constructs, and to what extent do other aspects of cognitive structure relate to this variable. This problem has only recently become a focus of active research in personal construct theory. This work will be examined primarily in Chapter 7.

Slater (1969) argues that neither constructs nor figures are logically prior, that is, constructs can be understood in terms of figures just as readily as figures can be understood in terms of constructs. He submits

What is methodologically important is that the data refer to two sets of entities interacting with one another. Giving one set any precedence over the other is not edifying. If construing is an operation which can only be performed when a set of elements is given, it might just as well be said that the elements are the operators and the constructs are the operands as *vice versa*, for the elements put the constructs into operation. (p. 1290)

To paraphrase Kant (1902) in the language of personal construct theory 'elements without constructions are blind; constructions without elements are empty'. On the other hand, Kelly (1955) himself makes it quite clear that he regarded constructs as logically (although not necessarily chronologically) prior: 'Rather the construct is the basis on which the elements are understood' (p. 109). As we shall see in the next chapter, Kelly's own emphasis upon the logical priority of constructs has led many investigators using his repertory grid technique to focus almost exclusively on relationships between constructs, and often overlook the importance of construct-figure interactions. For instance, Slater (1969, p. 1290) notes that 'they do not examine the relations between the elements or of the elements with the constructs'. This trend is especially evident in research concerned with the development of individual cognitive structures, which is the topic of the next chapter.

3

Conceptual Structures and Their Development

A major focus of research within the framework of personal construct theory has been the formal analysis of conceptual structures and their evolution. Consequently, an implicit model of individual cognitive development has gradually begun to emerge. Some recent attempts to formulate the principles of this model explicitly (Adams-Webber, 1970a; Salmon, 1970; Shotter, 1970) have emphasized the progressive differentiation and hierarchical integration of substructures, and the increasing permeability of superordinate structures to the introduction of novel elements. Pervin (1975, p. 307) summarizes this developmental perspective in the following terms:

According to this view, the normal course of development involves the addition of new and more elaborate concepts, the progressive differentiation of the system into organized subsystems, and increasing integration of subsystems within an overall framework. Thus, there is movement from a global, undifferentiated system into a differentiated, hierarchically arranged, integrated system.

DIFFERENTIATION

This model of the progressive evolution of a personal construct system has, as we noted in Chapter 1, several explicit parallels with the developmental principles of both Piaget and Werner. It was Bieri (1955), however, who first introduced into personal construct theory the notion of assessing the level of development of an individual's 'system of cognitive dimensions for construing behaviour' in terms of its relative degree of differentiation, which he called 'cognitive complexity'. In his initial study he employed Kelly's (1955) 'standard' binary repertory grid procedure to define this concept operationally. Each subject first nominated twelve of his personal associates on the basis of twelve role titles selected from Kelly's (1955) original list of nineteen, and then successively categorized these figures on a set of twelve personal constructs elicited from himself. Bieri compared each construct (row) in the resulting grid matrix with every other to determine the number of matches between them. His specific index of 'cognitive complexity' (differentiation) was derived as follows: (a) whenever two constructs matched perfectly, a score of -2 was assigned; (b) whenever there was only a single discrepancy between a pair of constructs, a score of -1 was assigned, and (c) all other comparisons were scored 0. Bieri then simply calculated the algebraic sum of these scores. The lower this total, the less 'cognitively complex' the subject. Bieri (1955, p. 265) reports a test-retest correlation of 0.78 (32 df) when this test was administered at the beginning and end of the same session. Bavelas *et al.* (1976) found a test-retest correlation of 0.67 (81 df) over intervals which averaged several weeks.

Thus, in general, subjects who tend to sort figures in an identical or near-identical way on several constructs are designated as 'cognitively simple' (undifferentiated); whereas those subjects who tend to sort figures differently on every construct are designated as 'cognitively complex' (differentiated) by Bieri's method of measuring individual differences in cognitive structure. As Leitner, Landfield, and Barr (1976) point out, this procedure assumes that when two or more constructs are applied to the same elements in an identical way, they can be considered 'functionally equivalent'. Kelly (1969, p. 108) asserts that 'there is an important theorem here to the effect that two constructs which produce an infinite series of identical operations are themselves identical'. It would seem to follow that the greater the degree of functional similarity among an individual's personal constructs, the less differentiated is his construct system as an operational whole. Bieri (1955, p. 263) reasons that 'inasmuch as constructs represent differential perceptions or discriminations of the environment, it would be expected that the greater the degree of differentiation among constructs, the greater will be the predictive power of the individual'.

He hypothesized specifically that his own index of differentiation ('cognitive complexity') would correlate positively with accuracy in predicting the behaviour of the other persons. Thus, he compared scores on his measure of cognitive complexity with the accuracy of subjects in predicting the social questionnaire responses of two acquaintances. Cognitive complexity scores were found to correlate significantly ($r = 0.35$; 32 df, $p < .05$) with the accurate prediction of differences between the subject's own responses on the questionnaire and those of the 'targets'; however, they did not relate significantly ($r = 0.02$) to the accurate prediction of similar responses. In addition, cognitively simple subjects predicted significantly more inaccurate similarities ('assimilative projection') between their own responses and those of others than did cognitively complex subjects, a finding which was replicated by Adams-Webber (1968).

In a subsequent study, based on Bieri's index of differentiation, Leventhal (1957) found that 'cognitively complex' subjects not only predicted fewer similarities between themselves and others (both accurate and inaccurate ones), but they also differentiated more among the persons whose responses they attempted to predict than did 'cognitively simple' subjects. Bieri (1955) also reports a significant correlation between his measure of 'cognitive complexity' and overall predictive accuracy ($r = 0.29$; 32 df, $p < .05$), but no significant relationship has been found in further studies (Honess, 1976; Leventhal, 1957;

Meaders, 1957; Morse, 1965; Sechrest and Jackson, 1961).

In reviewing the research based on Bieri's (1955) original operational definition of 'cognitive complexity' (differentiation), Crockett (1965, p. 64) concludes that it has been shown that 'subjects high in complexity, compared with lows, (a) distinguish more clearly between other individuals in the impressions they form of them, and (b) assume that others are less similar to themselves'. Nevertheless, Bieri's (1955) general hypothesis that the degree of functional differentiation between an individual's personal constructs relates to accuracy in predicting the behaviour of others has received very little direct experimental support. It is also not clear that this specific hypothesis logically follows from the principles of personal construct theory. From the standpoint of Kelly's model of interpersonal relations as defined by his sociality, commonality, and individuality corollaries the basic issue in 'person perception' is not whether one individual can predict the responses of another person in terms of any set of dimensions arbitrarily selected by the experimenter, as in Bieri's original study. Rather, the essential question from Kelly's point of view is whether he can identify the other's personal axes of reference as a basis for effective communication and mutual understanding.

More precisely, Kelly's (1970) sociality corollary specifically asserts that 'to the extent that one person construes the construction processes of another, he may play a role in a social process involving the other', where the term *role* is defined as a 'course of activity which is played out in the light of one or more other persons' construct systems'. It follows that individual social development involves the acquisition of increasing skill in (a) inferring the personal constructs of other in social situations; and, by implication, (b) in discriminating between persons on the basis of individual differences with respect to the form and content of their personal construct systems. Focusing on those subsystems of personal constructs which each individual customarily employs to interpret and anticipate his interpersonal experience, the ability to differentiate between a variety of unique personalities can be expected to develop as skill in inferring the personal constructs of other gradually increases.

In testing this hypothesis, Adams-Webber (1969) adopted Bieri's general approach to the measurement of individual differences in cognitive differentiation. The specific index used in this study was the average match between rows (reflected) in Kelly's (1955) 'standard' binary form of repertory grid test. This score was found to correlate 0.99 with the average match between figures (columns), also reflected. As we shall see in the next chapter, this measure of differentiation is a close structural analogue of Bannister's (1960) *intensity score* (Radley, 1974, discusses the relationship between these two indices). Adams-Webber (1969) found that the degree of differentiation in the repertory grid test related significantly to accuracy in identifying the previously elicited personal constructs of a new acquaintance following a brief conversation with him/her.

Honess (1976) suggests that the relationship observed between differentiation in the grid and accuracy in inferring the constructs of another person in Adams-Webber's (1969) experiment may be a spurious one. He points out that the specific task performed by subjects was to discriminate between the 'target's' own previously elicited personal constructs and an equal number of 'conventional' constructs supplied by the experimenter. Honess contends specifically that (p. 25) 'if high complex Js [judges] do seek diversity, then they would choose the more idiosyncratic personal constructs. In contrast, if low complex Js do prefer recurring uniformity, they will choose the 'conventional' constructs'. This hypothesis of Honess' would provide a plausible alternative explanation of Adams-Webber's (1969) results if it could be assumed that the personal constructs elicited from the 'targets' exhibited more 'diversity' than the common pool of supplied constructs. The latter, however, had been selected from a large set of constructs elicited from peers of the subjects and targets, and therefore are likely to have exhibited at least as much diversity as the constructs elicited from any one target.

Moreover, Honess' hypothesis cannot account for the results of a related experiment (Adams-Webber et al., 1972) in which differentiation scores related significantly to accuracy in discriminating between the previously elicited personal constructs of two new acquaintances following a short interaction with both of them. Whereas some of the subjects in the first experiment (Adams-Webber, 1969) could possibly have detected differences between the 'target's' constructs and the 'conventional' ones irrespective of whatever information they obtained during the interaction with the 'target' himself, this alternative is effectively ruled out by the design of the second experiment since all of the constructs used were elicited from the 'targets' themselves.

Adams-Webber et al. (1972) submit that the results of both of these experiments are consistent in showing that there is a relationship between the degree of differentiation of an individual's personal construct system and his skill in inferring the personal constructs of others from their behaviour. On the basis of this evidence, they hypothesize that 'sociality', or the ability to 'construe the construction processes of others', may play an important role in determining the extent to which an individual differentiates among persons in conceptually structuring his social environment. There are obviously many other attributes of people, apart from the particular constructs that they typically use, which can provide useful cues for distinguishing between them in forming impressions of their individual personalities. Nonetheless, a person who customarily notices differences between people in the ways in which they construe behaviour—his, their own, that of others—can make a wide range of distinctions between his acquaintances on this basis in interpreting his own interpersonal experiences.

Adams-Webber (1969) argues that the more differentiated ('cognitively complex') the structure of an individual's personal construct system, the more readily he may grasp the diverse points of view of the persons whom he encounters by virtue of his having potentially available within the context of his system a greater number of alternative lines of inference which he may pursue in interpreting their behaviour. Adams-Webber (1970a, p. 39) hypothesizes further that 'a person who can employ more than one set of related constructs in interpreting the same social situation is in a better position to see it in terms of two or more different points of view'. This hypothesis receives support from a recent study by Olson and Partington (1977) in which they compared Adams-Webber's index of differentiation from the 'standard' binary form repertory grid—the average match between rows—with the Role-Taking Task (Feffer, 1959).

The Role-Taking Task (RTT) requires the subject to make up a story for an ambiguous scene, and then retell his original story from the viewpoints of each of the three characters in the scene. The subject's performance on this task is evaluated in terms of four basic categories (Feffer and Suchotliff, 1966): (a) *simple refocusing* is cognitively the most primitive category, characterized by isolation between successive versions of the story; (b) *character elaboration* involves refocusing upon a particular character from more than one point of view; (c) *perspective elaboration* requires that successive descriptions of a given personage differ appropriately from role to role in that the description of each personage in his own role should have an 'inner' orientation as contrasted to an external description of him from a viewpoint other than his own; and (d) *change of perspective* occurs when the descriptions of at least two characters meet the requirements of 'perspective elaboration' and, in addition, the internal orientation of one is reflected in the external orientation of the other, and *vice versa*. There are different levels within each of these categories, yielding a total of twenty levels to which each RTT performance can be assigned.

Olson and Partington found a highly significant correlation between the differentiation scores derived from the repertory grids of twenty-four subjects (eleven women and thirteen men) and their total RTT scores ($r = 0.52$; $p < .05$; two-tailed test). They interpret this finding as reflecting a basic parallel between personal construct theory and Piaget's (1960) equilibration model of interpersonal cognitive development, as elaborated by Feffer (1970). The latter implies that mature social interaction requires the ability to reconcile simultaneously the perspectives of oneself and others. Olson and Partington (p. 13) suggest that 'the personal construct and equilibration models appear similar in that both conceptualize social effectiveness in terms of seeing the interpersonal event as another sees it'. In this context Adams-Webber's (1969) measure of differentiation was 'taken to reflect his (S's) ability to infer another's constructs' (Olson and Partington, p. 14). They conclude on the basis of the relationship between this index and RTT scores that 'an individual's ability to reconcile simultaneous different perspectives in an interaction is directly related to the complexity of organization of the constructs by which he structures his world' (p. 14). A recent finding by Craig and Duck (1977) is also consistent with this hypothesis. They report that when forty subjects chose trait words to describe a list of public figures, 'cognitively complex' (differentiated) subjects were more accepting than were 'cognitively simple' subjects of strangers who chose different dimensions.

An alternative approach to assessing the level of differentiation of an individual's construct system has been developed by Crockett (1965). He operationally defines the degree of differentiation in terms of the number of constructs which it contains. In his *Role Category Questionnaire* subjects nominate eight of their personal acquaintances on the basis of a list of brief role descriptions (e.g. 'an older man whom you dislike'). Four of these figures are older than the subject and four are his peers; four are liked and four disliked; four male and four female. The subject is instructed to 'describe each individual in writing as fully as you can within a three-minute time limit'. Judges then determine for each subject the total number of interpersonal constructs which he used across all eight characterizations. Adams-Webber and Benjafield (1976) found an inter-scorer correlation of 0.87 between two judges scoring the protocols of ten female and ten male subjects. Crockett (1965) reports a four-month, test-retest reliability of 0.95 for scores on this test. Thus, Crockett's measure of differentiation seems more reliable than both Bieri's (1955) index from the 'standard', binary form, repertory grid and Adams-Webber's (1969) measure (cf. Bavelas *et al*, 1976).

Following Werner (1957), Crockett assumes that cognitive differentiation increases as an individual gains experience with different aspects of his environment. Thus, he hypothesizes that the number of interpersonal constructs employed by an individual will depend primarily on the amount of social experience he has acquired in interacting with particular persons. It follows, for instance, that he will use more constructs to characterize people who are his own closest associates than those who are less familiar to him. In direct support of this hypothesis, Crockett and his students (cited in Crockett, 1965) have found that late adolescent subjects tend to use more constructs to describe their peers, persons of the same sex, and people whom they like than to describe older persons, those of the opposite sex, and disliked people. These three factors seem to interact so that subjects were found to produce their most differentiated descriptions when they characterized same-sex peers whom they liked and their least differentiated descriptions when they characterized older persons of the opposite sex whom they disliked. Presumably, most people spend far more time interacting with the former type of acquaintance than with the latter.

Research based on Bieri's repertory grid measure of differentiation, however, indicates that subjects discriminate more among 'negative' figures (real or fictional)—for example 'the person with whom you feel least comfortable', 'a disliked character in a play'—than among 'positive' ones—for example 'your best friend of the same sex', 'the protagonist of your favourite novel'. Miller and Bieri (1965) attempt to explain this finding, which is clearly inconsistent with Crockett's 'familiarity' hypothesis, in terms of their own 'vigilance' hypothesis, which implies that an individual tends to be more discriminating in construing negative, socially distant figures in his environment so as to isolate potentially threatening persons and keep an eye on them. Benjafield and Green (1978; see Chapter 7) suggest that such figures will constitute approximately 38 per cent of one's acquaintances. Irwin, Tripodi, and Bieri (1967) also report that subjects differentiate more between negative figures than positive ones.

This basic discrepancy between Crockett's and Bieri's interpretation of 'cognitive complexity' (differentiation) may be due, at least in part, to the fact that they employ different operational definitions of this variable. For instance, Seaman and Koenig (1974, p. 376) point out that 'with the Crockett procedure, it is possible for a subject to generate many interpersonal constructs in a free response exercise, and still use these constructs to construe different stimulus objects similarily'. Leitner *et al.* (1976) suggest that Crockett's test is 'contaminated by artifacts such as verbal fluency and writing speed'. Although this criticism seems plausible on the face of it, it is weakened by the fact that scores on Crockett's test do not correlate significantly with IQ (Crockett, 1965). In addition, they have been shown to correlate positively with a range of theoretically relevant variables, including (a) lack of susceptibility to recency effects in impression formation (Mayo and Crockett, 1964); (b) resolution of inconsistencies in information about the same person (Nidorff and Crockett, 1965); (c) ease in the assimilation of unbalanced social structures (Delia and Crockett, 1973; Press, Crockett, and Rosenkrantz, 1969); and (d) frequency of interaction with the people described (Zalot and Adams-Webber, 1977). In short, there is now considerable evidence in support of the construct validity of Crockett's measure of cognitive differentiation.

Bieri, Atkins, Briar, Leaman, Miller, and Tripodi (1966) have developed a modified form of repertory grid test to measure 'cognitive complexity'. In this test subjects rate ten of their personal associates on ten, 6-point scales (from − 3 to + 3 with no 0 point). These scales are based on a standard list of bi-polar constructs (e.g. *calm-excitable*) supplied to subjects rather than elicited from each of them individually as in Bieri's (1955) original test. An overall 'cognitive complexity' score is obtained by comparing each set of ratings with every other and assigning one point for every case in which the same figure is given an identical rating on two different constructs. Since there are forty-five possible comparisons between constructs and the same ten figures are rated on each construct, the total score can vary between 0 and 450. The higher this total, the less differentiated (more 'cognitively simple') the structure of the subject's 'system of cognitive dimensions for construing behaviour.' Kapp (1970) reports a one-week, test-retest reliability of 0.85 (28 df) for this score. It is not clear how this index relates to differentiation in the 'standard' repertory grid test (Kelly, 1955).

This instrument, unlike those used by Adams-Webber (1969) and Crockett (1965), relies on providing the same list of constructs to every subject. In order to assess the effects of this modification on complexity scores, Tripodi and Bieri (1963) asked subjects to rate a list of their acquaintances on five elicited constructs and five supplied ones. They found no significant difference between these two sets of constructs in terms of the distribution of 'cognitive complexity' scores. Moreover, the rank-order correlation between scores based on elicited constructs and those based on provided ones was 0.50 ($p < .05$). Tripodi and Bieri conclude that these results 'indicate that for research purposes provided constructs are comparable to own constructs in measuring cognitive complexity' (p. 26). Leitner *et al.* (1976) question this inference. They contend that 'with seventy-five percent of the variance unaccounted for, a more accurate interpretation of the data would be that there is a significant relationship between the two measures, but they are not interchangeable' (p. 12). Other studies which have some bearing on this problem are reviewed by Adams-Webber (1970b), and Metcalfe (1974).

Crockett (1965, p. 51) suggests that 'we assume these two variables—the number of constructs (Crockett's index) and the extent to which constructs differentiate among the subject's associates (Bieri's index)—are highly correlated'. Nonetheless, in the few studies in which scores on Crockett's test have been directly compared with those from Bieri *et al.*'s (1966) test, no significant relationship has been found (Irwin *et al.*, 1967; Miller, 1969; Epting and Wilkins, 1974). On the other hand, there could be some indirect connection between these two aspects of cognitive differentiation in terms of the relation of each of them to *identification*. We saw in the last chapter that identification—the extent to which the *self* and others are characterized as similar—correlates highly with several repertory-grid-based measure of 'cognitive complexity'. Not only does identification account for more than 50 per cent of the variation in many of these measures, but also the correlation between identification and several of these other indices is higher than the test-retest reliability of the latter (cf. Adams-Webber, 1970c; Bavelas *et al.*, 1976).

Crockett (1965, p. 64) puts forward the hypothesis that 'subjects high in complexity, compared with lows, assume that others are less similar to themselves'. This implies that subjects who are relatively 'cognitively complex', in the sense that they employ a large repertory of interpersonal constructs, are more sensitive to differences between themselves and others than are subjects who use fewer interpersonal constructs. Thus, Crockett's hypothesis specifically predicts a negative relationship between scores on his *Role Category Questionnaire* and identification scores from Kelly's (1955) 'standard' repertory grid test. However, Adams-Webber and Benjafield (1976) found that the relationship between these two indices is both significant and negative only when figures with negative valences (e.g. 'the coldest person you know') are categorized in terms of elicited constructs. Since Crockett's measure is itself based entirely on elicited constructs, it is not surprising that it relates more closely to the distribution of interpersonal judgements involving elicited constructs than to those involving supplied ones. On the other hand, this factor does not account for why Crockett's hypothesis seems to hold only when *negative figures* are judged on the basis of elicited constructs.

Perhaps relatively 'cognitively complex' subjects tend to elaborate the specific implications of negative information in terms of their own personal constructs more extensively than do less 'cognitively complex' subjects. This hypothesis, which is admittedly *ad hoc,* would explain the finding that subjects with relatively high scores on Crockett's test make a greater number of distinctions between themselves and negative figures on elicited constructs than do subjects with relatively low scores on this test. This hypothesis is also consistent with the 'vigilance hypothesis' (Miller and Bieri, 1965; Irwin *et al.*, 1967), which implies that 'complex' modes of construing the behaviour of others may derive from a form of perceptual vigilance in which 'negative persons' are differentiated more than positive ones (see Chapter 7).

Nevertheless, the evidence does not support Crockett's (1965) assumption that his own index of the relative number of constructs employed by a subject to interpret his interpersonal experience relates directly to the extent to which he generally differentiates among his associates on various forms of repertory grid test. This fact seems especially problematic when we consider that both types of measure are presumed to reflect the same aspect of conceptual structure, that is, its degree of differentiation. There is, however, some evidence that Bieri's measure and related repertory grid indices may also tap 'integration', a second important aspect of conceptual organization.

INTEGRATION

Bannister and co-workers (Bannister, 1960; 1962b; Bannister and Fransella, 1966, 1967; Bannister and Salmon, 1966; Bannister, Fransella, and Agnew, 1971; Bannister, Adams-Webber, Penn and Radley, 1975) have demonstrated that schizophrenic patients who are judged to be clinically thought-disordered exhibit a high degree of statistical independence between constructs in both binary and rank-order forms of repertory grid test. However, their personal judgements seem more random than 'cognitively complex' in organization in that they are highly unstable and inconsistent from one occasion to another. Bannister and Fransella (1966) interpret this finding as evidence that thought-disordered schizophrenics are limited to an overly loose system of constructs for interpreting and predicting the behaviour of persons—in more conventional terms, their ideas about people are poorly related to one another.

Bieri's (1955, 1966) and Adams-Webber's (1969) indices of differentiation between constructs in the repertory grid are more or less structural analogues of Bannister's own measure of clinical thought disorder. More specifically, Bannister's *intensity* score, which is based on the degree of statistical association between constructs in the repertory grid and is interperted as an index of 'integration', is quite similar to Bieri's (1955) measure of functional similarity between constructs, which he terms 'cognitive simplicity'. Langley (1971, p. 11) submits that 'it is unknowable whether cognitive complexity, for example, reflects high differentiation, as Bieri suggests, and/or low integration, as implied by research based on Kelly's personal construct theory'. As Radley (1974, p. 325) points out, 'it seems unlikely that the degree of functional independence of constructs is a sufficiently comprehensive measure to encompass such disparate modes of thinking'. Thus, the fact that scores on Crockett's *Role Category Questionnaire* do not correlate significantly with measures of statistical independence between constructs in various forms of repertory grid test could be viewed as evidence of its discriminant validity as a measure of differentiation rather than as indicating a lack of convergent validity.

A further problem with repertory-grid-based measures of differentiation is that they do not exhibit 'developmental' changes in the expected direction. For example, Barratt (1977a) hypothesized that the average correlation between constructs in a repertory grid test in which children rated a list of their peers on elicited constructs would decrease (indicating increased differentiation) between ages eight and fourteen. This would have provided evidence of a 'progressive organizational differentiation of the peer construct system' as children grow older and acquire more social experience. Barratt made similar predictions for the number of significant correlations between constructs, and the explanatory power of the first three components extracted by Slater's (1969) principal component analysis (described in Chapter 2). Although he found no significant differences between groups of children aged eight, ten, twelve, and fourteen in terms of any one of these indices, all of the observed trends were in the opposite direction to that expected, i.e. there was a higher degree of construct relationship in the grids of older children. Barratt (pp. 12–13) suggests that 'the possibility that grid technique itself is the problem and is inappropriate for the developmental investigation of structural issues must be seriously considered'. (cf. Hayden, Nashby, and Davids, 1977; discussed in Chapter 8.)

On the other hand, if we consider the alternative possibility that correlations between constructs primarily reflect the degree of integration of conceptual structures, rather than lack of differentiation, then the trends reported by Barratt are consistent with the results of an earlier study. Applebee (1975) administered a repertory grid test to four groups of children aged six, nine, thirteen, and seventeen. First, he elicited the titles of eight stories from each child using a set of categories such as 'moving', 'disliked', 'favourite', 'difficult', etc. Then, every child rated each story on nineteen supplied constructs and one elicited one. Applebee calculated the correlation between all possible pairs of constructs, and found that both the proportion of significant ($p < .05$) construct relationships and the explanatory power of the first component in the pooled grid matrix for each age group showed significant increases across the whole age range from six to seventeen. The largest jump occurred between the ages nine and thirteen. Applebee interprets these results as evidence of a rise with age in the degree of social consensus for patterns of relationships between constructs. As in an earlier study by Bannister (1962a), there was far more agreement about construct relationships than about the rating of particular elements on each construct. In short, as Applebee notes (p. 478), 'there is more agreement about the structure of the construct system than about its implications'.

The outcome of a short-term 'longitudinal' study (Adams-Webber and Mirc, 1976a, b, c) also suggests that the degree of integration of a construct system is reflected by the extent to which constructs are related in use. Following Lemon (1975, see Chapter 2), it was assumed that experience in a particular sphere of activity will lead to increases in the degree of interrelationship between constructs which are specifically relevant to that domain. A repertory grid test was used to monitor the development of student teachers' conceptions of their future professional roles during their first six weeks of classroom experience. They completed a series of 'experimental grids' in which various role figures important in the school (e.g. *teacher, pupil, principal*) were successively rank-ordered on a set of supplied constructs directly relevant to their classroom activities (e.g. instruction, counselling, testing, etc.); and a series of 'control grids' in which the same figures were ranked-ordered on interpersonal constructs elicited from themselves. As predicted there were significant increases in the level of correlation between constructs in the experimental grids, but not in the control grids, during six weeks of practice teaching. Prior to any teaching experience, the student teachers exhibited significantly less relationship between constructs in the experimental grids than did a sample of regular classroom teachers; however, after only six weeks of practice teaching, there was no difference between the students and experienced teachers. Some further implications of this study will be considered in Chapter 8.

Additional evidence that the correlations between constructs in repertory grid data may reflect integration of cognitive structures, and not merely lack of differentiation, is provided in a recent experiment by Bodden and James (1976). They developed a 'Cognitive Differentiation Grid' in which twelve occupational titles (e.g. *physician*) are rated on 6-point, Likert-type scales based on twelve 'vocationally relevant', bi-polar constructs (e.g. *high status-low status*). This test was administered on two occasions both to an experimental group of sixteen male and twelve female undergraduates and to a control group of thirteen male and eleven female undergraduates. The subjects in the experimental group were given 'occupational information' which was 'designed specifically to contain data relevant to the 12 construct dimensions on the grid' (p. 281). The control group received no relevant information during the interval between the two administrations of the test. Bodden and James explain the rationale of their grid test in the following terms: 'if the subject uses the constructs in the same way with different occupations, then his constructs have considerable overlap and receive a high score, reflecting low differentiation' (p. 280).

They found that the subjects who received the information relevant to the occupations being judged became significantly lower in differentiation between constructs. This finding is interpreted as indicating that 'occupational information-giving results in a reduction of cognitive complexity or differentiation in the vocational realm' (p. 281). An alternative explanation of their results might be that supplying information about occupations to people leads to an increase in the level of relationship (integration) between constructs which are relevant to vocational choice, just as classroom experience produces increases in the level of relationship between constructs used by student teachers to structure their roles in the school and studying geography in English leads to increases in the degree of relationship between English constructs used by Tanzanians to characterize foreign nations (Adams-Webber and Mirc, 1976a, b, c; Lemon, 1975; see Chapter 2). Cochran (1978) has shown also that university students exhibit more intercorrelation between constructs when they rate future career possibilities on elicited constructs than when they rate them on supplied constructs.

In addition, one effect of 'sensitivity training' seems to be an increase in the level of relationship (integration?) between the participants' interpersonal constructs. For instance, Baldwin (1972) used Bieri's (1966) grid test of cognitive complexity to assess the outcome of a five-day training group experience for twenty-five subjects. The grid test was administered on the first day (pre-test) and late on the last day (post-test). Baldwin found that the 'changes were in the direction of greater cognitive simplicity' (p. 935). Parallel results were obtained by Benjafield *et al.* (1976), who monitored changes in cognitive structure during a weekend 'basic encounter marathon' group.

The evidence considered above lends fairly strong support to Bannister's (1960, 1962b) general assumption that the degree of statistical association between constructs in repertory grid data primarily reflects the level of integration of subjects' conceptual structures. In a theoretical analysis of the concept of 'cognitive complexity', Zimring (1971) argues that differentiation and integration are separate but equally necessary processes in the evolution of an individual's personal construct system. This is consistent with Kelly's (1955) own view of cognitive development as involving not only functional differentiation of substructures, but also a progressive integration of constructs both within and between these substructures (see Chapter 1, pp. 9–14).

SUBSYSTEM SPECIALIZATION

Langley (1971, p. 10) points out that differentiation serves the specialization of subsystems, whereas integration primarily serves the integrity and unity of the system as a whole. There is also evidence that separate subsystems within the same construct system can differ from one another in terms of their degree of internal organization. For example, Williams (1970) employed a series of repertory grid tests to assess the level of organization of three distinct subsystems—'occupational, social and political'—within the construct system of one university student. He reports that 'a distinct *primary* structure was found encompassing three subsystems—academic, social and political—each subsystem bearing a distinct relationship with each of the others within the primary system' (p. 11). He notes that the academic subsystem exhibited a higher level of organization than the other two, suggesting 'a distinction in the degree of development of different cognitive systems for the individual' (p. 11). Although we cannot base any generalizations on the repertory grid assessment of a single subject, this 'case study' clearly illustrates the principle of subsystem specialization.

Kelly's model of conceptual organization requires that we take into consideration not only relationships between constructs, but also 'superordinate' relationships between separate subsystems of interrelated constructs. For instance, Crockett (1965) proposes that the degree of development of an individual's 'cognitive system with respect to other people', is reflected in both its level of differentiation, operationally defined in terms of the number of constructs, and its degree of hierarchical integration, operationally defined in terms both of the pattern of relationships between constructs within subsystems and of the extent to which subsystems are interrelated by superordinate constructs. Some data supporting Crockett's thesis have been supplied by the work of Makhlouf-Norris, *et al.* (1970), who have developed a method of inferring the 'topographical organization of constructs' from the pattern of correlations in individual repertory grid protocols.

Two major types of conceptual structure have been identified by this topographical technique: 'articulated' and 'non-articulated'. Articulated structures each contain several different clusters of interrelated constructs which are joined by 'linkage' constructs. Makhlouf-Norris *et al.* define a cluster as a set of constructs which are all significantly intercorrelated, and a 'linkage construct' as one which correlates significantly with constructs in two or more different clusters. They found that this kind of conceptual organization is typical of normal adults. The non-articulated structures were found to be more characteristic of patients diagnosed as obsessive-compulsive neurotics. There are two main subtypes of non-articulated structures: 'monolithic' and 'segmented'. The former involves one large primary cluster of interrelated constructs, and perhaps an unrelated secondary cluster, with a few isolated constructs. The latter contains several separate clusters of interrelated constructs with no linkages between these clusters.

The monolithic system, integrated primarily in terms of a single set of construct relationships, is prototypical of Bieri's (1966) notion of 'cognitive simplicity' (or unidimensionality). Regardless of the number of constructs constituting the system, events must be assimilated to one specific pattern of organization. As Schroder *et al.* (1967) point out, it is not the number of dimensions in a system which determines the level of complexity in information processing. Makhlouf-Norris *et al.* did not find any significant differences between normal adults and obsessive-compulsive neurotics in terms of the degree of statistical independence of their constructs *per se* in the repertory grid. However, these two groups did differ significantly with respect to the number of 'linkage constructs'. This suggests that the patients do not differ from normals with respect to the extent to which their constructs are related directly to one another *within* subsystems, but only in terms of the degree to which separate subsystems are interrelated as integral parts of the same overall construct system.

It can be argued that in both articulated and non-articulated systems the information processing which takes place within each subsystem is a direct expression of the relationships between constructs which define the 'logical' structure of that particular subsystem. On the other hand, only in the articulated type of system can each subsystem be viewed as performing a specific function, which is integrated with other functions, within the total structure of the construct system as an operational whole (cf. Adams-Webber, 1970a).

HIERARCHICAL ORGANIZATION

Several studies have adopted a hierarchical approach to assessing the structure of an individual's personal construct system. For instance, Smith and Leach (1972) have developed a method of 'hierarchical analysis' based on a repertory grid format. Each subject first nominates thirteen figures—the *self* plus twelve acquaintances—and then rates them successively on each of thirteen elicited constructs using a 5-point scale graded from -2 to $+2$. The correlation between each row (construct) and every other one is computed, as well as that between each column (figure) and every other. Both of these matrices of correlations are then separately 'mapped' employing Johnson's (1967) procedure for hierarchical cluster analysis to indicate how both constructs and figures group together.

The next step involves locating all pairs of constructs whose correlations are significant ($p < .05$) and collapsing them into a single dimension. Then, all the correlations between columns are recalculated and subjected to a second cluster analysis. The greater the observed change in the groupings of figures between the first and second cluster analysis, the higher a subject's 'cognitive complexity' score. The specific index of the amount of change in the grouping of the figures is based on a non-parametric node count, which is too complicated to describe here. The theoretical rationale of this approach to measuring 'cognitive complexity' derives from Smith and Leach's (1972, p. 564) assumption that 'the fine details of the construct system will be more important for a "complex subject" than for a "simple subject", so that impoverishing the structure will have a more dramatic effect on the relationships between people for the more complex subject'.

Smith and Leach have carried out extensive comparisons between this measure of complexity and Bieri's (1966) index based on the same repertory grid protocols. In their initial sample, the observed correlation between these two scores was positive, but not significant ($r = 0.10$). In their second sample, it was found to be both negative and significant ($r = -0.34$). A third sample of subjects completed a repertory grid test based on twenty-one figures and fourteen constructs, which was administered on two occasions one week apart using the same list of figures. On the first occasion, the observed correlation was $r = -0.10$, and on the second, it was $r = -0.26$. Smith and Leach conclude on the basis of these findings that their own measure of cognitive structure is 'looking at a different aspect of the construct system' than is Bieri's measure (cf. Honess, 1976). They report a one-week, test-retest reliability of $r = 0.76$ for their own index, and one of $r = 0.46$ for Bieri's score, which is considerably lower than the one-week, test-retest correlation of 0.85 which Kapp (1970) reports for Bieri's index.

Smith and Leach also found that subjects with relatively high scores on their own measure of 'cognitive complexity' tend to be classified as 'abstract' on the basis of Harvey's (1966) *This I Believe Test*, which is a widely used measure of the 'integrative complexity' of conceptual structures (cf. Harvey, Hunt, and Schroder, 1961). Scores on Harvey's test were not found to relate significantly to Bieri's (1966) measure of 'cognitive complexity' in Smith and Leach's study, which is consistent with recent findings reported by Epting and Wilkins (1974) and Slane and Barrows (1974). The main advantage of Smith and Leach's procedure for assessing 'hierarchical complexity' seems to be that it does not correlate too closely with Bieri's index of differentiation between constructs based on the same repertory grid data. Although this provides some evidence for discriminant validity with respect to other aspects of grid structure (cf. Adams-Webber, 1970b), we shall not be in a position to evaluate its general validity until we have more information concerning its positive correlates.

A method for assessing the 'hierarchical integration' of an individual's personal construct system, also derived from repertory grid technique, was developed by Hinkle (1965) and elaborated by Fransella (1972) and Crockett and Meisel (1974). In his original validational study (summarized by Bannister and Mair, 1968), Hinkle asked twenty-eight American university students to nominate ten persons whom they knew well, including themselves. Kelly's (1955) 'method of triads' (described in Chapter 2, p. 21)—including the *self* in every triad—was used to elicit ten bi-polar constructs from each subject. Then, every subject was asked to indicate which pole of each of the constructs elicited from himself was 'clearly descriptive of the kind of person he would prefer to be'.

Next, Hinkle employed a 'laddering technique' to elicit a further ten 'superordinate' constructs from each subject. This involved taking one of the original ten constructs elicited from a subject and asking him to explain why he preferred the pole which he had previously chosen for himself; for example, why he preferred being 'outgoing' to being 'reserved'. This usually resulted in the subject's evoking another construct, which was 'superordinate' to the first one, to justify his initial preference; for instance, persons who are 'outgoing' seem to him to be more 'interested in others' (as he himself is) while 'reserved' persons, in his judgement, tend to be 'wrapped-up in themselves'. This procedure was used by Hinkle to help each subject to 'climb up' his supposedly hierarchically structured construct system until ten 'superordinate' constructs had been elicited from him in addition to the original ten (cf. Fransella, 1972).

The next step in Hinkle's procedure was to rank-order all twenty constructs—the ten original 'subordinate constructs' and the ten 'superordinate constructs' elicited by means of laddering technique—on the basis of their 'resistance to change'. He presented the twenty constructs to each subject in all possible pairs, and for each pair the subject was asked to specify which of the two constructs he would prefer to remain the same with respect to, if he had to change in terms of only one of them. All twenty constructs were then rank-ordered from highest to lowest with respect to 'resistance to change' according to the number of times each construct had been designated for no change across its nineteen pairings with other constructs.

Finally, Hinkle constructed a twenty-row by twenty-column 'implication grid' matrix using the same twenty constructs. This involved presenting constructs to the subject one at a time and asking him, if he were to change on that particular construct, from one pole to the other, on which of the other nineteen constructs would a change also be necessary. In this procedure each construct is paired successively with every other one twice, with any one of four possible outcomes:
(1) a change in Construct A implies a change in Construct B, which is recorded as one 'superordinate' implication for A and one 'subordinate' implication for B;
(2) a change in B implies a change in A, which is recorded as a 'superordinate'

implication for B and a 'subordinate' implication for A; (3) a change in either construct implies a change in the other, which is recorded as a 'reciprocal' implication for both constructs; and (4) a change in either construct has no implications in terms of the other, in which case nothing is recorded. The resulting data are entered into a symmetrical grid matrix to facilitate the tabulation of the number of 'superordinate', 'subordinate' and 'reciprocal' implications for each of twenty constructs (see Figure 4).

At this point some further clarification of the rationale of Hinkle's scoring system might be helpful to the reader. If the subject indicates that he thinks that a change in Construct A would necessitate a change in Construct B (case 1 above), then we can infer that A is a necessary condition for B. It follows that B is a sufficient condition for A. Thus, we can assert that (a) if not-A. then not-B; and (b) if B, then A. These two propositions define case 2 of the possible relationships between any two constructs outlined by Adams-Webber (1970a) and listed in Chapter 1 (p. 9) (case 2 is also represented in Figure 1), that is, Construct B defines a subset of the set defined by Construct A. In this sense, Construct B can be considered to be 'subordinate' to Construct A, and Construct A is 'superordinate' to Construct B. Thus, Hinkle quite rightly classifies this particular case as involving a 'superordinate' implication for Construct A and a 'subordinate' one for Construct B. It is important to bear in mind that it is the 'subordinate' construction which implies the 'superordinate', and not the other way around. In Hinkle's 'case 3', each construct is both a sufficient *and* a necessary condition for the other one, and therefore, neither is 'superordinate' in the relationship between them.

Hinkle found that the higher the rank-order of a given construct with respect to its measured 'resistance to change', the greater the number of 'superordinate' implications which it carried. Moreover, the 'superordinate' constructs which were elicited by means of his 'laddering' technique had significantly more 'superordinate' implications than those elicited by Kelly's method of triads, while the latter had significantly more 'subordinate' implications than did the former. Finally, the 'superordinate' constructs were ranked significantly higher than the 'subordinate' ones in terms of resistance to change. Hinkle interprets these results as supporting his hypothesis that 'there will be a higher level of resistance to change on superordinate constructs, because any change at this level will necessarily involve a great number of related changes' (Bannister and Mair, 1968, p. 82). Nevertheless, his findings do not provide unequivocal evidence in favour of this hypothesis because of two methodological problems.

The first of these problems stems from the fact that in Hinkle's 'laddering' procedure, some of the original sample of 'subordinate' constructs (elicited by means of Kelly's method of successive triads) were used as the starting points in 'climbing up' to 'superordinate' constructs by a sequence of inferences which took the form of a series of conditional syllogisms (*sorites*) of the type 'if A, then B; if B, then C . . . etc'. This method of deriving 'superordinate' constructs from a sample of 'subordinate' constructs is definitely biased in favour of the hypothesis that 'superordinate' constructs will have, on average, more 'superordinate' implications than will 'subordinate' ones, and the latter will have more 'subordinate' implications than will the former. This is because each 'super-ordinate' construct will have, by definition, at least one 'superordinate' implication in terms of the particular 'subordinate' construct (and often several intermediary constructs) from which it was derived. Conversely, each 'sub-ordinate' construct will have at least one 'subordinate' implication for every 'superordinate' construct derived from it. The second problem arises from the fact that for most subjects all ten 'superordinate' constructs were derived from only a few of the original sample of 'subordinate' constructs—in the limiting case, only one of them. Therefore, it is not clear that, according to Hinkle's operational definition of 'superordination', all of his 'superordinate' constructs were in fact superordinate to even the majority of his 'subordinate' constructs.

Nevertheless, the construct validity of 'implication grid' procedure does not rest entirely on the results of this one experiment. Crockett and Meisel (1974) employed implication grids to explore the effect of the degree of connectedness among a subject's personal constructs in terms of changes in his impressions of another person. They hypothesized specifically that 'individual differences in the impressions that are formed from a standard set of information should reflect not only differences in the constructs the information elicits directly, but also differences in the pattern of relationships among constructs' (p. 291). More precisely, they predicted that not only the degree of difficulty in inducing change in current impressions, but also the extent of whatever changes take place, will depend on the degree of interconnectedness of the subject's personal constructs. 'These considerations may be summarized formally in the following hypothesis: when subjects' impressions are strongly disconfirmed there should be a direct relationship between the extent to which the impressions change and the degree of connectedness of the subjects' construct systems . . . when impressions are weakly disconfirmed, there should be an inverse relationship between change and degree of connectedness' (p. 291). This hypothesis is generally consistent with Hinkle's (1965) finding that subjects' 'resistance to change' with respect to a particular construction relates to the number of superordinate implications which it carries within their own personal construct systems.

Crockett and Meisel adopted Kelly's (1955) method of successive triads to elicit twenty constructs from each of forty-five American undergaduates (all males), and then employed implication grid technique to determine both the pattern and strength of the interrelationships among these constructs in-dividually for each subject. All subjects were then asked to record their initial impressions of the personality of a hypothetical figure named 'Larry' on the basis of their own constructs, given 'minimal' information about him. They were also asked to make a set of predictions about his behaviour in various situations.

Subjects were assigned randomly to three experimental conditions in which they received bogus 'feedback' on their performances. Subjects in the 'weak disconfirmation' condition were told only that their initial impressions of 'Larry' were relatively inaccurate. Subjects in the 'strong disconfirmation' condition were told that, not only were their initial impressions of 'Larry' relatively inaccurate, but also they were incorrect in their inferences concerning their own most central constructs. Each subject's 'central construct' had been previously identified as that 'which could be reached by the maximum of other constructs in the system'. Finally, subjects in the 'predictive disconfirmation' condition were told that their initial impressions were relatively inaccurate and also their predictions concerning 'Larry's' behaviour in a situation closely related to their most central constructs were incorrect. Every subject, irrespective of what condition he had been assigned to, was given an opportunity to revise both his initial impression of 'Larry' and his predictions about his behaviour following the 'feedback' on his earlier performance.

Crockett and Meisel report that the observed relationship between the degree of connectedness among a subject's personal constructs and impression change under conditions of invalidation was significantly positive ($r = 0.54$) in the 'strong disconfirmation' group and significantly negative ($r = -0.78$) in the 'weak disconfirmation' group. They offer the following explanation for their results:

For a subject whose personal constructs are massively connected, a change in inference along one construct dimension demands a change on many others, especially if the changed construct is a central one. Unless his impressions of other people are to vacillate continuously as he obtains new information about them such a subject must show little or no response to relatively weak disconfirmation of his impressions . . . it is interesting to note that more than one subject in this condition was heard to remark, 'If I change this, I'll have to change practically everything', and then was observed not to change the central construct. Only when their inference on a central construct was directly disconfirmed, did such subjects show much change. (p. 298)

Thus, persons who manifest relatively high levels of interrelationship among their constructs in the implication grid tend to revise their impressions of others more in response to strong disconfirmation than following weak disconfirmation. In contrast, people with relatively low levels of relationship within their construct system as measured by implication grid technique, change fewer of their impressions after strong disconfirmation than after weak disconfirmation. As Crockett and Meisel point out, these findings are consistent with the assumptions of personal construct theory, and they provide support for the validity of implication grid procedure for assessing patterns of relationships between the personal constructs elicited from a subject. Some further aspects of this question will be considered in Chapter 6 in relation to Fransella's (1972) use of implication grids to predict changes in the construct systems and speech of clients undergoing treatment for stuttering.

INTEGRATION VERSUS CONFUSION

We can conceptualize two structural extremes as limiting conditions for the development of each individual's personal construct system. One extreme would be a system so tightly organized that all lines of implication which he might pursue in deriving inferences from the information given must converge upon the most 'central construct' (Crockett and Meisel, 1974) in his system. Such a construct system can be viewed as the ideal prototype of Bieri's (1966) definition of 'cognitive simplicity', that is, lack of functional differentiation between constructs. Makhlouf-Norris *et al.* (1970) have shown that this kind of 'monolithic' conceptual structure is more characteristic of obsessive-compulsive neurotics than of normal adults. In general, the more 'monolithic' the structure of an individual's personal construct system, the fewer the alternatives which are available to him in interpreting a given sequence of events because all his constructions have to 'fit' the constraints of a single fixed pattern of 'logical relations' between constructs.

Thus, it is not surprising that the more highly interrelated all of an individual's personal constructs, the less he is able to reinterpret the same situation from the diverse points of view of several other persons while maintaining continuity between the successive versions, and construe his own behaviour from different perspectives (Olson and Partington, 1977). As Crockett and Meisel (1974) have shown, in such a tightly organized system, even a few minor revisions of his initial impressions of an event may have sweeping implications throughout his system as a whole. Schroder *et al.* (1967) note, 'the more absolute the rules of integration, the greater the generalization of functioning within a certain range, and the more abrupt or compartmentalized the change when it occurs' (p.17).

The opposite extreme would be the total absence of connections between a person's constructs rendering organized thought an impossibility. For instance, Bannister (1963, 1965b) submits that the genesis of clinical thought disorder is characterized by a progressive 'serial invalidation' of a person's inferences about events in the course of which one subsystem of interrelated constructs after another 'loosens' in structure and eventually collapses. Ultimately, the entire personal construct system—'reduced steeply by the loss of possible combinations'—ceases to function effectively as an operational whole. Research on this hypothesis, which is the topic of the next chapter, has shown that a decrease in the level of connections between constructs in the repertory grid is characteristic of patients who have been clinically diagnosed as thought-disordered schizophrenics (e.g. Bannister and Fransella, 1966).

Leitner *et al.* (1976) offer an explanation of how these two structural extremes might relate logically to two fundamentally different ways of construing events. They point out that the theoretical basis for Bieri's (1955) original operational definition of cognitive complexity in terms of the degree of functional differentiation between constructs was derived directly from Kelly's (1955) own distinction between 'propositional' and 'constellatory' constructs. According to this distinction, a propositional construct is one which 'leaves its elements open to constructions in all other respects' (p.155); whereas a constellatory construct 'permits its elements to belong to other realms concurrently, but fixes their membership'. An example of propositional construing is the following statement: 'a roundish mass may be considered, among other things, a ball'. Constellatory constructions are usually of the following kind: 'anything which is a ball must also be something which will bounce'.

An early attempt to operationalize Kelly's distinction between propositional and constellatory constructions was undertaken by Levy (1956), whose research can be viewed as a forerunner of the experiment of Crockett and Meisel (1974) discussed in the last section. Levy elicited a sample of constructs from subjects and used grid technique to determine the relationships between these constructs for each subject individually. He then conducted a conventional factor analysis of the resulting matrix of relationships for every subject. By means of this analysis he was able to isolate five 'constellatory' constructs, operationally defined as constructs which load on a general factor, and five 'propositional' constructs, none of which, by definition, loaded on a general factor.

Subjects were then given information about two hypothetical persons and asked to form impressions of their personalities. They were subsequently informed that their inferences about one of these figures were below average in terms of their accuracy and above average for the other one. They were then given an opportunity to revise any of their original impressions. Levy found that subjects changed their impressions more in terms of constellatory constructs than in terms of propositional constructs when they believed that their intitial impressions had been relatively inaccurate. They made very few changes on either kind of construct when they thought that they had been fairly accurate in their first impressions.

Leitner *et al.* argue that 'in theory, an individual who uses propositional constructs will tend to construe events in a more complex manner than an individual who uses constellatory constructs, due to his greater freedom to place alternative constructions on events.' (p. 4). As Schroder *et al.* (1967) point out, given flexible combinatory rules, the extent to which one event can be discriminated from another will increase as the number of dimensions increases. For example, in the 'articulated' construct system illustrated by the 'maps' of Makhlouf-Norris *et al.* (1970), there are several different subsystems, each of which can be viewed as providing one of several alternative lines of 'constellatory' inferences which can be applied to the same events. As we saw in Chapter 1, this form of conceptual organization is implied by Kelly's (1970) 'fragmentation' corollary, which asserts that 'a person may successively employ a variety of construction systems which are inferentially incompatible with each other'. We noted also that this kind of functional differentiation among independently organized subsystems can increase the level of overall efficiency in information processing (cf. Adams-Webber, 1970a).

On the other hand, as we shall see in the next chapter, an individual's construct system can become so fragmented in structure that, even though he may still have a large repertory of different constructs available (Crockett's operational definition of cognitive complexity), there may not be sufficient connections between them to enable him to relate one aspect of events to another (cf. Bannister, 1960, 1962b). Adams-Webber (1970a) and Maklouf-Norris *et al.* (1970) propose that superordinate constructs at the highest level of hierarchical organization within an individual's construct system provide a thread of coherence throughout the system as a whole by integrating the various functions of different subsystems at higher levels of abstraction. In short, subsystems which are functionally differentiated at lower levels of organization can be integrated at higher levels when they are 'abstractly cross-referenced' within the context of superordinate constructs. Leitner *et al.* (1976) submit that

Although it may be more adaptive to be complex when one is using subordinate constructs, one also needs hierarchical integration if one is to make decisions about how and when to apply certain constructs. It can be argued that high complexity, in the absence of higher order integration, may be correlated with chaos and confusion.

In the next chapter we shall consider research which deals with the gradual disintegration of conceptual structures within the framework of the same basic model of individual cognitive development as that discussed in this chapter. It will be argued there that whenever superordinate aspects of a person's construct system are not sufficiently well-defined or are too impermeable to subsume structural variations and still maintain overall consistency, fragmentation under the impact of events in an ever-changing environment will be haphazard rather than systematic, and can lead to the total or partial collapse of the system. Kelly (1955, p. 89) himself describes this process of decompensation as follows:

The variety of construction subsystems which are inferentially incompatible with each other may, in the train of rapidly moving events, become so vast that he is hard put to find ready-made superordinate constructs which are sufficiently permeable and open-ended to maintain overall consistency. He starts making new ones. While he has very little successful experience with concept formation at the permeable level, these are the kinds of constructs which he tries to develop. They may turn out to be generalized suspicions of the motives of other people. They may have to do with the reevaluation of life and death. They may lead him to anticipate reality in bizarre ways.

In summary, clinical thought disorder—which Bannister (1960) defines as loosening of conceptual structures in the face of invalidating feedback from the environment—can result from the failure of superordinate constructions adequately to subsume progressive changes in the rest of the system. A less drastic outcome might be the kind of 'segmented' conceptual structure which Makhlouf-Norris *et al.* (1970) found to be characteristic of some obsessive-compulsive neurotics, who in Kelly's (1955, p. 89) own words, 'need a separate pigeonhole for each new experience'.

4

Fragmentation and Thought Disorder

Kelly (1955) assumes that change within a personal construct system occurs only in response to 'validation' or 'invalidation' of an individual's anticipations. He contends that validational 'feedback' from the environment affects a person's construct system at various levels which follow a gradient. Constructs which are closely related to the construct upon which the original expectation was based will be more affected by a predictive failure than constructs which are more remotely related to it. This implies that the more closely related all of the constructs within an individual's system, the greater will be the potential impact of any invalidating experience in terms of its range of 'implications' (Crockett and Meisel, 1974; Hinkle, 1965).

Bannister (1963, 1965a) proposes that in the face of repeated predictive failure—'serial invalidation'—an individual will loosen the definition of his constructs in terms of their specific linkages with other constructs in order to minimize the 'reverberatory' effects of further predictive failure. Although this loosening is undertaken to conserve the system, the progressive loosening of construct relationships must, by definition, lead ultimately to the collapse of all conceptual organization. As Bannister *et al.* (1975, p. 170) note, 'invalidation is thus avoided at the cost of living subjectively in a fluid and largely meaningless universe'. Bannister's 'serial invalidation' hypothesis has provided the theoretical basis for an extensive programme of research concerned with the assessment, simulation, and experimental modification of clinical thought disorder.

LOOSENED CONSTRUING

Bannister's (1960, 1962b) initial studies involved the development of a form of repertory grid technique to define operationally the concept *loosened construing*. All the experimental subjects in this research were patients in British psychiatric hospitals who had been diagnosed clinically as 'thought-disordered schizophrenics'. The term *thought disorder*, as Bannister (1960) points out, was originally a concept derived by psychiatrists from their own experiences with schizoid patients (cf. Kretschmer, 1936). As defined by Mayer-Gross, Slater, and Roth (1954) thought disorder involves the following characteristics of the speech, and presumably of the thought patterns, of 'schizophrenics': (1) inconsequential following of side issues; (2) tendencies for the thought to be directed by alliterations, analogies, clang associations, associations with accidents of the speaker's environment, symbolic meanings, and condensations of several (perhaps mutually contradictory) ideas into one; (3) words used out of context, for example concrete meanings taken where abstract meanings would be more appropriate; (4) clinging to unimportant detail; (5) the use of laconic answers, for example 'I don't know, maybe, perhaps . . .' indicative of emptiness and vagueness of ideas; (6) thought is generally marked by gaps, poverty, indefiniteness, and vagueness; (7) indications of thought blocking; and (8) indications of pressure on thoughts.

Bannister (1960) notes that all these features represent abnormalities of the *form*, as opposed to the *content*, of thought, and thus are theoretically distinct from merely delusional ideas. In psychiatric practice, patients exhibiting some or all of these features are identified as a subgroup of the total population of schizophrenics which is labelled 'thought-disordered'.

It was Kelly (1955) himself who first suggested that 'schizoid' thinking was characterized essentially by 'loosened construction'. According to his theory, a loose construct is one which leads to varying predictions (cf. Maher, 1966). Bannister (1960, p.1241) refined this notion further by suggesting that 'the varying predictions of a loose construct are consequent upon the construct's having weak relationships with surrounding constructs in the hierarchical system; its predictions are made specific or focussed by a constellation of associated construing patterns'. As Lemon and Warren (1974, cited in Chapter 2) point out, the meaning of any construct in use by a particular individual is defined in part by the specific implications which that construct carries by virtue of its linkages with other constructs within the explicit framework of his own personal construct system. As we noted in Chapter 1, each construct in this system tends to imply a set of predictions about each of the persons or objects to which it is applied in terms of the particular constructs which are either directly or indirectly related to it for that individual. Thus, any loosening of the relationships between constructs will leave the meaning of each of them less well-defined and the individual's expectations will become increasingly vague.

In his initial study, Bannister (1960) developed an operational definition of 'loosened construing' in terms of Kelly's (1955) binary repertory grid procedure. He administered two repertory grids in succession to a sample of sixty adult subjects, including twenty normals, ten neurotics, ten depressives, and twenty schizophrenics. Eight of the schizophrenics were judged to be clinically thought-disordered by the psychiatrists primarily responsible for them, and twelve of them were diagnosed as not exhibiting symptoms of clinical thought disorder. There were no significant differences among these five groups in terms of either age or IQ. Bannister first elicited the names of thirty-six acquaintances from every subject. Then, each subject was asked to categorize eighteen of these figures—randomly selected—successively on the basis of each of ten adjectives: (1) *likeable*, (2) *serious*, (3) *good*, (4) *prejudiced*, (5) *aggressive*, (6) *lazy*, (7) *sincere*, (8) *uneducated*, (9) *religious*, and (10) *unreliable*. Subjects were instructed to select the nine figures who were best described by each of these adjectives in turn. Finally, they were asked to categorize the remaining eighteen figures in terms of the same set of ten adjectives.

The grid test results of each subject were analysed individually as follows. First, the degree of agreement of ratings between all possible pairs of adjectives was computed separately for each set of eighteen figures. Then, the estimate of the extent of agreement for each pair of adjectives (constructs)—the 'matching score'—for the first set of eighteen figures (Grid A) was added to that for the second set (Grid B), and the deviation of this total matching score for each pair of constructs from a 'chance' expectancy of eighteen was recorded. This procedure assumes that the *a priori* probability that a subject will allot a given figure to the 'same' pole of both constructs is equal to the probability that he will allot it to 'different' poles (i.e. 1/2). The implications of this assumption are examined in Chapter 7. The deviation scores were then summed separately for each subject to yield a total *intensity* score. This score is presumed to reflect the degree of interrelationship between a subject's constructs. It was found that the thought-disordered schizophrenics exhibited significantly lower intensity scores than all the other groups. Bannister interprets this result as indicating that 'it is possible operationally to define schizophrenic thought disorder in terms of weakened construct relationships as measured by this form of repertory grid technique, and indicate that this phenomenon could be isolated both between diagnostic categories and within the overall category of schizophrenia' (p. 1245).

A second 'structural' index—the realtionship consistency score—was also derived from the same repertory grid data. This score was discussed at length in Chapter 2. It was extracted from each subject's grid test protocol individually by calculating a Pearson product-moment correlation coefficient between the set of matching scores derived from forty-five separate construct (row) comparisons in Grid A and the corresponding set of scores from Grid B, squaring the resulting value of r, and multiplying it by 100. It was found that the thought-disordered schizophrenics also exhibited significantly lower relationship consistency scores than all other groups, including non thought-disordered schizophrenics. This is a very important finding in terms of Bannister's specific model of the genesis of clinical thought disorder because it indicates that the judgements of the thought-disordered patients are not only more fragmented in structure than those of other populations, but also, they are less stable. Bannister *et al.* (1975) point out that

The grids of thought-disordered subjects were characterized by low correlations between constructs and low consistency of the pattern of relationships between constructs, when grid measures were repeated.

Thought disorder is thereby defined as grossly loosened construing (a loose construct is one which leads to variable predictions) and the *simultaneous* lowering of both intensity and consistency is seen as inevitable. If you are certain today that *decency* is essentially *British* (high intensity, tight construing) then you may well be certain of this tomorrow, but if you become vague as to whether *decency* is related at all to *British* (low intensity, loose construing) then tomorrow you may toy with the notion that decency may relate to *foreign* (low consistency, loose construing). (p. 170)

In short, Bannister's hypothesis implies that the organization of the judgements of thought-disordered patients is not just more mathematically complex than that of other populations—it is essentially *random*. Thus, the experience of such persons, in so far as we can imagine it, must seem hopelessly kaleidoscopic.

Bannister's (1962b) second study was a replication and refinement of the first one. It was based on a sample of 110 subjects, which included thirty normal adults, twenty depressives, twenty neurotics, and forty schizophrenics. There was unanimous agreement between a consultant psychiatrist, registrar, and psychologist that twenty of the schizophrenics manifested clear signs of thought disorder as defined by Mayer-Gross *et al.* (1954), and that the remaining twenty schizophrenics exhibited no symptoms of thought disorder. All five groups contained equal numbers of men and women, and they did not differ significantly in terms of either mean age or IQ. The same repertory grid test was administered individually to each subject in which he categorized two sets of twenty passport-type photographs of strangers successively on the basis of nine adjectives: (1) *likeable*, (2) *mean*, (3) *good*, (4) *unusual*, (5) *narrow-minded*, (6) *sincere*, (7) *selfish*, (8) *unreliable*, and (9) *kind*. Only four of these adjectives were repeated from the first study. Subjects were asked to apply each adjective to exactly half of the photographs in each set. Both intensity and consistency of relationship scores were computed using the same procedures as those used in the previous study.

Once more, it was found that the thought-disordered schizophrenics exhibited significantly lower intensity and relationship consistency scores than all other groups. Moreover, the discriminating capacity of both of these indices was observed to have improved substantially over the first occasion, which Bannister attributes to his substitution of photographs of strangers for actual acquaintances. He reasons that 'if they (thought-disordered schizophrenics) were faced with completely novel stimuli the inability of their current construing system and the consequent sorting performance to manifest pattern would be more apparent' (p. 837). This particular point has provided the focus of some recent criticism of his research. For instance, Frith and Lillie (1972) argue that the inability of thought-disordered schizophrenics to sort figures consistently on this test may be due primarily to their being unable to discriminate between complex stimuli such as photographs of faces rather than to a state of weakened relationships between their constructs. On the other hand, as Radley (1974) notes, Frith and Lillie's alternative explanation of Bannister's results is inconsistent with McPherson and Buckley's (1970) finding that thought-disordered schizophrenics are as consistent as normals when they sort photographs of people in terms of their physical attributes (e.g. *old-young*), but are more random than normals when they attempt to sort the same photographs on the basis of psychological constructs (e.g. *generous-mean*).

Adams-Webber (1977a) shows that when the matching scores on Bannister's

(1962b) repertory grid test are summed separately for positive adjectives, such as *good* and *sincere*, and negative ones, such as *mean* and *selfish*, thought-disordered schizophrenics, as well as all the other populations sampled in Bannister's study, exhibit significantly higher intensity of relationship scores for the positive adjectives than for the negative ones. This is consistent with other evidence that judgements involving negative adjectives are more difficult to formulate and remember than those involving positive adjectives (Adams-Webber and Benjafield, 1972; Benjafield and Doan, 1971; Benjafield and Giesbrecht, 1973). This finding also suggests that in Bannister's (1962b) grid test the thought-disordered schizophrenics do attempt to make specific comparisons among the photographs on the basis of the adjectives provided to them and do not simply sort them in an entirely haphazard manner. In short, there is at least one source of systematic variation in the repertory grid performances of thought-disordered schizophrenics which is also reflected in the grid performances of normals and other clinical populations.

An extremely provocative reinterpretation of the results of Bannister's (1960, 1962b) first two studies of thought disorder has been recently offered by Radley (1974). He suggests that some of Bannister's data, summarized in Table 1 below, indicate that (p. 317) 'variability in the extent to which constructs are related within a person's system may also be associated with the problem of thought disorder'. He points out that in the second set of data (line 4 Table 1) both subgroups of schizophrenics show less *variability of intensity* scores than do normals. This is basically an index of variability among constructs in terms of the extent to which they relate to all other constructs in the same grid.

Radley (p. 318) infers from these data that 'normal subjects have, overall, a system of closely related constructs, but within the system there is high variability in the extent to which constructs relate to one another'. He argues further that this hypothesis is consistent with Makhlouf-Norris *et al.*'s (1970) finding—discussed in Chapter 3—that the personal construct systems of normal

Table 1. Mean intensity and mean variability of intensity scores

		Thought-disordered schizophrenics	Non-thought-disordered schizophrenics	Normals
Figures abstracted from Tables V and VI (Bannister, 1960)	Intensity	209.62	258.66	281.65
	Variability of intensity	26.04	30.12	29.6
Figures abstracted from Tables 5 and 7 (Bannister, 1962)	Intensity	170.5	273.6	271.5
	Variability of intensity	20.9	20.9	24.9

(Reproduced by permission of the British Psychological Society from Radley, A. R., 'Schizophrenic thought disorder and the nature of personal constructs', *Brit. J. soc. clin. Psychol.* (1974), **13**, p. 318, published by Cambridge University Press.)

adults are typically composed of a number of separate subsystems of highly interrelated constructs which are 'articulated' by means of several 'linkage' constructs, which are not themselves closely related to the constructs within any one subsystem. Radley points out that within the framework of a construct system with this kind of differentiated and abstractly 'cross-referenced' structure, relatively independent judgements can be derived within the context of separately organized subsystems, but they can also be rendered coherent within the range of convenience of the 'superordinate' linkage constructs (cf. Adams-Webber, 1970a).

Radley also argues on the basis of Bannister's (1962b) data that the non-thought-disordered schizophrenics have construct systems in which all constructs are highly interrelated to one another, because they have significantly higher mean intensity scores than the thought-disordered schizophrenics, but also significantly lower variability of intensity scores than the normals. Thus, they can be viewed as having what Makhlouf-Norris *et al.* (1970) term 'monolithic' (undifferentiated) systems. Radley contends further that 'as opposed to the invariably tight constructs of the non-thought-disordered schizophrenic, Bannister's figures show that thought-disordered schizophrenics have systems of weakly interrelated constructs which are relatively invariable in the intensity of relationship, i.e. they have homogeneously loose systems' (p. 319).

This series of hypotheses does not follow strictly from the data summarized in Table 1. The observed differences in variability of intensity scores among the three subgroups are all relatively small, and are significant only in the second set of data. Nonetheless, this model does have wide-ranging implications and may provide a basis for extending Bannister's theory in terms of the fundamental principles of construct theory. Specifically, it suggests the possibility that a thought-disordered individual may be floundering in the wreckage of what was once a highly 'monolithic' or 'cognitively simple' system of constructs. In such a system all constructs are, as we saw in the preceding chapter, concretely pyramided so that at any given level in the hierarchy the rules of organization are inflexible. Regardless of the number of constructs constituting the system, events will be interpreted in rigid accordance with one fixed pattern of expectations defined by the common intersect of all lines of inference from one construct to another. Kelly (1955, p. 121) offers the example of the 'old maid' who never met the 'right' man: 'there are all too many dimensions involved and nobody ever lands on the precise point where all of them converge. Her long standing anticipation is never fulfilled'.

Since the rules of organizing one's experience in terms of a 'monolithic' construct system are inflexible, there is no way to assimilate events which do not 'fit' the constraints of current construct relationships. Thus, as Radley (1974) notes, the individual will not be able to resolve inconsistencies in his experience. It was hypothesized in Chapter 1 that it is the ambiguity of new experience in the context of existing structure which normally leads to change in the organization and content of a construct system throughout its development. An event can be said to be ambiguous when it emerges as the focus of anticipations which are inconsistent in terms of specific relationships between constructs which define the current structure of one's system. In short, when confronted with events which do not fit the 'interweaving of construed likenesses and differences' (Kelly, 1955, p. 304), an individual may recognize a need to make changes in the structure of his system in order specifically to accommodate those events. Kelly points out, however, that an individual whose construct system is 'monolithic' rather than differentiated in structure, because of his great dependence on a single pattern of construct relationships, cannot risk adjustments at any level within the structure of his system in the face of invalidating feedback from the environment for fear that this will place him in an even more ambiguous position with respect to the anticipation of events.

The experiment of Crockett and Meisel (1974)—discussed in the preceding chapter—provides an excellent illustration of this problem. In such a tightly organized system, each predictive failure, because of the inflexibility of present structural relations, will present the prospect of impending chaos. Makhlouf-Norris et al. (1970) report that 'monolithic' conceptual structures are found primarily in the personal construct systems of obsessive-compulsive neurotics. Marked decompensation processes are frequently observed in the thinking of these patients on a clinical basis. In the face of increasing ambiguity, they constrict the range of application of each of their constructs more and more, until the range of convenience of every construct becomes so narrow that there can be very little overlap between different constructions of events. Kelly (1961, p. 46) describes this outcome in the following terms: 'schizoid persons have a complex repertory, but their constructs lack sufficient ranges of convenience to enable the person to relate one of them to another'. He observes further that when schizoid individuals apply their personal constructs thus narrowly they retain some degree of precise meaning. It is in this sense that 'loosening' relationships between his constructs may allow the schizoid person to preserve at least some coherence in his own experience (cf. Radley, 1974). That is, he withdraws more and more into a narrow, constricted, but still predictable world. However, all events outside the impoverished range of convenience of his highly truncated system will remain 'meaningless' to him in the sense that he cannot abstract palpable features of regularity from them.

For example, Radley (1974) suggests that when the schizoid individual's constructs are applied to his immediate family they may exhibit more specificity and stability of meaning than when they are applied to new figures in his life. In support of this hypothesis, he cites Bannister's (1959) finding that thought-disordered schizophrenics are more precise and more consistent in categorizing the behaviour of their own personal acquaintances than when they are asked to describe photographs of strangers.

Fragmentation, when it does occur in the face of increasing ambiguity and predictive failure, may be sudden and lead rapidly to further variation, thereby precipitating a major shake-up in the brittle organization of the system. As this rigid structure begins to collapse under the impact of massive invalidation, even the most superordinate constructs in the system will gradually begin to lose definition as their relationships of 'implication' with other constructs at various levels become increasingly vague and unstable (Lemon and Warren, 1974; Crockett and Meisel, 1974). Thus, the individual may eventually have to abandon his superordinate constructs altogether and fall back on a more primitive and less effectual system in which constructs are related not to other constructs, but directly to concrete events.

SERIAL INVALIDATION

Personal construct theory implies that if Construct A relates to Construct B, and if predictions based on this relationship are consistently confirmed or disconfirmed, then the relationship between A and B will be enhanced or diminished accordingly. If the predictions are consistently disconfirmed, eventually the individual will abandon the strategy of attempting to predict B from A, and *vice versa*. As the relationships between any given construct and other constructs fall off ('linkage invalidation') or require revision (e.g. 'reversal') its range of convenience will be progressively restricted to fewer and fewer events and its meaning will become increasingly vague. Eventually, it will probably be abandoned as a basis for anticipatory constructions.

In his first experiment designed to test the implications of this model for the genesis of clinical thought disorder, Bannister (1963, p. 681) tried to 'produce the condition of weak conceptual structure in normal subjects under controlled conditions'. He assumed that any one of a person's anticipations may have one of three possible outcomes—'validation', 'invalidation', or 'no feedback'. He developed a 'laboratory game' for assessing the differential effects of these three types of feedback on the degree of relationship between an individual's constructs.

His basic hypothesis was that 'if a person is repeatedly invalidated in his construing of an element, then his *initial* reaction may be to reconstrue this element on the opposite pole of the construct (e.g. this person is not a "loving" person, he is a "hating" person), but after shuffling a person to and fro across the poles of the construct, the eventual response (aimed at avoiding further invalidation) may be to loosen or weaken the relationship of this construct with constructs constellated around it' (Bannister, 1963; p. 681). Therefore, predictions and anticipations arising from the construct in question will become increasingly vague and multi-directional instead of specific and unidirectional. Further invalidation may thus be avoided at the expense of an inability to formulate testable predictions. For example, 'if we loosen the relationship of the construct *loving-hating* with those normally constellated around it, then we cease to anticipate from a "loving" person say "kind", "sincere", "dependable", etc. behaviour since these constructs are no longer closely linked together and invalidation is thereby avoided' (p. 681).

In the initial experiment, ten normal adults, five men and five women, completed the same repertory grid test on each of ten successive days. On each occasion they were asked to rank-order a different set of ten photographs of strangers on the basis of a list of ten adjectives (*likeable, mean, good*, etc.). On every occasion following the first, each subject was informed that he had been very successful in judging the photographs in terms of five of the adjectives (randomly selected), and very unsuccessful in terms of the remaining five adjectives. Supplementary 'evidence' in the form of fake biographies and bogus score sheets was used to back up this information. The correlations between sets of rankings of the same photographs on different adjectives were divided into three separate classes: (1) those between two validated constructs, (2) those between two invalidated constructs, and (3) those between one validated construct and one invalidated construct. This analysis was carried out separately for each subject.

Bannister predicted that the first set of correlations would gradually increase over the ten trials and that the second set would gradually decrease. Only the first prediction was confirmed by his results. He suspected that the second prediction may have failed to be confirmed because subjects were able to avoid collapse in structure through changes in the pattern of relationships between their constructs. In support of this hypothesis it was observed that there were significantly more 'reversals' in the direction of the correlations between the invalidated constructs from one trial to the next than for those between validated constructs.

This experiment was repeated with only a single change in the basic design. This time one group of five subjects were told after every trial that they were doing poorly in all of their judgements, and another group of five subjects were assured that they were doing well in all of their judgements. The result was that the second group showed significant increases in the overall level of correlation between their constructs, as expected; however, there were no significant changes in the grids of the 'invalidated' group. Also, the latter did not differ from the 'validated' group in terms of the number of 'reversals' of construct relationships.

On the other hand, there was one unexpected finding. Those subjects who exhibited relatively high intensity of relationship scores on their initial 'base-line' performance on the grid test 'showed catastrophic reactions to validational experience by zig-zagging from very high to very low strengths of structure while the low intensity group were markedly less affected' (p. 685). This finding is consistent with Kelly's (1955) assumption, discussed in the previous section, that the more closely related all of an individual's constructs, the greater will be the impact throughout his personal construct system of any validational feedback from the environment. It is consistent also with the results of Crockett and Meisel (1974) and Levy (1956), reviewed in the last chapter. Bannister's (1963, p. 685) tentative conclusion is that 'the length and slope of the curve of weakening of conceptual structure may differ depending on the *initial* degree of structure (and) vary as a function of the position in the total construct system of the subsystem under attack'.

Bannister (1965a) carried out two further experimental tests of his 'serial invalidation' hypothesis. The first of these experiments was designed not only to demonstrate loosened construing, but also to define the specific conditions under which it takes place. A sample of eighteen normal adults, nine women and nine men, rank-ordered a different set of ten photographs of people on the basis of the same list of six adjectives on each of twenty separate trials. Six subjects—randomly selected—were informed after every trial that they had performed exceptionally well on this task, another six subjects that they had done extremely poorly, and the remaining six subjects received no feedback of any sort. Once more, the 'validated' group significantly increased their intensity of relationship scores over the twenty trials, but neither of the other two groups showed any change in terms of intensity. However, as Bannister predicted on the basis of the results of his first experiment described above, the 'invalidated' group exhibited significantly more 'reversals' of the relationships between constructs across trials than either of the other two groups. Thus, the results of this experiment are essentially consistent with those of his two previous studies, that is, 'serial validation produced a significant increase in the strength of correlational relationships between constructs and serial invalidation produced radical changes in the pattern of these relationships' (Bannister, 1965a, p. 379).

In his fourth experiment in this series, Bannister explicitly acknowledged the importance of the principle of functional differentiation between subsystems, elaborated in the preceding chapter. Specifically, he supplied his subjects with a list of constructs 'which fall into constellations which are relatively independent of each other' (p. 379). Ten normal adults (five women, five men) rank-ordered a different set of ten photographs of persons on the basis of a list of eight adjectives on each of twenty successive trials. Four of these adjectives represented 'moral constructs'—*kind, sincere, mean,* and *selfish*—and four of them represented 'intellectual constructs'—*clever, simple, educated, stupid.* Following each trial, five subjects (randomly selected) were informed that they were doing well on the basis of the moral constructs and poorly in terms of the intellectual ones. The remaining five subjects were told the opposite. The average correlation between the moral constructs across all ten subjects was 0.72, while that between intellectual constructs was 0.71. The 'cross-correlations' between moral and intellectual constructs averaged 0.46. This evidence suggests that these two sets of constructs did function as separate subsystems during the experiment.

Bannister reports that the correlations within the 'validated' subsystem increased significantly from the first to the last trial, as observed in all the previous experiments. There was also a significant decrease in the level of correlations between constructs within the 'invalidated' subsystem over trials. In addition, there were significantly more 'reversals' in relationships between constructs within the 'invalidated' subsystem than within the 'validated' one. Bannister concludes that 'it was finally shown that if two separate constellations of constructs are available to normal subjects and one is serially validated and the second is serially invalidated then intercorrelations in the former will rise while in the latter the pattern of construct relationships will repeatedly change and the strength of correlations will ultimately fall' (p. 381–382).

This study provides the first experimental demonstration of the principle of subsystem specialization in the organization of an individual's conceptual processes. Bannister notes that in his earlier experiments the failure of differences between validated and invalidated constructs to show up may have been because all constructs within a single subsystem tend to be directly related. As we saw in the preceding chapter, Crockett and Meisel (1974) have shown that constructs which are related to many other constructs are relatively resistant to the type of non-specific invalidation such as that provided to subjects in Bannister's four experiments. Bannister also points out that it is difficult to invalidate some constructs while validating others within the same subsystem since the validation of any construct in the network will have 'reverberatory effects' in terms of providing support for all constructs constellated around it in spite of the fact that some of these are being specifically invalidated.

The evidence from all four of Bannister's 'serial invalidation' experiments, considered together, suggests that the differential effects of validation and invalidation on an individual's personal construct system will be most pro-nounced when that system is 'articulated' in terms of relatively independent subsystems, between which there is some degree of 'cross-linkage' (Adams-Webber, 1970a; Radley, 1974). This general hypothesis is also illustrated by the 'maps' of conceptual structures derived from the repertory grid data elicited from normal adults by Makhlouf-Norris et al. (1970).

As Rehm (1971) points out, Bannister's (1963; 1965a) 'serial invalidation' procedure may have conveyed either of two different kinds of information to his subjects, or both at once: (a) information concerning the accuracy of their judgements about the photographs themselves, and (b) information concerning the relationships between constructs. The former can be viewed as validation of specific constructions, and the latter as 'linkage' validation. Rehm herself conducted an experiment which was designed 'to differentiate between the effects of linkage validation and construct validation alone' (p. 267).

She initially asked 104 American undergraduates to rate photographs of people on the basis of two bi-polar constructs: constrained-free and objective-subjective. Eighty subjects who applied these two constructs to photographs in a relatively independent way in this pre-test were selected for her experiment. They were assigned randomly to four separate experimental groups. Group I received a high percentage of positive feedback for responses linking the two constructs in a positively correlated manner in rating photographs of unknown people. Group II received the same percentage of positive validation as Group I, but in the opposite direction. That is, a negative correlation between the constructs was being validated for this particular group. Group III received a percentage of validation which was identical to that provided for subjects in the first two groups in a yoked design. Thus, subjects in Group III were essentially validated for each construct independently; that is, they were told they were correct more often than could happen by chance, as were subjects in Groups I and II, but the pattern of validation for subjects in Group III was random in terms of the direction of the relationship between the two constructs. Group IV received no feedback of any sort.

As predicted, subjects in Group I were found to show an increase in the degree of positive correlation between the constructs; whereas subjects in Group II showed a corresponding increase in the degree of negative correlation between them. Both Groups I and II differed significantly in the amount of increase in the correlation between the two constructs from both Groups III and IV, which did not differ significantly from one another. Rehm also found that the differences in the direction of the correlation between the two constructs observed for Groups I and II transferred to their ratings of their own personal acquaintances on these constructs, direct construct to construct ratings in the *Semantic Differential*, and indirect *Semantic Differential* ratings based on similarities in connotative meanings. She argues on the basis of these findings that 'the linkage between two constructs can be modified directly by validation of the linkage and that the modification occurs in the validated direction as a function of the amount of validational experience' (p. 270). Rehm notes also that 'validation of constructs alone had no significant effect on linkage, contrary to Bannister's (1963, 1965) conclusions regarding his data' (p. 270).

Rehm's results are not at all inconsistent with Bannister's 'serial invalidation' hypothesis. In Bannister's fourth experiment, described above, 'validation' was not contingent upon the subject's using constructs as related to one another. It was simply indicated to each subject that one set of constructs had been applied to the photographs correctly and the other set had been applied to them incorrectly. Rehm implies that Bannister's subjects could have understood this 'feedback' in either of two different ways. They could have interpreted it either as validation of their specific judgements of the photographs or as a validation of the 'linkages' between their constructs (or possibly both). Rehm's experimental procedures clearly differentiate between validation of specific judgements only (Group III) and validation of linkages between constructs in addition to validation of specific judgements (Group I and II). Thus, she was able to demonstrate that only when some form of 'linkage validation' was provided did the correlations between constructs change systematically in the predicted direction. This finding implies that 'linkage validation' may be a necessary condition for modifying relationships between constructs.

In Rehm's experiment, validation of specific judgements alone produced no significant changes in construct relationships; however, her procedures differed in two important respects from those of Bannister. First, she carefully selected subjects who evidenced no relationship between the relevant constructs during pre-testing; whereas Bannister used sets of constructs with fairly high levels of interrelationship at the outset of his experiment. Secondly, Bannister recorded all changes in the magnitude of the correlations between constructs irrespective of direction, whereas Rehm did not. It is possible that in her experiment some changes in the size of correlations between constructs in both directions may have occurred and cancelled one another out in Group III. Thus, it is conceivable that in Rehm's experiment the validation of specific judgements alone could have produced systematic changes in the degree of relationship between constructs which were obscured by her method of recording and analysing her data. Finally, since Rehm's experiment involved validation only, while Bannister's experiments included both validation and invalidation procedures, it is not clear that Rehm's findings have any direct bearing on the 'serial invalidation' hypothesis itself.

In an earlier study (Poch, 1952), a group of American undergraduates tried to predict how their classmates would respond to a specific questionnaire item. When their predictions were directly disconfirmed, they tended to abandon the constructs on which the predictions had been based in favour of other constructs, although there was a 'failure of invalidation to show a statistically significant relationship to changes in constructs' (p. 86). Mischel (1964, p. 182) cites Poch's experiment in support of his own hypothesis that 'it is not logically possible for the facts ever to falsify my construct—not even subjectively'. Mischel seems to overlook Kelly's (1955) assumption that in the strict sense it is always the specific construction (which is anticipatory in nature) which is either confirmed or disconfirmed by subsequent events, and not the construct which serves as the basis for the prediction. In short, constructions can be judged as either correct or incorrect while constructs can only be judged as predictively useful or pre-dictively useless. Warren (1964, p. 12) points out that Mischel (1964) seems to disregard Kelly's basic distinction between construct and construction: 'clearly Mischel agrees that a *construction*, i.e. the classification of a person as "hostile", can be invalidated . . . what he wishes to know is how, in Kelly's terms, can the generic *construct* of "hostile-submissive" be invalidated'. As Warren explains, this is something which may come about gradually over a period of time as the result of repeated predictive failures.

There is not yet enough experimental and clinical evidence to evaluate the 'serial invalidation' hypothesis. In Bannister's own experiments some subjects were observed to show decreases in the relationships among one set of constructs when all of their constructions based on these specific constructs were diffusely invalidated. The results of other experiments (Levy, 1956; Crockett and Meisel, 1974)—discussed in Chapter 3—suggest that some constructs, depending on their position in the subject's own network of interrelated constructs, are more resistant than others to change, following invalidation. Maher (1966) points out that 'there appears to be little doubt that thought-disordered schizophrenics exhibit looser and less consistent constructs as these are defined by Kelly . . . however, this remains a descriptive hypothesis. The processes that underlie it are still a matter of speculation (p. 425).

Kelly (1955) assumes that whatever changes take place in the content and structure of an individual's personal construct system in the course of its validational history, he will attempt to integrate his experience as far as possible within his current conceptual framework. Kelly's theory also implies that structural changes within a construct system normally involve the further evolution of that system as an operational whole, rather than simply grafting new components onto it from the outside. He emphasizes this point in his assertion that 'progressive variation must itself take place within a system . . . one's personal constructs can only be changed within subsystems of constructs and subsystems only within more comprehensive systems' (Kelly, 1955, p. 79). As we saw in Chapter 1, Kelly's 'modulation corollary' stipulates that 'variation within a person's construct system is limited by the permeability of the constructs within whose range of convenience the variants lie'. This proposition implies that the extent to which orderly change can take place within an individual's personal construct system is ultimately limited by the permeability of his most superordinate constructs (Adams-Webber, 1970a).

According to Kelly (1955), a construct is permeable if it is so constituted that 'new experience and new events can be discriminately added to those which it already embraces' (p. 81). He contends that 'it is under the regency of such constructs that the more subordinate aspects of one's construction system can be systematically varied without making his whole psychological house fall down' (Ibid.). Conversely, when superordinate constructs are relatively impermeable, they cannot be used to cope with new situations or to readjust to old ones, because new substructures cannot be organized under them. Thus, the modulation corollary clearly implies that, the more permeable the most superordinate constructs within an individual's personal construct system, the greater the amount of systematic change which can occur within the substructures which they subsume. Although Kelly's (1955) 'fragmentation corollary' explicitly permits the progressive differentiation of a construct system into relatively independent subsystems, the extent of this differentiation will be limited by the degree of permeability of superordinate constructs.

It follows that when an individual's most superordinate constructs, that is, those which are the highest 'up the ladder' (Hinkle, 1965), are relatively permeable, they can provide a thread of coherence throughout most of his personal experience. As we noted in the preceding chapter, constructs and subsystems of constructs which are functionally differentiated at lower levels of organization can be reintegrated with one another at higher levels when they are 'abstractly cross-referenced' within the context of relatively permeable superordinate constructs. Nevertheless, it is only in the context of the most permeable aspects of superordinate structures that overall coherence can be sustained. In order systematically to incorporate new components of substructure into his system it is essential that the individual be able continually to readjust his superordinate constructs so as to minimize incompatibilities and inconsistencies at the highest level of abstraction.

Thus, clinical thought disorder as operationally defined by Bannister (1960) in terms of 'loosening' of conceptual structure could result from a failure of superordinate constructions to integrate changes at lower levels of organization. Bannister et al. (1971) suggest that thought disorder could represent the endpoint in a process in which, in the early stages, there may be abrupt changes in the usual pattern of construct relationships. This hypothesis is consistent with Bannister's (1963, 1965a) finding that there are 'considerable changes in construct patterning as the *primary* reaction to the experience of being repeatedly wrong' (Bannister et al., 1971, p. 150). Whenever an individual's superordinate constructs are relatively impermeable, such changes in the structure of his system cannot be readily integrated at higher levels of abstraction and can prove disruptive, and even traumatic, when they are forced upon him by events. Kelly (1955, p. 89) observes that

There is no clearer example of the limitation of one's ability to adjust to the vicissitudes of life due to the impermeability of his superordinate constructs than the case of the compulsion neurosis client who is undergoing a marked decompensation process . . . frequently on a clinical basis we can see the so-called 'decompensation' taking place in a client in the space of a few days or weeks. We are able to see how the brittleness and impermeability of his construction system failed to support the alternations which he was finding it necessary to make.

This illustration suggests that the impermeability of superordinate constructs may underlie the development of the 'non-articulated'—either 'monolithic' or 'segmented'—conceptual structures identified by Makhlouf-Norris *et al.* (1970) as characteristic of obsessive-compulsion neurosis. Given highly impermeable superordinate constructs little can take place in the way of systematic differentiation between substructures and their reintegration at higher levels of organization. Thus it will be difficult to resolve inconsistencies in one's experience or cope with novel situations (Adams-Webber, 1970a; Radley, 1974).

Bannister (1963, 1965a) implies that repeated predictive failure alone can lead an individual to loosen the definition of his constructs in terms of their relationships with other constructs to the point where he is no longer capable of ordered thought and action. This hypothesis, as it stands, leaves open the fundamental question of why the person who gradually becomes more and more thought-disordered in response to 'serial invalidation' is unable to make the necessary adjustments in the structure and content of his construct system in order to accommodate to novel events. For instance, Bannister *et al.* (1971) suggest that a 'deviant' construct system (e.g. 'delusional beliefs') 'is a bus stop on the way to thought disorder (albeit a bus stop at which some get off and remain)' (pp. 148–149). We must then ask why it is that some persons first get on the wrong bus, and then are unable to get off it before the end of the line.

Perhaps it is the impermeability of the superordinate aspects of their personal construct systems which continually arrests the changes which are a necessary condition for adaptation in the face of environmental variation. That is, the more impermeable a person's superordinate constructs, the less his daily commerce with events in terms of anticipation and feedback will produce the changes in his construct system required for extending its range of convenience to meet new circumstances. This implies that whenever superordinate structures are too impermeable to subsume variations and still maintain overall coherence in the system, fragmentation under the pressure of events will tend to be chaotic and may lead eventually to the partial or total disintegration of the system (Adams-Webber, 1970a).

THE SPECIFICITY HYPOTHESIS

Bannister and Salmon (1966, p. 215) pose the question of 'whether the thinking of schizophrenics is generally disordered across all subsystems (i.e. are they equally confused whatever topic they think about) or whether it is more specifically disordered in thinking about some areas than others'. They hypothesize that, in general, schizophrenics hold more loosely structured anticipations about persons than about objects: 'we often observe thought-disordered schizophrenics confidently handling doors, cutlery, and shoelaces but failing to distinguish friend from foe' (p. 216). They refer specifically to the work of Bateson, Jackson, Haley, and Weakland (1956), Laing and Esterson (1964), and Lidz (1964) as also suggesting that interpersonal events can be more confusing to the schizophrenic than his experience in other spheres.

In order to test this 'specificity hypothesis', Bannister and Salmon administered both a 'people grid' and an 'object grid' to eleven thought-disordered schizophrenics and twelve normal adults. The people grid was the *Bannister–Fransella Grid Test of Thought Disorder* (described more fully in the following section), in which eight photographs of people (four men, four women) were successively rank-ordered on six trait adjectives (*mean, kind,* etc.). In the object grid, the names of fifteen common objects (e.g. loaf of bread, drawing pin, washing machine) were rank-ordered successively on six 'physical' constructs (e.g. *large-small, heavy-light, long-short*). There was unanimous agreement among consultant, registrar, and psychologist concerning the diagnosis of thought disorder for all eleven schizophrenic patients, while the twelve normals had no psychiatric histories.

It was predicted that the 'thought-disordered schizophrenics would not differ significantly from normals in their degree of stability in construing objects but would manifest significantly less stability in construing photographs of people' (p. 217). They found that normal subjects exhibited significantly more stability in construing *both* people and objects, which disconfirmed their main hypothesis. They found also that both groups exhibited more stability across object grids than across people grids.

Bannister and Salmon re-examined their data in terms of 'the *relative* loss of reliable structure as between objects and people as elements for thought-disordered schizophrenics as compared with normals' (p. 218). The overall percentage of loss of stability across grids was calculated separately for object and people grids individually for each subject. It was observed that thought-disordered schizophrenics lost significantly more stability in construing when shifted from objects to people than did the normals. They also counted the 'number of individuals who achieve a statistically significant degree of stability in construing objects but produce only a non-significant level of correlation in construing people' (p. 218). Seven thought-disordered schizophrenics and only one normal fell into this category ($p < .001$).

Fianlly, they compared schizophrenics and normals in terms of 'social deviation'. Social deviation was operationally defined as the degree to which the pattern of construct relationship for each individual agrees with a 'normal' pattern, that is the mean pattern for the normal group. It was found that (a) schizophrenics exhibited a significantly higher level of social deviation for both objects and people, and (b) 'thought-disordered schizophrenics have lost relatively more social agreement in people construing when compared with normals and show more cases of insignificant levels of social agreement' (p. 218).

Bannister and Salmon (p. 218) interpret the outcome of this study as 'clearly consistent with the view that the area of *maximal* damage for thought-disordered schizophrenics as between object— and people-construing is people-construing'.

The findings of Salmon, Bromley, and Presley (1967) based on Heim and Watts' (1958) *Word-in-Context Test* also lend support to the 'specificity hypothesis'. In this test subjects are asked to infer the meanings of words with which they are unfamiliar from contexts extracted from published prose. Subjects' responses are evaluated in terms of how closely they approximate the 'correct' meanings of the words. Salmon *et al*. administered this test to twenty-four schizophrenics, eleven of whom were diagnosed as thought-disordered by the consultant responsible for them. The remaining thirteen were judged by their consultants to be completely free of thought disorder. Scores on the *Word-in-Context Test* correlated significantly with IQ for the non-thought disordered group, but not for the thought-disordered group.

The main finding of this study was that these two groups did not differ significantly in terms of their accuracy in inferring 'non-psychological' words from contexts, that is 'words referring to the physical world of time and space'; however, the non-thought-disordered schizophrenics were significantly more accurate in inferring the meanings of 'psychological' words that is 'words referring to the world of human thought, feeling, and judgement'. Also accuracy in identifying psychological meanings correlated negatively with severity of thought disorder as measured by the *Bannister–Fransella Grid Test* (discussed in the next section). Salmon *et al*. conclude, 'the fact that schizophrenics with thought disorder seem to be relatively impaired in acquiring "psychological" as against "non-psychological" concepts, implies that it is specifically within the area of concepts relating to psychological processes and attributes that their conceptual breakdown has occurred' (p. 258).

Further work on this problem has been carried out by McPherson and Buckley (1970), who point out that, since Bannister and Salmon (1966) varied both elements and constructs in their grid tests, 'it is not possible to distinguish the effects of using different classes of construct (psychological versus physical) from any effects due to different elements being construed (people versus objects)' (McPherson and Buckley, 1970, p. 380). McPherson and Buckley administered two forms of grid test on successive days to twelve psychiatric patients all diagnosed as schizophrenic, and independently rated by two psychiatrists who knew them as showing clear signs of clinical thought disorder, and twelve normal adults. One grid test was the *Bannister–Fransella Grid Test of Thought Disorder* used by Bannister and Salmon (1966); and the second grid test employed the same set of eight photographs of people and six constructs 'descriptive of the physical features of people' (e.g. *healthy, well-built, slow-moving*).

It was found that thought-disordered patients differed significantly from normals in terms of both intensity and consistency of relationships between constructs only on the grid test based on psychological constructs. McPherson and Buckley (p. 381) argue that their results 'clarify those of Bannister and Salmon (1966) by showing that thought-process-disordered schizophrenics, when construing people, are less disordered when doing so according to objective (physical) criteria than to psychological criteria'. They suggest further that, when both studies are taken into consideration, the evidence indicates that formal thought disorder can affect separate subsytems of consructs within the same overall construct system in different ways. This conclusion is consistent with Kelly's (1955) assumption that 'a person's total construct system comprises several subsystems characterized by relatively strong relationships between constructs within each subsystem, but by relatively weak relationships between constructs from different subsystems' (McPherson and Buckley, 1970, p. 380). Their conclusion is also consistent with the findings of Bannister (1965a), discussed in the preceding section.

Williams (1971), on the other hand, argues that cues relating to physical dimensions are more easily extracted from photographs of people than cues relevant to their personality characteristics, and this consideration could explain why thought-disordered patients do not differ significantly from normals in terms of either intensity or consistency of relationship when they rank-order photographs of people on the basis of 'physical' constructs. Heather (1976) points out, however, that if subjects were asked to rank-order people personally known to them rather than photographs of strangers in the grid test, then the effects of differences in 'cue-availability' between physical and psychological characteristics hypothesized by Williams should be smaller.

Heather (p. 132) specifically hypothesizes that 'thought-disordered schizophrenics will be less disordered relative to non-thought-disordered schizophrenics and normals when using physical constructs than when using psychological constructs, irrespective of whether photographs of strangers or known people are used as elements to be construed'. In order to test this hypothesis, Heather devised four versions of the grid test based on all possible combinations of 'psychological' and 'physical' constructs with known persons and photographs of strangers as elements. All four grid tests were administered to each of twenty-four subjects, including eight schizophrenics judged to be thought-disordered by their respective junior doctors, consultants and the experimenter himself, eight schizophrenics judged to be non-thought-disordered on the same basis, and eight normal adults without psychiatric histories. Each type of grid was administered only once, and consequently, consistency of construct relationships was not measured.

Thought-disordered schizophrenics were found to have significantly lower intensity of relationship scores averaged across all four grid tests than either normals or non-thought-disordered schizophrenics. Also, overall intensity scores were observed to be significantly higher for psychological constructs than for physical ones. The predicted interaction between constructs and groups was not significant; however, multiple comparisons between the three groups did reveal that, in both grid tests in which photographs were used as elements, the observed differences with respect to intensity scores between the thought-disordered schizophrenics and the other groups were significant in terms of psychological constructs ($p < .01$), but not in terms of physical constructs.

Similarly, when people known personally to the subjects themselves were employed as elements, the difference between thought-disordered and non-thought-disordered subjects was significant ($p < .01$) for psychological constructs, but not for physical constructs.

Heather argues that these results provide support for his general hypothesis in so far as they indicate that 'thought-disordered schizophrenics should obtain significantly lower scores than non-thought-disordered subjects on grids employing psychological constructs but *not* on grids employing physical constructs, irrespective of elements' (p. 135). This argument would have considerably more force if the expected interaction between constructs and groups had reached significance; however, the results of separate t-tests between groups were fully consistent with McPherson and Buckley's (1970) finding that thought-disordered subjects obtain significantly lower intensity scores than non-thought-disordered subjects on grid tests involving psychological constructs, but not on grid tests involving only physical constructs. Heather's experiment extends this generalization to grid tests employing persons known to the subjects themselves as elements. This is also consistent with the results of an earlier study in which McFayden and Foulds (1972) showed that intensity scores based on grid tests in which subjects rank-ordered known persons on elicited constructs relate significantly (rho $= 0.52$) to clinical ratings of thought disorder.

Heather has also made an important distinction between the 'strong' and 'weak' forms of Bannister and Salmon's 'specificity hypothesis'. The strong version implies that schizophrenic thought disorder should be specific to 'psychological' subsystems, and therefore, thought-disordered patients should exhibit no 'cognitive deficit' when they use physical constructs. Heather argues that the strong version of the specificity hypothesis is more closely related to Bannister's 'serial invalidation' hypothesis, 'which locates the genesis of schizophrenic thought disorder in a type of confusing interaction between the future schizophrenic and significant others in his environment' (Heather, 1976, p. 131). In its weaker form, the specificity hypothesis merely implies that thought-disordered schizophrenics will show more disorganization than normals in processing information in terms of physical constructs, and the difference between these two populations will be even greater when psychological constructs are used. Heather (p. 136) concludes that 'in the absence of significant differences on physical construct grids (between thought-disordered and non-thought-disordered subjects) there is no reason to reject the strong version'.

Nevertheless, McPherson, Armstrong, and Heather (1975) contend that all previous experiments concerned with the specificity hypothesis—including Heather (1976)—have produced ambiguous results. For instance, they point out (p. 303) that Bannister and Salmon (1966) used different types of elements in their psychological and physical grid tests 'allowing the possibility that some factor other than content might have accounted for the results'. For example, photographs of people may be more complex as stimuli, or include more distracting features than the names of various common objects. McPherson and Buckley (1970) tried to eliminate this problem by using the same set of photographs on both versions of the test. Nonetheless, McPherson *et al.* (1975) point out that there are at least four alternative explanations of the results of McPherson and Buckley (1970) and Heather (1976). Firstly, the observed differences between thought-disordered and non-thought-disordered subjects on psychological grid tests, and the absence of any differences on physical grid tests, could have resulted from 'the *control* groups having performed differently on the two versions, whereas the thought-disordered groups performed similarly on both, e.g. more or less randomly' (p. 304). Secondly, the psychological and physical versions of the test may have differed with respect to their test-retest reliabilities, that is, the physical version may have been less reliable, and therefore failed to discriminate accurately the real differences between thought-disordered and non-thought-disordered subjects. Thirdly, the psychological test may have involved a more 'difficult' cognitive task apart from its specific human content. Thus, the results of previous studies may reflect merely a general conceptual deficit on the part of thought-disordered schizophrenics. Finally, the results of all previous experiments can be explained on the basis of Bannister and Salmon's specificity hypothesis. In their own study, McPherson *et al.* attempted explicitly to rule out the first three explanations outlined above.

They reasoned that the first explanation could be strictly ruled out in terms of differences in intensity scores between thought-disordered and non-thought-disordered subjects 'only if psychological and non-psychological versions of the grid test are constructed so that a normal control group have similar intensity scores on the two versions' (p. 304). As Heather (1976) points out, when psychological and physical constructs are matched with respect to intensity scores for a normal population, the specificity hypothesis predicts that thought-disordered schizophrenics will exhibit lower intensity scores in terms of psychological constructs than in terms of physical constructs. McPherson *et al.* attempted to rule out the second possible explanation by ensuring that both versions of the test were comparable with respect to their test-retest reliabilities. In order to exclude the third potential explanation, they attempted to construct different versions of these tests which were comparable in terms of their levels of 'difficulty'. They suggest that the relative difficulty of a set of constructs can be operationally defined 'by comparing the amount of agreement shown by a criterion group in their ranking of a set of elements in terms of the constructs, a low level of consensual agreement indicating that the construct is 'difficult', *used with these specific elements*' (p. 305).

They constructed two versions of the grid test including the same elements, one based on psychological constructs and the other based on non-psychological constructs. These two versions were matched with respect to 'difficulty' (amount of consensual agreement); and also, for subjects free of thought disorder, with respect to test-retest reliability (element consistency) and mean intensity and consistency of relationship scores. In addition, two other grid tests were constructed, one 'difficult' and one 'easy'.

All four grid tests were administered to three groups each consisting of ten subjects: (1) three women and seven men who had been judged to be thought-disordered by the consultants and registrars who knew them best, (2) six women and four men diagnosed as neurotic with no history of thought disorder, and (3) four female and six male hospital employees without psychiatric histories. It was found that the thought-disordered group exhibited significantly lower intensity scores than either group of non-thought-disordered subjects on the psychological version of the test. There were no significant differences among these groups on the non-psychological version of the test. The thought-disordered group also obtained significantly lower consistency of relationship scores than either of the other groups on both versions of the test. Finally, it was found that varying the level of 'difficulty' of the tests produced no significant effects in terms of either intensity or consistency of relationship scores. McPherson *et al.* (p. 313) conclude that 'the present results appear to provide strong evidence for the notion that thought disorder does not entail a generalized breakdown across all areas of thinking, but rather it is maximal in the area of psychological construing'.

The evidence, reviewed in this section, which favours Bannister and Salmon's 'specificity hypothesis' within the framework of personal construct theory, also lends support to other general theories which emphasize the role of social factors in the genesis of clinical thought disorder, for example Bateson *et al.* (1956), Laing and Esterson (1964), and Lidz (1964, 1968). For instance, Lidz (1968) argues that the so-called 'schizophrenogenic' family is one in which children are rewarded by their parents for denying reality and thinking illogically. In a recent experiment, using a procedure very similar to that of Rehm (1971), described above, Higgins and Schwarz (1976) reinforced ('validated') subjects for applying two 'typically related constructs' (*kind* and *sincere*) to people in 'an atypical, inversely related manner'. That is, subjects were reinforced whenever they described someone as either sincere and unkind or as kind and insincere. It was found that this procedure produced a progressive loosening of the initially high degree of relationship between these two constructs. It was also observed that this effect was most pronounced for those subjects who were identified as 'schizotypic' on the basis of the *Sc* scale of the MMPI. Higgins and Schwarz suggest that this experiment provides an 'analogue to what Lidz (1968) described as the day to day demands of a schizophrenic environment, which insidiously inculcates disordered thinking through the reinforcement of agreement with atypical and illogical statements' (p. 805).

Lidz's theory also implies that the parents of thought-disordered patients are themselves more thought-disordered than the parents of individuals who are not thought-disordered (cf. Lidz, Wild, Shafer, Rosman, and Fleck, 1962). In order to examine this implication of Lidz's model, Romney (1969) administered the *Bannister—Fransella Grid Test of Thought Disorder* to fifty-one relatives of schizophrenics patients, thirty-four relatives of neurotic patients and thirty-four relatives of non-psychiatric patients. Although the results failed to confirm his hypothesis that the relatives of schizophrenics are more thought-disordered than those of normals and neurotics, he suggests (p. 1002) that 'it is probable that had more subjects been tested the differences would have become significant'.

Winter (1975) contends that Romney's study 'can be criticized for its inclusion of siblings, and of parents as old as 85 years in the groups of relatives as differences between the groups might thus have been obscured' (p. 280). Muntz and Power (1970) were able to show that significantly more parents of thought-disordered schizophrenics than those of non-thought-disordered patients were identified as thought-disordered themselves on the basis of the *Bannister–Fransella Grid Test*. Winter (1975) also found that the parents of schizophrenics exhibited significantly lower intensity scores on this test than did the parents of non-schizophrenic, psychiatric patients. In addition, he found a significant correlation ($r = 0.55$) between the intensity scores of schizophrenics and those of their parents, which is parallel to the correlation he found between the intensity scores of his control patients and those of their parents ($r = 0.65$). Winter (p. 288) notes that his own findings are consistent with Lidz's general hypothesis that schizophrenics, as well as other populations, 'learn their mode of general organization of conventional constructs from their parents'.

Higgins and Schwarz (1976) contend that Kelly 'generally minimized the importance of reinforcement in discussing the way people learn to use constructs . . . [and] adherents of his theory, such as Bannister, also ignore the potential role of social reinforcement in the development of pathological construing' (p. 805). It is true that both Kelly and Bannister eschew the concept of *reinforcement* in favour of that of *validation* in accounting for progressive changes in the structure and content of personal construct systems. It is not accurate to say, however, that Bannister overlooks the importance of 'feedback' from other people in the genesis of clinical thought disorder. On the contrary, Bannister and Salmon's (1966) 'specificity hypothesis' assigns 'social validation', or more precisely, the lack of it, the central role in causing the gradual disintegration of conceptual structures in thought-disordered schizophrenics. There is still insufficient evidence to evaluate fully their specificity hypothesis, but there is no doubt concerning its implications in terms of Bannister's 'serial invalidation' hypothesis. The interpersonal experience of thought-disordered patients has now become the primary focus of research within the context of this model (cf. Bannister *et al.*, 1975).

VALIDITY AND CLINICAL UTILITY

Bannister and Fransella (1966, 1967) have developed a standardized instrument for the assessment of clinical thought disorder, which they have named the *Grid Test of Schizophrenic Thought Disorder*. They devised a new repertory grid format in which eight passport-type photographs of people, four women and four men, are successively rank-ordered by the subject on the basis of each of six adjectives (constructs): *kind, stupid, selfish, sincere, mean*, and *honest* (in that order). This entire task is completed by the subject twice in immediate succession. Two scores—intensity and consistency of relationship—are derived from the test protocol of each subject.

In computing the overall intensity score, Spearman rank-order correlations are calculated for all possible pairs of adjectives in both *Grid I* (first administration) and *Grid II* (second administration) separately. Each of these correlations is squared and multiplied by 100 (retaining the sign of the original correlation for computing the consistency score) to yield the coefficient of determination for each pair of constructs. The absolute values of these coefficients are summed across both grids to yield a total intensity of relationship score for each subject. Although it would be easier to estimate overall intensity by calculating a single coefficient of concordance for the entire twelve by sixteen matrix composed of both grids, both the magnitude and direction of the correlation between each construct and every other from each separate grid is needed later in computing the consistency of relationship score. The fifteen correlations between the six constructs in each grid are separately rank-ordered from the highest positive one down to the highest negative one, and a single Spearman correlation is computed between these two sets of rankings to yield an index of consistency in the pattern of relationships between constructs across grids.

In their original validational study, Bannister and Fransella (1966, 1967) administered their test to a sample of 188 subjects, which included thirty normal adults, thirty depressives, twenty neurotics, twenty organics, twenty-eight subnormals, thirty thought-disordered schizophrenics, and thirty non-thought-disordered schizophrenics. As in Bannister's (1960, 1962b) two earlier studies, the thought-disordered schizophrenics exhibited significantly less statistical association among constructs (intensity) and less consistency in the pattern of relationships between constructs from the first to the second administration (consistency of relationship) than did any other group (including non-thought-disordered schizophrenics), except the organics. Neither intensity nor relationship consistency scores were found to correlate significantly with IQ within any of these groups; however, intensity and consistency of relationship were observed to be significantly related to each other within every group except the neurotics. Bannister and Fransella suggest that the latter finding is not really problematic, since 'by no means all the discriminating variance of the two measures is held in common and the capacity of the test to detect thought disorder is substantially improved if both measures are used' (p. 98).

As we saw in Chapter 2, a second measure of consistency can be derived from the repertory grid, which was not included in Bannister and Fransella's study. This is an index of the extent to which the same elements are ranked in the same order on the basis of the same constructs from the first administration of the test to the second one. It can be argued that this index provides an estimate of the 'true' test-retest reliability of this instrument (cf., Slater, 1972). This measure is generally referred to as the *element consistency* score, to distinguish it from Bannister's index of the consistency of relationship. The fact that element consistency was not assessed by Bannister and Fransella (1966), or in previous related studies (Bannister, 1960; 1962b), has provided the major focus of doubt concerning the construct validity of the *Grid Test of Schizophrenic Thought Disorder*.

For instance, Frith and Lillie (1972) contend that element consistency discriminates thought-disordered schizophrenics from other clinical populations and normals more accurately than either intensity or consistency of relationship. They submit evidence which indicates that when element consistency is itself partialled-out, both intensity and consistency of relationship scores fail to discriminate between thought-disordered and non-thought-disordered subjects. In addition, Haynes and Phillips (1973), using an instrument which closely resembles a repertory grid test, report that, when element consistency is partialled-out, intensity scores do not significantly discriminate between thought-disordered schizophrenics and other populations. They argue that, since there is some evidence that element consistency itself discriminates more accurately between thought-disordered and non-thought-disordered subjects than does either intensity or consistency of relationship, 'an alternative interpretation of his [Bannister's] results is that thought-disordered schizophrenics are simply more inconsistent than other groups' (p. 209). They submit further that, 'it does not require the elaborate conceptual apparatus of personal construct theory to tell us that thought-disordered schizophrenics are inconsistent' (p. 215). Frith and Lillie (1972, p. 78) also argue that 'inconsistency' as an explanatory concept is 'at a lower level of abstraction' than is Bannister's notion of loosened construing, and thus, the former is presumed to be more consistent with the principle of parsimony in scientific explanation.

These criticisms of the rationale of the *Bannister—Fransella Grid Test* are not consistent with all the data which are now available. For instance, McPherson, Blackburn, Draffan, and McFayden (1973) report that Bannister and Fransella's (1966) intensity and consistency of relationship scores correlate significantly with clinical ratings of the severity of thought disorder of a sample of patients diagnosed as schizophrenic. Moreover, when the effects of intensity and consistency of relationship were themselves partialled-out, they observed no significant relationship between element consistency alone and clinical judgements of the severity of thought disorder. Finally, both intensity and consistency of relationship scores were found to correlate with clinical ratings of thought disorder with element consistency partialled-out. McPherson *et al.* (p. 420) argue on the basis of these findings that 'not only has the Bannister–Fransella test been successfully cross-validated as a measure of thought disorder, but the results also support Bannister's explanation that low scores on this test reflect a loose construct system'.

It would seem now that the best policy would be to follow Radley's (1974) recommendation of calculating both element consistency and relationship consistency, in addition to intensity, whenever repertory grid tests are used to assess thought disorder. Radley points out, for example, that subjects might 'show a marked reallocation of elements over successive occasions, but maintain the intensity of relationships' (p. 316), which is essentially what Bannister (1963, 1965a) observed to be his subjects' initial response to 'serial invalidation'.

Fransella and Bannister (1977, p. 114) argue that

The essential weakness of the 'element inconsistency' way of conceptualizing what is going on is that it is so close to the concrete data that it amounts essentially to a re-naming of the process rather than an explanation of it. Certainly thought-disordered schizophrenics change their mind about the judgements they make (as do many of us drunk or sober), but the problem remains—why do we change our minds? Construct theory, in terms of its description of construing processes and arguments from the nature of validation and invalidation, offers an explanation. It is this explanation which is embodied in the notion of loose construing which underlies the grid test of thought disorder. To retreat to a kind of conceptual pointing to the concrete data of grids is literally to make them good for nothing.

In other words, the 'alternative explanation' proposed by Frith and Lillie (1972) and Haynes and Phillips (1973) seems simply to beg the question concerning the construct validity of the grid test of thought disorder. Construct validity is not assessed entirely in terms of the correlation between scores on a test and a single criterion. It is basically a question of the 'meaning', or correct interpretation, of these scores. Frith and Lillie (1972) and Haynes and Phillips (1973) imply that the observed inconsistency of thought-disordered schizoph-renics on the grid test of thought disorder can be accounted for in terms of their being unable to discriminate among complex visual stimuli such as photographs of faces. Bannister (1972), in reply, argues that this is 'exactly what would have been predicted from a "loose construing" argument and the proposed con-ceptualization is the same notion at a lower level of abstraction' (p. 413). He claims that their 'reinterpretation' of inconsistency on his grid test is therefore not a clear alternative to his own 'loose construing hypothesis', but rather 'a specific sub-hypothesis derivable from the loose construing hypothesis' (p. 412). For example, Bannister (1962b, p. 841) suggests that 'schizophrenic thought disorder is experienced subjectively as living in a fluid, unfocused, and *undifferentiated* world'.

Bannister (1972) also contends that the term *loose construing* has little or no meaning 'unless it is seen in relation to the theoretical framework within which it was derived' (p. 413), that is, personal construct theory as a whole. Its specific theoretical meaning can be elaborated in relation to other hypotheses concerning the development and organization of conceptual processes within the context of this theory. Radley (1974) also points out that the position maintained by Frith and Lillie (1972) and Haynes and Phillips (1973) 'not only fails to account for why thought-disordered schizophrenics might be inconsistent, but also throws open the whole question of how normal people establish and maintain consistency in their thinking' (p. 316). It is a major advantage of Bannister's 'loose construing' hypothesis over the alternative hypothesis advanced by his critics that it is not based on either implicit or *ad hoc* assumptions concerning 'normal' conceptual processes, but rather is logically derived from a specific model of individual cognitive development which attempts to explain both 'normal' and 'abnormal' thinking on the basis of the same set of theoretical principles.

Within the explicit framework of personal construct theory, the implications of Bannister's loose construing hypothesis are becoming increasingly clear. One of the most important of these, discussed at some length in the preceding chapter, is that the opposite logical extreme to 'cognitive simplicity' (monolithic conceptual structure) is not organizational complexity, but rather *chaos*. An individual's personal construct system can become so fragmented that, although he may still have a relatively large repertory of constructs available (Crockett's (1965) operational definition of differentiation), there may be insufficient linkages between his constructs to enable him to relate one aspect of his experience to another. He may thereby avoid specific invalidation of his anticipations, but only at the cost of living in a mostly fluid and meaningless world. It clearly follows that it cannot be the number of constructs (differentiation) alone which determines the level of efficiency of an individual's construct system in processing information. This implies in turn that the development of conceptual structure involves not only differentiation between substructures, but also a progressive reintegration of relatively independent substructures at increasingly higher levels of abstraction.

The most extensive validational study based on the grid test of thought disorder was carried out simultaneously at three different National Health Service hospitals in the UK by Bannister, *et al.* (1971). The main objective of this research was to cross-validate the results of the original standardization study (Bannister and Fransella, 1966, 1967). A total sample of 316 psychiatric patients across three hospitals, 172 women and 144 men, completed the test. The overall mean intensity and consistency of relationship scores were found to be 1084 (SD = 499) and 0.66 (SD = 0.43) respectively. Neither score correlated significantly with either age, sex, or verbal IQ, which is consistent with all previous findings (Bannister and Fransella, 1966; Bannister, 1960, 1962b).

A subsample of 200 patients had been specifically examined for clinical signs of thought disorder by their own psychiatrists prior to testing. In the remaining 116 cases clinical judgements of thought disorder and grid test scores could have been contaminated. Out of the subsample of 200, thirty-two patients were judged by their own psychiatrists to be clinically thought-disordered and 168 were judged to be free of thought disorder. Intensity and consistency of relationship scores were 'cut' at 1000 and 0.49 respectively (cf. Bannister and Fransella, 1967). All subjects scoring below these cut-off points on both indices were identified as thought-disordered with respect to their grid test performances. The test was found to agree with the psychiatric judgements in 152 out of 200 cases ($\chi^2 = 12.261$; 1 df; $p < .001$).

Nevertheless, the proportion of 'false positives', that is, patients identified as thought-disordered by the test but judged to be free of thought disorder by their own psychiatrists, was thirty-one out of forty-six, or slightly more than two-thirds of those scoring below the designated cutting scores on the test. On the other hand, the proportion of 'false negatives', that is, those judged to be thought-disordered by their own psychiatrists but not identified as such by the test itself, was seventeen out of 154, or only 11 per cent. A major problem in this study was that the distribution of the criterion, that is, psychiatric diagnosis of thought disorder, deviated markedly from a 50/50 split in favour of the 'non-thought-disordered' category. Out of the total sample of 200 patients 168 were identified by their psychiatrists as being free from thought disorder (84 per cent).

Thus, predictions made without the test, that is, in terms of the 'base rates' alone, could have been expected to be correct 84 per cent of the time. On the other hand, predictions made on the basis of the test scores alone were found to be correct only 76 per cent of the time.

In general, given a test of less than perfect validity (i.e. 100 per cent accuracy), this kind of maldistribution of the criterion variable will lead to an increase in the proportion of false positives (cf. Meehl and Rosen, 1955). A fair test of the efficiency of the instrument would require a situation where the distribution of the criterion approached more closely to a 50/50 split. For instance, Salmon et al. (1967) administered the grid test of thought disorder to twenty-four schizophrenics, eleven of whom had been diagnosed as thought-disordered by the consultant psychiatrist responsible for them. The remaining thirteen were judged to be completely free from thought disorder by their own consultants. The test agreed with the psychiatrists in twenty-one out of twenty-four cases. From the standpoint of test scores, there were only two false positives and one false negative, which is indeed quite encouraging. However, these assessment conditions may be somewhat artificial in terms of the 'natural' incidence of thought disorder in a typical hospital population. The data presented by Bannister et al. (1971) were based on randomly selected admissions in three different hospitals. Therefore, the proportion of thought-disordered patients in their sample probably did not differ significantly from that in the relevant clinical population.

Poole (1976) reports the results of a further attempt to cross-validate the test in a situation where 'the base rate for thought disorder is 50 per cent, so without testing and simply pronouncing all patients as being non-thought-disordered, the probability of a psychologist being correct is 0.5' (p. 184). He administered the test to seventy-five patients, forty-three men and thirty-two women, thirty of whom were clinically assessed by their own psychiatrists to be thought-disordered, and thirty of whom were judged to be free from thought disorder. The remaining fifteen cases were considered doubtful, and were excluded from the analysis. The test and the psychiatrists agreed in thirty-eight out of sixty cases ($\chi^2 = 4.1761$, 1 df; $p < .05$). Of the sixteen patients who scored below the stipulated cut-off points for intensity and consistency of relationship, twelve were clinically assessed to be thought-disordered by their own psychiatrists. Thus, there were four false positives (25 per cent). Of the forty-four patients who were not identified as being thought-disordered on the basis of their test scores, eighteen were judged to be thought-disordered by their own psychiatrists, indicating that the proportion of false negatives was .41. Thus, the overall percentage of misclassification based on test scores was observed to be 37 per cent in a situation wherein the criterion was ideally distributed. Poole concludes that 'a psychologist, by using the test, would improve on the misclassification rate obtained by employing the base rate (alone)' (p. 184). He does question, however, whether his own sample is representative with respect to the distribution of thought disorder in relevant clinical populations.

In the original standardization study, Bannister and Fransella (1967) decided to set their cutting scores so as to minimize the number of false positives (less than 7 per cent). The results of Bannister *et al.* (1971) and Poole (1976) are quite disappointing in this respect; although those of Salmon *et al.* (1967) seem more encouraging. Bannister *et al.* (1971) suggest that the unreliability of psychiatric judgement in general may have militated against the accuracy of the test producing 'a relatively harsh context for cross-validation' (p.144). In Bannister and Fransella's (1966) original sample, the presence or absence of thought disorder was determined by three judges—the responsible consultant psychiatrist, the junior doctor dealing with the case and the psychologist. Bannister *et al.* (1971) and Poole (1976) both employed only one psychiatrist to assess clinically the presence of thought disorder, which could have decreased the reliability of the criterion, and thereby caused some 'drift' in the validity of test scores. On the other hand, as Poole points out, 'there is a remarkable degree of similarity between the results of the present investigation (Poole, 1976) and those of other published studies (Bannister *et al.*, 1971; Frith and Lillie, 1972, see below; and McPherson *et al.* 1973), and all yield considerably higher rates of mis-classification than did Bannister and Fransella's (1966) standardization study' (p. 185). Finally, it may be relevant that Poole's sample was made up entirely of patients referred for assessment because of doubts concerning their diagnostic status; whereas the original standardization sample reported by Bannister and Fransella (1966) included only undisputed cases.

McPherson *et al.* (1973) employed a sample of 111 psychiatric patients, including thirty-six thought-disordered schizophrenics, twenty-four non-thought-disordered schizophrenics, eighteen manics and thirty-three depressives. They found that the thought-disordered schizophrenics exhibited significantly lower intensity and consistency of relationship scores than any of the other groups. Using the cutting scores prescribed by Bannister and Fransella (1967), twenty-one out of thirty-six thought-disordered schizophrenics (clinically diagnosed) were correctly identified as such on the basis of their performance on the test. This represents a 'hit' rate of 58 per cent. There were seventeen false positives (45 per cent), and fifteen false negatives (21 per cent) on the test. The overall agreement between test scores and psychiatric diagnosis was seventy-nine out of 111 cases (71 per cent) ($\chi^2 = 13.74$; 1 df; $p < .001$).

As in all the previous studies reviewed above, neither intensity nor consistency of relationship correlated significantly with age, sex, or verbal IQ. The distribution of the criterion variable deviated markedly from a 50/50 split in this study, but not so widely as in the data reported by Bannister *et al.* (1971). In the (1973) study we could expect predictions made in terms of the base rates alone to be correct 68 per cent of the time. Therefore, as in Poole's study, the test exhibited some degree of 'incremental' validity (Sechrest, 1963). That is, a clinician using the test could be expected to make a correct prediction 71 per cent of the time, whereas he could expect to be right 68 per cent of the time if he used only the base rates in making his predictions. Nevertheless, this represents a rather modest increment in predictive efficiency over the base rates alone.

Frith and Lillie (1972) administered the test to ninety-five psychiatric patients, including eleven schizophrenics diagnosed as thought-disordered. Another twelve patients were excluded from the analysis because they were either diagnosed as organic or had IQs below 80. When Bannister and Fransella's (1967) cut-off points were used to identify thought disorder, the test and psychiatric diagnoses agreed in seventy out of eighty-three cases (84 per cent) ($\chi^2 = 9.93$; 1 df; $p < .001$). Nonetheless, in this particular sample, predictions made with the base rates alone could have been expected to be correct 87 per cent of the time. The proportion of false positives was eight out of fourteen cases (57 per cent); whereas the proportion of false negatives was only five out of sixty-nine cases (7 per cent). Again, there were no significant correlations between either intensity or consistency of relationship and either age, sex, or IQ.

Hill (1976, p. 251), after reviewing the studies summarized above, concludes that 'it is clear that the Grid Test has substantial statistical validity in the sense of correlating beyond chance level with clinical judgements of schizophrenic thought disorder [however] the test, at least in its present form, has no appreciable utility'. He points out that a clinically useful test should generate more accurate predictions than can be derived from the base rates alone, and the proportion of false positives should not exceed that of false negatives. Bannister and Fransella (1966) attempted to find cutting scores which would serve to minimize the proportion of false positives. The rationale underlying this objective is that being mistakenly diagnosed as thought-disordered may have more serious consequences for the patient himself than actually being thought-disordered and not having it recognized.

In some of the studies reviewed above, predictions made on the basis of the test were better than could fairly be expected using the base rates alone (Bannister and Fransella, 1966; McPherson et al. 1973; Poole, 1976; Salmon et al., 1967), and in others the base rates would have been more useful than the test (Bannister et al. 1971; Frith and Lillie, 1972). It might be argued that Poole's data, representing the accuracy of the test when the criterion is ideally distributed (i.e. 50/50) provide the fairest test of the 'true' clinical utility of the test. However, even under ideal conditions, as Poole (p. 186) points out, 'the rate of mis-classification is too high to justify the diagnostic use of the test'. As we noted earlier, whenever the distribution of the criterion deviates markedly from a 50/50 split, we can expect the proportion of false positives to increase. Thus, it is not surprising that Poole's is the only sample in which the proportion of false positives did not exceed that of false negatives. This is not at all encouraging, since, as Hill (1976) notes, we can expect the incidence of thought disorder in the settings in which the test is used to be typically far less than 50 per cent. Hill himself estimates approximately 10 per cent.

Bannister (1976, p.93), in replying specifically to the points raised by Hill (1976), questions whether clinical judgements themselves have any clinical utility. He argues that Hill arbitrarily assumes that clinical judgement is to be the criterion and the grid test is to be the predictor which is to be evaluated in terms of its correlation with clinical judgement. Bannister raises the following objection to this procedure:

The only virtue in the grid is that it has what Hill refers to as a 'clear and appealing rationale', whereas clinical judgement has little by the way of rationale, it is a descriptive response which says nothing as to the 'why' or the 'how' or the 'what do we do about' of schizophrenic thought disorder. (p. 93)

He concludes that, since neither the grid test nor clinical judgement provides us with a means of actually helping the patients themselves, neither grid nor clinical judgement has 'clinical utility'. Nonetheless, since Bannister himself originally chose to validate his test using clinical judgement as a criterion (Bannister and Fransella, 1966; Bannister et al., 1971), he can hardly lay this problem at the feet of Hill. It is simply a specific instance of the general lack of close correlations between diagnoses and methods of treatment in psychiatry (cf. Bannister, Salmon, and Lieberman, 1964), and is not peculiar to schizophrenic thought disorder.

A second major problem in evaluating the validity and clinical utility of the grid test of thought disorder is that most of the available evidence comes from 'retrospective' studies in which psychiatric diagnoses preceded grid testing. Therefore, this evidence strictly relates only to the concurrent validity of the test, that is, the extent to which test scores correlate with the current status of subjects with respect to the criterion variable. None of these data provides a basis for directly evaluating the predictive validity of this instrument, that is, the degree to which predictions made on the basis of this test are confirmed by subsequent events. For instance, the probability that a subject who has already been diagnosed as thought-disordered will obtain scores below the prescribed cutting points (Bannister and Fransella, 1967) on this test is not necessarily equivalent to the probability that a patient who obtains similarly low scores will at some time in the future be clinically diagnosed as thought-disordered (i.e. in general, the probability of A contingent upon B is not necessarily equal to the probability of B contingent upon A).

Bannister et al. (1971) did attempt to make some predictions about patients on the basis of their grid test performances. It was hypothesized (p. 147) that 'patients who have very low scores on the grid test might have a dubious prognosis in that thought disorder is deemed to represent a major breakdown in the integration of the person'. Two prognostic indices were found to relate significantly to test scores in the expected direction.

The 128 patients who were rated as being in good condition upon discharge from the hospital exhibited a mean intensity score of 1097; whereas the twenty-seven rated as being in relatively poor condition at the time of their discharge had a mean intensity score of 880. This difference is statistically significant ($p < .025$). It was found also that the average number of previous admissions for seventy-three patients who were identified as thought-disordered on the basis of their test scores was 1.67, while that for other patients was 1.16. Although this difference is also significant ($p < .05$), it is based on 'postdiction' rather than prediction. Three other prognostic indicators—length of current stay in the hospital, number of admissions in the year following testing, and total admissions up to one year following testing—did not correlate significantly with test performance.

Bannister *et al.* note (p. 148) that 'these results add only marginally to evidence of validity for the grid test but are of a kind worth seeking in that they are evidence different from, and independent of, the *psychiatrist's* judgement of 'thought-disordered'.

SOCIAL DEVIATIONS

In his first two studies concerned with the measurement of clinical thought disorder, Bannister (1960, 1962b) explored the question of whether or not thought-disordered patients differed from other populations in terms of the specific pattern of relationship between constructs as well as in terms of structural indices. Fransella and Bannister (1977) point out (p.87) that 'for a given group of constructs a large number of grids could be averaged and the resulting matrix of relationships between constructs looked on as a kind of normative map'. In his initial study Bannister (1960) found non-thought-disordered schizophrenics were significantly more 'socially deviant' than normals with respect to the specific patterns of inter-relationships among their constructs. In his second study, Bannister (1962b) employed a correlational measure of 'deviancy' which partialled-out the effects of individual differences with respect to intensity scores. This time, he found that 'thought-disordered schizophrenics appeared to be more deviant in whatever pattern they had managed to retain' (Bannister *et al.* 1971, p.148).

In the light of the results of Bannister (1962b), Bannister *et at.* (1971) focused primarily upon the 'content' of the residual conceptual structure in the grids of thought-disordered patients, that is, 'the question of which constructs relate to which positively or negatively' (p. 148). A single measure of 'social deviation' was derived from each subject's grid test protocol by means of the following procedure. Each of the fifteen correlations between pairs of constructs was assumed to have a 'modal direction positive or negative, for any normal population, this being (for the constructs in the order in which they are used in the test) $- - + - + + - + - - + - - + -$' (p. 148). It was then determined for each subject individually the extent to which the pattern of correlations in his own grid test performance deviated from the modal pattern. Correlations of zero were simply ignored, and any given correlation was identified as 'deviant' only if it was greater than 0.50, and was in a direction opposite to the 'norm'. The resulting index of social deviation was found to correlate 0.00 with intensity of relationship scores, indicating that 'deviant' patterns of construct relationships are probably not simply the product of 'random' responding. Social deviation scores also did not correlate with either age or intelligence. Interestingly, male patients were observed to be significantly more socially deviant as a group than female patients. Bannister *et al.* suggest that the latter finding may relate to the fact that a higher proportion of men than women are diagnosed as schizophrenics by psychiatrists.

The main finding of this study with respect to social deviation was that thirty-two patients who were judged by their own psychiatrists to be clinically thought-disordered exhibited significantly higher social deviation scores than did patients judged to be free of thought disorder ($p < .05$). A parallel finding was that those patients who were identified as thought-disordered on the basis of their grid test performances showed significantly higher social deviation scores than did patients who were non-thought-disordered in grid terms ($p < .01$). The latter finding, together with the fact that social deviation scores correlate zero with intensity scores, implies that social deviation scores can be expected to correlate negatively with consistency of relationship scores. The observed correlation between these two indices was -0.21 ($p < .01$), which suggests that 'deviant' patterns of construct relationships might be relatively unstable. This seems consistent with Bannister's (1963, 1965a) finding that there are frequent 'reversals' of construct relationships under conditions of 'serial invalidation', which he presumes to be a determinant of thought disorder. Bannister *et al.* conclude (p. 149) that 'the data support the general argument that a breakdown in structure may be initiated by deviant patterning. Ideas become odd before they become chaotic and lose their linkages'. The results of Higgins and Schwarz (1976), previously discussed, also lend support to this hypothesis.

McPherson *et al.* (1973), employing the same measure as Bannister *et al.* (1971), found that the social deviation scores of thirty-six thought-disordered Schizophrenics were significantly higher than those of twenty-four non-thought-disordered schizophrenics ($\chi^2 = 10.04$; $p < .01$); eighteen manics ($\chi^2 = 6.00$; $p < 01$), and thirty-three depressives ($\chi^2 = 8.08$; $p < .02$). None of the differences between the non-thought-disordered groups was significant. They also compared the social deviation scores of nineteen schizophrenics with the independent ratings of two psychiatrists concerning severity of thought disorder. The observed correlation was 0.58 ($p < .01$). As in Bannister *et al.*'s (1971) study, social deviation scores did not relate significantly to either age or IQ. McPherson *et al.* were unable to replicate Bannister *et al.*'s finding that men exhibit more social deviation than women. They conclude that their results 'confirm the main finding of Bannister *et al.* (1971) that clinically thought-disordered patients have abnormally high Social Deviation scores' (p. 424).

The finding that thought-disordered patients exhibit significantly more 'social deviation' in the grid test than other clinical populations is also consistent with Radley's (1974, p. 324) hypothesis that 'although the schizoid person retains construct labels which denote highly abstract concepts in public use, he uses these labels within the context of constructions which are now idiosyncratic and of *a different form* to those he might have originally employed'. For instance, in the grid test itself, the adjectives *kind, stupid*, etc. are perhaps no longer understood by the thought-disordered subject as referring to the public, or 'lexical', meanings of these words. On the other hand, the finding that even thought-disordered schizophrenics obtain higher intensity scores on the grid test when they rank-order photographs of people on E + adjectives than when they use E − ones (Adams-Webber, 1977a) suggests that their judgements are still influenced to some extent by the 'public' connotative meanings of these adjectives. (see Chapter 7).

Radley (p.324) speculates further that 'the thought-disordered person's language no longer adequately serves to synthesize his thought and symbolize his conceptual processes'. This line of inference brings us up against the difficult, if not insoluble, problem of trying to specify the relation between thought and language in schizophrenic speech and writing (cf. Maher, 1966). In our attempts to explain the lack of 'communicability' of the utterances of schizophrenics it is never clear whether the data with which we are dealing represent a garbled transcript of a more or less coherent thought process, a relatively clear transcript of incoherent thinking or, worst of all, a garbled transcript of incoherent thoughts. There may be no point in trying to differentiate between 'psycho-linguistic' and 'cognitive' factors in interpreting the speech of thought-disordered schizophrenics.

Bannister's own loose construing hypothesis can subsume the finding that thought-disordered patients exhibit a higher degree of social deviation on his grid test than do other groups. Specifically, this hypothesis implies that as the ranges of convenience of constructs diminish, and the relationships between them begin to reverse and eventually fade away, the pattern of one's judgements will become progressively more unstable. Therefore, as patients become more 'inconsistent' in the pattern of relationships between their constructs, their judgements will, by definition, tend to deviate from any 'modal pattern' of meaning. Thus, it is not surprising that social deviation scores correlate negatively with consistency of relationship scores in the grid test of thought disorder.

As Fransella and Bannister (1977) point out, an important question is that of the reliability of the 'normative maps' of patterns of construct relationships derived from group grid test data. Bannister (1962a) presents evidence that 'though there are considerable variations in individual construct relationship pattern, it may be that from samples of a relatively limited size, reliable *normative* estimates can be established' (Fransella and Bannister, 1977, p. 87) (see Chapter 7).

Finally, a secondary finding of Bannister *et al.* (1971) was that fourteen patients with a wide variety of different diagnostic labels, who were described in their case notes as having a 'clear precipitating factor for their illness', had a mean social deviation score of 2.50 (SD = 2.50), while those twelve patients who were described as having 'no precipitating factor' had a mean of .33 (SD = 1.16), yielding a significant difference ($p < .02$). They suggest (p. 149) that 'the precipitating factor here may refer to some single event, traumatic enough to require a special and peculiar adaptive patterning of his constructs on the part of the confronted person'. This is consistent with Cochran's (1976a) general hypothesis that traumatic situations facilitate change on core concepts, which, in turn, can lead to extensive revisions of construct relationships, perhaps in extremely deviant ways.

There are basically two general approaches which can be adopted in assessing Bannister's model of the genesis of clinical thought disorder. The first approach, the one which is usually undertaken by experimental psychopathologists, is to continue to derive predictions from this model concerning how thought-

96

disordered patients will differ from normals and other clinical populations on a variety of different 'criterion' variables, and systematically test these predictions one by one so that the evidence for and against the model can be gradually built up. We can evaluate the model, either as a whole or in piecemeal fashion, against these accumulated 'facts'. The alternative approach, the one which is clearly favoured by Bannister and co-workers, is to derive a way of helping thought-disordered patients from the principles of the model, trying it out and evaluating the outcome (Bannister, 1976, p. 93). Such an experimental treatment pro-gramme is reported by Bannister *et al.* (1975).

SERIAL VALIDATION

Bannister (1965a), himself points out that his own experiments do not really provide a direct test of the 'serial invalidation' hypothesis as an explanation of the genesis of clinical thought disorder because 'the link between the condition in its clinically dramatic form and the laboratory manipulation is missing' (p.381). He notes further that an experiment in which the clinical features of thought disorder can be modified through the application of the basic principles of his model would provide a much stronger test of his hypothesis.

Bannister *et al.* (1975) attempted to reverse the process of thought disorder by means of a 'serial validation' procedure. This experiment was carried out in two phases. In the first phase, the existing patterns of construct relationships for individuals identified as clinically thought-disordered were 'mapped' by means of extensive clinical interviews and repertory grid testing in order to locate some areas of residual structure in what was still left of their conceptual frameworks. In the second phase of the experiment, the environment of individual patients was systematically engineered in an attempt to provide mostly validating evidence for the linkages between their constructs. They were retested at regular intervals throughout the experiment in order to assess whether any changes had occured in the level of integration of their construct systems in response to this validating experience. In short, the serial validation procedure employed in this experiment is essentially the logical converse of the serial invalidation procedure used in Bannister's (1963, 1965a) earlier experiments. That is, 'the serial invalidation hypothesis was simply inverted, and it was argued that the experience of repeated validation might result in a progressive strengthening of the links between constructs, a reordering of thought' (Bannister *et al.*, 1975, p. 171).

The results of two previous studies, discussed above (Bannister and Salmon, 1966; Salmon *et al.*, 1967) suggested that it is people who particularly confuse the thought-disordered patient and that it is his subsystem of psychological constructs which is especially loose. Thus, the experimental regime set up for each thought-disordered patient by Bannister *et al.* (1975) primarily involved 'interpersonal' situations:

The content his loose construing system was to be investigated in considerable detail using varying forms of grid and by the analysis of long tape-recorded conversations. It was hoped to discern the nature of his vague expectations and then repeatedly engineer situations in which these expectations would be fulfilled. Thereby the links between the constructs which had generated the expectations would gradually be strengthened and other constructs which were part of the same loose constellation might be drawn in, so that eventually the whole subsystem (specifically his subsystem of constructs about people and interpersonal relationships) might be strengthened and elaborated. Just as it was shown by Bannister (1963, 1965a) that repeated validation tightens the construct system starting from a normal base, it was argued that the same might be true for a construct system starting from an abnormally loose base. If the vague and probabilistic bets of a person's interpretative system begin to pay off, then bets might be made with increasing confidence and the theory which generated those bets may be strengthened and developed. (p. 171)

It is important to note that no attempt was made to validate directly the linkages between constructs, as in Rehm's (1971) laboratory experiment (discussed above). Rather, the patient's constructions of people, which were presumed to have been derived on the basis of the existing linkages between constructs within his own system, were consistently validated in the hope that this would indirectly validate those linkages and strengthen them. As Rehm points out, this represents the same rationale as that underlying the validational procedures in Bannister's (1963, 1965a) earlier serial invalidation experiments.

A sample of twenty four severely thought-disordered patients was randomly divided into experimental and control groups of twelve patients each (one member of the control group died before the end of the experiment). Each of these patients had originally been selected for the study on the basis of the following four criteria: (1) two psychologists independently detected clear signs of thought disorder (e.g. vagueness, irrelevance, poverty of thought, clang associations, neologisms, word-salads, blocking, etc.) during separate clinical interviews with the patient; (2) intensity and consistency of relationship scores were below the stipulated cut-off points of 1000 and 0.49 respectively on the grid test of thought disorder (Bannister and Fransella (1967); (3) the Mill Hill verbal IQ was above 80; and (4) the patient's age was between 18 and 60. Most of these patients were described as 'chronic schizophrenics' in their case notes. They had all been hospitalized continuously for at least two years at the beginning of the programme. There were no significant differences between the experimental and control group with respect to either age, IQ, length of hospitalization, or grid test scores.

In order to minimize the possible effects of any differences between the experimental and control patients in terms of the overall amount of attention paid to them by staff during the period of the experiment, the control patients were identified as 'experimental' to the doctors, nurses, and occupational therapists responsible for them. It was specifically suggested that they should be treated as special patients and subjected to a so-called 'total push' regime. The experimental patients were assigned randomly in groups of three to each of the four psychologists on the research team. Each patient was seen by the same psychologist approximately once a fortnight for a total period of two years and three months. Firstly, the personal construct system of each patient was assessed

98

by means of extensive grid testing and clinical interviews in order to locate clusters of interrelated 'psychological' constructs, which were viewed as 'islands of meaning in the generally chaotic and poorly structured fabric of the systems of constructs which the patient used for viewing himself and other people in interpersonal and psychological terms (p. 172)'. Figure 2 presents a diagram of a constellation of interrelated psychological constructs extracted from the repertory grid protocol of one male patient—'Bill'.

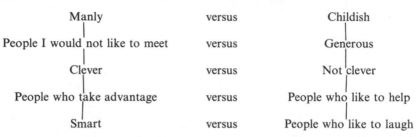

Figure 2. (Reproduced by permission of the British Psychological Society from Bannister *et al.*, 'Reversing the process of thought disorder: a serial validation hypothesis', *Brit. J. soc. clin. Psychol.* (1975), **14**, 173, published by Cambridge University Press

When one or more such clusters of interrelated constructs had been identified for each patient, she or he was encouraged to formulate some differential predictions about persons in the immediate environment, using these constructs. An attempt was then made to provide evidence confirming these predictions. For example, a nurse whom Bill construed as 'a person who likes to help' might have been instructed to give him cigarettes, thereby providing potential validation for the linkage between his constructs *generous* and *people who like to help* (see Figure 2). However, the experimenters often found that in their attempts to set up specifically validating experiences they had initially misunderstood the concrete meaning ('operational definition') and implications of the target constructs. For example, consider again the cluster of interrelated constructs represented in Figure 2 above:

The problem is that the system pivots on the construct *manly-childish* but this construct is destructively ambiguous. In conversation *manly* was sometimes operationally defined as *going to work, aggressive, punctual, being taken notice of, loving your family*, while *childish* was *record-playing, being happy, eating sweets, dancing, watching T.V.*. Bill's dominant relative was a sister who 'wanted to help me' and 'treats me like a child' and who Bill sometimes claimed was really his mother. Bill *both* wanted to be a child and hated being treated as a child. The psychologist was seen as *manly* (therefore *taking advantage*) and the system proved singularly difficult to validate in any meaningful way. (p. 173)

Bannister *et al.* observe that it became increasingly clear in the course of this experimental treatment programme that the construct systems of thought-disordered patients were not simply weakened forms of 'normal' conceptual systems, but rather dilute forms of construct systems which had been grossly distorted before they had weakened. This observation is consistent with Bannister's (1963, 1965a) finding that in his serial invalidation experiments normal subjects, when confronted with repeated predictive failure, initially alter the pattern of linkages between their constructs with the result that some of their constructs acquire rather peculiar implications (e.g. *sincere* being negatively related to *honest*). Another relevant finding, discussed in the previous section, is that the constructs of patients clinically diagnosed as thought-disordered are more 'socially deviant' in the ways in which they are related to one another than are the constructs of other psychiatric patients (Bannister *et al.*, 1971). In addition, the case histories of the patients in the serial validation project were found to include frequent references to 'deluded' and 'paranoid' behaviour, suggesting that 'gross disturbances of *content* had taken place before the final disintegration of structure' (Bannister *et al.*, 1975, p. 178).

Thus, an adequate serial validation programme may require more than simply discovering still existing clusters of interrelated constructs for each patient and then assuming that the patient 'operationally defines' his constructs in the same way as every one else. To get from the patient's own verbal labels for his constructions to the actual discriminations which he is able to make may involve a complicated code-breaking procedure. Bannister *et al.* suggest that 'a failure to interpret the code correctly may mean that what is intended as validation is experienced as further mystification' (p. 179). Kelly (1955, p. 587) summarizes this general problem in the following terms:

Now a good therapist must frequently, among other things, be accepting of the client. He should attempt to anticipate events in the way the client anticipates them. He should try to employ the client's vocabulary in thinking about the issues which the client sees himself as facing. He should give words the meaning that the client gives them, rather than the meanings the dictionary gives them or the personal or professional meanings he has himself customarily given them.

Kelly considered that this form of 'support' is an important aspect of psychotherapy with all clients; however, it may be especially crucial in working with clients who are thought-disordered.

Another major problem which arose in the course of the serial validation project was 'a clear failure to achieve the necessary degree of control over the environments of the 12 thought-disordered people in the experimental group' (p. 177). A fairly high level of control would be a necessary condition for a strict experimental test of the serial validation hypothesis itself. First of all, it clearly calls for something more than simple kindness and sympathy from everyone surrounding the patient. Indeed, it may require relatively 'harsh' treatment of the patient on the part of particular individuals if that is what he specifically *expects* from them. It also differs from even the most comprehensive operant conditioning regime in that it is based on fulfilment of expectation rather than reward as such. In short, 'the aim is to create a meaningful relationship between the behaviour of other persons toward the patient and the view and expectations of the patient about those particular people—specifically it is an attempt to make their behaviour meaningful to the patient in his own terms' (p.173).

It was possible for the psychologists and nurses in immediate contact with the patients to provide direct 'validational' evidence of the type required. Nevertheless, these contacts represented only a small sector of the patient's full sphere of interpersonal experience during the period of the experiment. Each patient was also surrounded by other patients, who 'whatever they might have been doing, were certainly not serial validating him' (p. 178). Also, the experimenters were largely unsuccessful in their attempts to persuade parents and relatives to modify their behaviour towards the patients in a 'validational' direction. For instance, 'apparent gains in the structure of the patient's thinking were abruptly and catastrophically swept away after a visit by a mother or other relative' (p. 178). Bannister *et al.* suggest that the entire project should have been organized from the outset around a single specialized unit wherein most of the patient's interpersonal interactions could have been carefully structured and observed, and the 'total world of the patient made more validating' (p. 178).

The main criterion of improvement employed in this experiment was discharge from the hospital by psychiatrists unaware of the patient's status with respect to the experiment itself, and remaining outside the hospital for a substantial period after the end of the treatment programme. A follow-up two years after the treatment programme had been concluded revealed that five out of the twelve experimental patients and two out of the eleven control patients had been discharged from, and were still out of, the hospital. Chronicity and IQ bore no relation to discharge. The difference between the experimental and control groups in terms of this criterion is not statistically significant, but as Bannister *et al.* point out (p. 177), 'it is interestingly tilted' in favour of the experimental group'.

An extensive battery of psychological tests was also administered to all patients at the beginning of the experiment and on three further occasions, at approximately eight-month intervals. This battery included the Bannister–Fransella (1967) *Grid Test of Schizophrenic Thought Disorder*; the *Hospital Adjustment Scale* (Ferguson, McReynolds, and Bellachy, 1951), the *TAT, Word-in-Context Test* (Werner and Kaplan, 1963), the *Structured Clinical Interview* (Burdock and Hardesty, 1969), and an analysis of speech samples. Significant changes over the four occasions of testing are summarized in Table 2. The experimental group showed significant improvement on nine of these indices and deteriorated on two of them, whereas the control group showed little change, improving on three indices and deteriorating on two of them.

This project cannot be called an experiment in the strictest sense of the term. It is more akin to programme evaluation research than to a laboratory test of a hypothesis. In the first place, although the general strategy of serial validation was carefully defined in formal terms, the actual procedures employed in this programme did not resemble laboratory manipulations. For example, it was impossible to specify the 'amount' of validation received by any patient. The treatment programme essentially consisted of long-term, close, interpersonal relationships between psychologists and patients. Secondly, a wide range of so-called 'background' variables, including most of the patients' hospital routines, as well as their contacts with relatives, were neither controlled nor systematically

Table 2. Significant changes over four occasions of testing

Measures	Experimental group
Grid Consistency (1–2)	$p < 0.01$ (deterioration)
Hospital Adjustment Scale total (1–2)	$p < 0.05$ (improvement)
HAS Communication and Relationship (1–2)	$p < 0.01$ (improvement)
Word-in-Context Semantic Unique (1–2)	$p < 0.01$ (improvement)
Structured Clinical Interview—Incongruous Behaviour (1–3)	$p < 0.01$ (improvement)
SCI Conceptual Dysfunction (1–4)	$p < 0.01$ (improvement)
SCI Self-Depreciation (2–3)	$p < 0.05$ (improvement)
HAS Work and Recreation (2–4)	$p < 0.02$ (improvement)
Speech Sample—psychological/non-psychological ratio (2–4)	$p < 0.02$ (deterioration)
Word-in-Context—Literal Unique (2–4)	$p < 0.05$ (improvement)
SCI Incongruous Ideation (2–4)	$p < 0.01$ (improvement)
Control group	
Word-in-Context—Number correct (1–3)	$p < 0.01$ (deterioration)
SCI Lethargy-Dejection (1–3)	$p < 0.05$ (improvement)
SCI Anger-Hostility (1–4)	$p < 0.01$ (improvement)
SCI Incongruous Behaviour (1 4)	$p < 0.02$ (improvement)
Word-in-Context—Semantic Unique (2–4)	$p < 0.01$ (deterioration)

(Reproduced by permission of the British Psychological Society from Bannister, D., Adams-Webber, J., Penn, W., and Radley, A. R., 'Reversing the process of thought disorder: a serial validation experiment,' *Brit. J. soc. clin. Psychol.*, (1975), **14**, p. 177, published by Cambridge University Press.

observed and recorded. Thus, it cannot be argued that this investigation produced any 'hard' evidence against which the serial validation hypothesis can be evaluated. On the other hand, when this project is viewed as a preliminary pilot investigation, the results do provide some fairly clear indications of how this hypothesis might be refined and tested more adequately:

Further research into the serial validation hypothesis might firstly require the establishment of a very much closer contextual control over the environment of the experimental patients than was achieved in the study reported. Secondly, it would demand a great deal more exploration, both in terms of grids and more informal methods to work out appropriate operational definitions of patients' constructs so that what is done in relation to the patient is indeed personally meaningful to him and validating for him. It may be that some areas of the patients' construing have to be ignored because, even though they have apparent structural potential, they offer their meanings so obscurely that it is impossible to relate to the patient on the basis of such construct clusters. (Bannister *et al.*, 1975, p.179)

In Chapter 6 we shall consider other specific procedures for facilitating conceptual reorganization and change which have been derived from the principles of personal construct theory. However, since the interpersonal relationship between client and therapist is a basic factor in all forms of psychological 'treatment', it is necessary to examine Kelly's model of role relationships in general and related research, which is discussed in the next chapter, before it is possible to appreciate his unique approach to psychotherapy.

5

Sharing the Perspectives of Others

Kelly (1955) assumes that each individual relies on his own personal constructs to plan, regulate, and explain his own actions. It follows that specific information about the content and structure of a person's construct system will provide a source of useful cues to anyone—friend, spouse, therapist, or even a stranger—who attempts to interpret or anticipate his or her behaviour. This general hypothesis has served as the basis for a considerable body of research concerned with effective communication and mutual understanding within the framework of personal construct theory. This work has focused upon a variety of interpersonal relationships including the initial encounter between strangers, friendship formation, marriage, and psychotherapy.

FORMING IMPRESSIONS

Shoemaker (1952) submits that if an individual customarily employs his own personal constructs to interpret his interpersonal experience, then the content of his construct system should manifest itself at some level in his social behaviour. Shoemaker hypothesized specifically that judges observing a subject during an interpersonal interaction would be able to pick out those constructs which had been elicited from the subject himself from a list which also included constructs elicited from other persons. It was found that judges were able to identify correctly the personal constructs elicited from twenty-one different subjects beyond chance expectation ($p < .02$) after having observed a sample of their behaviour in a social situation. Shoemaker was, however, unable to replicate this finding with a second group of twelve subjects.

In a subsequent experiment involving the forming of impressions of strangers, Adams-Webber (1968) asked judges to predict the self-ratings of thirty subjects (fifteen women and fifteen men) on a set of forty-four bi-polar dimensions, following a brief conversation with them. Half of these dimensions had been elicited previously from the subjects themselves and the other half were selected randomly from a pool of dimensions which had been elicited from peers of the subjects attending the same American university. Judges were able to predict the subjects' self-ratings significantly more accurately on the basis of the constructs which had been elicited from the subjects themselves ($F = 11.482$; 1/24 df; $p < .001$). No sex differences or interactions involving sex in terms of accuracy were observed. The results of this study and those of Shoemaker, considered together, indicate that judges are able to infer specific information about the content of an individual's personal construct system on the basis of his behaviour in a social situation. Research discussed later in this chapter suggests that this form of 'sociality' plays an important role in both friendship formation and psychotherapy.

This relationship seems to work the other way around as well. That is, access to the particular constructs elicited from an individual can significantly enhance the accuracy of judges' attempts to predict his behaviour. For instance, Payne (1956) asked subjects to try to predict the behaviour of each of two persons whom they had not met before. Every subject was supplied with a list of fifteen constructs previously elicited from one of these 'targets' and fifteen descriptive statements about the other formulated by a group of his own peers. Subjects attempted to anticipate the responses of both of their 'targets' on the same social questionnaire. Payne found that the predictions which were made on the basis of the constructs which had been elicited from 'targets' themselves were significantly more accurate. This evidence indicates that specific information about the content of an individual's personal construct system may be quite useful to others in anticipating his behaviour.

CONVERSATIONS AND OTHER EXCHANGES

Mair (1970a,b) has developed within the context of personal construct theory an elaborate 'conversational' technique by means of which two (or more) persons can explore together and share to some extent their own psychological perspectives. Suppose that two persons, A and B, wish to 'sit down together to undertake an exploratory study of how they each and together "theorize" and "experiment" about themselves, each other and others in general' (Mair, 1970a, p. 170). Mair approaches this problem from the point of view of the sociality corollary and Kelly's (1955, 1970) definition of a role relationship as a course of activity carried out in the light of one's understanding of another person's outlook.

Mair's conversational technique can be implemented in several clearly differentiated stages. During the initial 'formulations' stage, A first writes a brief character sketch of himself, putting down as candidly as possible what he thinks of himself. This 'private' self-characterization will never be seen by anyone else. Then, he prepares a second 'public' sketch of himself, in which he includes only those things which he feels perfectly comfortable about sharing with B. B also writes both 'private' and 'public' self-characterizations using the same set of 'ground rules' as those followed by A. Next, A creates two short character sketches of B. One of these, which he writes for himself alone, expresses a completely private view of B which the latter will never see. The second sketch is for B himself to read, and so its contents consist only of those impressions and judgements which A is comfortable about communicating to B. B also constructs two sketches of A, one for A to read and the other for himself alone.

Mair refers to the second stage of the interaction between A and B as 'confrontation and consequences'. It begins with an exchange of their 'public' sketches of one another. First, they record their own initial reactions to the new information which has been given them about themselves; 'what they feel, think, want to do, say, reject, accept, avoid or welcome about it' (Mair, 1970a). A period of discussion then follows in which A and B take turns in questioning each other in order to clarify for themselves what the other really said about them and to obtain further elaboration of points which they feel that they have not fully understood. During this discussion A and B also note down something about their own personal strategies for assimilating and discarding new information about themselves.

The third stage, called 'grounds for belief', is the point at which A and B question one another in turn about what evidence each has for the specific statements which he has made about the other, and what criteria he employed in each of his judgements. Mair (1970b, p. 252) suggests that 'in the course of this procedure each of us might find that there were some things which we did not want to tell the other'. Neither partner, however, should pressure the other 'to come clean' and reveal all his private thoughts and feelings about him.

In the fourth stage, termed 'inference about the other' both partners 'examine the description of themselves presented to them by the other and analyse it in terms of what it seems to suggest about the interests, ideas, strengths, limitations, tactics and such like of the person who wrote it' (Mair, 1970a, p. 170). Each partner may also question the other concerning the specific grounds for his inferences about himself (the questioner) as writer of a sketch. Finally, all four stages described above for dealing with the sketches of the other can be repeated for the sketches of the self. Then the initial face-to-face encounter is concluded, perhaps with an agreement to meet again at some point in the future to continue the experiment.

Mair points out that this entire cycle of encounter and withdrawal can be repeated an indefinite number of times or concluded at any point by mutual agreement, depending on the purpose of the experiment and the interests of the participants. In any event, he suggests that the 'conversation' will have some long-term consequences for both participants:

As they go, however, the study goes with them. In the encounter just completed many personal issues will have been touched on and stirred; each participant may find, whether he wishes it or not, that he continues to ruminate on, act out, experiment with, attempt to disconfirm or confirm in a variety of imaginary or practical ways some of the issues and possibilities raised. (Mair, 1970a, p. 171)

In this approach to 'interpersonal exploration' each partner serves as both 'experimenter' and 'subject'. They may not both entertain the same hypotheses concerning the outcome of their venture, and they may employ somewhat different strategies of enquiry; however, 'their status and functions are indistinguishable' (p. 178). Both participants are equally engaged in enacting a 'role' in Kelly's (1955, 1970) sense of the term, that is a course of activity carried out in the light of one's understanding of the point of view of the other.

Thomas (1977) argues that 'sociality', that is, construing the construction process of another person as a basis for participating in a role relationship with him, involves far more than simple verbal agreement or even behavioural prediction: 'it is a question of exchanging patterns of meaning, of being able to hold similar and elaborate sets of relationships in close juxtaposition'. Ultimately, what is needed, according to Thomas, is the ability to hold in mind simultaneously different systems of meaning, exploring each in relation to the other and identifying common areas of reference. This hypothesis is consistent with the general assumption that the person who is able to bring more than one set of related constructs to bear on the same social interaction is in a better position to interpret if from the point of view of another person and make accurate inferences about the other's construct system (Adams-Webber, 1970a; Olson and Partington, 1977).

Thomas (1977) has developed an 'exchange grid' technique for structuring the process of communication of the personal constructions of one individual to another and then assessing the effectiveness of this exchange of information. This approach has several parallels to Mair's 'conversation model' discussed above; however, Mair's approach relies primarily on Kelly's (1955) 'self-characterization' procedure (described further in the next chapter) while Thomas makes use of repertory grid methodology (summarized in Chapter 2). The basic mechanics of Thomas' technique are quite easily understood by anyone familiar with grid methods.

Person B is asked to perform a repertory grid test as if he were person A; and then A completes the same grid test as himself. The two resulting grid protocols are then directly compared with each other and any areas of mismatch are located and then discussed by A and B together. This entire procedure can be repeated several times until some predetermined level of agreement is eventually reached. To this extent, we can say that B is sharing that component of A's point of view that can be defined in terms of the specific constructs and elements included in the exchange grids. Meanwhile, A can also undertake a series of 'like-B' grid tests, until he also arrives at the desired level of understanding.

In the simplest form of exchange grid technique, A nominates a list of figures or some other type of elements, which are used in eliciting a set of constructs from him. A then rates every figure on each construct in turn. The 'verbal content' of A's figures and constructs is transcribed onto a blank form, which is then presented to B. B is asked to pretend to be A and to fill in the ratings on the grid form as he thinks A would do it. When B has completed his version of A's grid test performance, the two grid protocols are superimposed and a single matrix of difference scores is derived by subtracting the entry in each cell of one of the grids from the entry in the corresponding cell of the other grid, and squaring the result.

The sum of these squared difference scores across all rows serves as the overall measure of the extent of the disagreement between the two grids. Reference back to the original matrix of difference scores allows us to locate specific areas of both agreement and disagreement. The identification of the major points of disagreement in relation to particular constructs and elements provides a concrete focus for subsequent discussions between A and B in which contexts of meaning can be explored together and mutually understood.

Thomas suggests that the quality of such exchange discussions depends primarily upon the ability of the participants to take the constructs and elements apart, that is, move down through the hierarchy of meanings until all misunderstandings are identified and resolved in terms of direct references to particular people and events in the common experience of both partners. He points out that although metaphor, simile, and analogy are often helpful in the intermediate stages, specificity is necessary in the crunch points of the discussion. Thomas recommends further that A be B while B is A because then each partner will be committed to his own grid and must establish a specific pattern of meanings for himself before attempting to construe the meanings of the other. He indicates that his own experience with this exchange grid technique has shown that it is possible to recognize a 'good' exchange discussion. For example, he reports that many couples have found that the processes of exchange grid discussion result in greater refinement of shared meanings and often produce the experience of reconstruing the same events in a different way with an increase in mutual understanding.

Thomas' exchange grid procedure is designed to provide a more specific focus for discussion than is Mair's conversational approach. The latter involves a rather open-ended, global, and diffuse process of communication compared with the former's emphasis on particular constructs and elements. It would seem possible to combine the two techniques, using the exchange grid procedure to assess the effectiveness, and perhaps further refine, the processes of communication and interpersonal understanding initiated by means of the conversational model. There is not yet sufficient data available, however, for a systematic comparison of the two methods in terms of their relative ranges of convenience.

COUPLES

The ability to share the perspectives of others, while enhancing and facilitating day-to-day interactions with people in general, may be crucial to the well-being of a permanent role relationship. There has been some research within the framework of personal construct theory on the level of mutual understanding achieved by couples.

For instance, Ryle (1975) has developed a 'double dyad grid' which can be completed jointly by two persons. This procedure is based on his single 'dyad grid' technique, which is similar in structure to the standard repertory grid except that the elements are not individual people, but rather relationships between two persons: for example, 'yourself in relation to your father' and 'your father in relation to you'. In eliciting constructs for this type of grid test, elements are presented to subjects in pairs rather than in triads, as in Kelly's original technique (described in Chapter 2). The following form of elicitation is commonly used: 'Can you tell me ways in which your relationship to your father resembles or differs from your relationship to your mother?' (Ryle, 1975, p. 29). The subject is asked to phrase his construct in such a way that it depicts an interaction between two persons, for example, the construct *exploitive* could take the form *exploits*, or *is exploited by*. Each pair of figures is always used to generate two relationship elements, for example 'self-to-therapist' and 'therapist-to-self'. Typically the *self* is included in a number of different pairings in order to obtain evidence of how the subject perceives his own role as different in relation to various significant figures in his life.

Ryle (1976, p. 71) suggests that 'the dyad form of grid is of particular value where relationships are the main focus of interest, as for example, in the investigation of couples or in the investigation of role relationships'. The 'double dyad grid' has been employed by Ryle and Breen (1972a,c) to explore the role relationships between couples. It is completed jointly by both partners, and typically includes among the elements the relationship between them under two conditions: 'when it is going well' and 'when it is going badly'. The relationship of each partner with his or her own parents, and the relationship between both sets of parents are often included as well. In addition, other couples might be brought in, for example some friends who are viewed as having a very good relationship and others who seem to have a relatively bad one.

Four versions of the grid test are constructed, and each partner completes two of these—one for the self and one trying to anticipate the responses of the partner. Comparisons can be made between their two 'self-grids' as yielding a measure of similarity between their personal construct systems and revealing specific areas of difference. The 'self-grid' of each partner can also be compared with his partner's predictions, as in Thomas' (1977) 'exchange grid' technique, providing an index of 'accurate empathy' (cf. Ryle, 1976, p. 72) and locating 'misconstructions' (Ryle, 1975). We can also compare each partner's own 'self-grid' with his predictions of the other's responses to assess the extent to which she or he tends to overestimate the degree of similarity between them ('assimilative projection').

Ryle and Breen (1972a) employed their double dyad grid procedure to compare a group of seven 'maladjusted' couples, one or both partners having consulted for problems centring on their relationship, with seven 'control' couples. The purpose of this study was to determine 'how far this method could aid the understanding of the problems of couples experiencing difficulties and how far it could identify features distinguishing disturbed from non-disturbed relationships' (p. 375). All fourteen couples completed the same double dyad grid test in which each partner filled out a single dyad grid for the 'self' and a 'prediction' grid for the other. Both elicited and supplied constructs were used in this test. The similarities and differences between the grid matrices generated by each couple were analysed separately, and then the incidence of certain grid features was systematically compared between the 'maladjusted' and 'control' groups. It was hypothesized that the maladjusted couples would be 'more likely to see their relationship in parent-child terms, and this tendency would be more apparent when the relationship was rated "when it is going badly" than "when it is going well"' (p. 378).

The results indicated that the maladjusted group tended to perceive the relationship of 'self-to-partner' as resembling that of 'self-to-parent', and the relationship of 'partner-to-self' as resembling that of 'parent-to-self' to a greater extent than did the control group. The two groups also contrasted with respect to differences between the 'going well' and 'going badly' versions of their relationships. For the maladjusted couples, the shift from the former to the latter perspective led to an increase in the perceived similarity between 'self-to-partner' and 'self-to-parent' relationships, while the resemblance between the 'parent-to-self' and the 'partner-to-self' relationships was seen to decrease. In summary, the maladjusted group exhibited a greater tendency than the control group to cast the partner in the parental role and the 'self' in that of a child; and when the relationship was viewed as 'going badly', the former appeared to see the partner as becoming less parental as the 'self' became more childish—'a situation likely to be experienced as doubly depriving' (Ryle, 1975, p. 102).

The Middlesex Hospital Questionnaire (Crown and Crisp, 1966) was also administered to all twenty-eight subjects to assess their 'personal maladjustment'. Scores on this test were found to correlate positively with accuracy in predicting the partner's dyad grid responses for female subjects ($r = 0.38$), but negatively for male subjects ($r = -0.51$). Ryle and Breen (p. 381) propose that 'this suggests that neurotic females may be *more* able and neurotic males *less* able to predict the other accurately'. Although with only 12 degrees of freedom, neither correlation is significant, their hypothesis is consistent with two previous findings when these are considered in relation to one another.

Ryle and Breen (1972b) report that male neurotics were observed to have significantly greater loadings of the *self* on the first and second components extracted from their 'standard' grid test protocols by principal component analysis (Slater, 1972) than a normal control group. Adams-Webber *et al.* (1972) found that accuracy in making inferences about the personal constructs of others ('accurate empathy') is related to the extent to which the *self* is differentiated from other figures in the standard grid test. Given the finding that neurotic men differentiate less between themselves and others in the standard grid test (Ryle and Breen, 1972b), we might expect them to be more inaccurate in making inferences about their partners' constructions in the light of the results of Admas-Webber *et al.* (1972). The fairly strong negative correlation of -0.51 ($.05 < p < .10$) between 'maladjustment' and 'accurate empathy' for male subjects in Ryle and Breen's (1972a) study lends some support to this hypothesis.

Ryle and Breen (1972c) also present a detailed case history of a couple undergoing conjoint therapy as an illustration of how the clinical interpretation of double dyad grids 'can demonstrate general neurotic features and specific problems for each individual; can indicate areas of similarity and/or difference; and can indicate areas of misperception and communication failure' (p. 385). Ryle (1975) describes a range of methods for scoring and statistically analysing double dyad grids.

Bannister and Bott (1973) also present a case history of conjoint psychotherapy with a couple in order to illustrate the usefulness of repertory grid technique in marriage counselling. This couple had been married for several years but had never engaged in sexual intercourse and 'apart from a brief and unhappy encounter at the beginning of the marriage, had no kind of sexual relationship' (p. 168). Both of them were still virgins at the beginning of therapy. At the outset, both husband and wife completed the same grid test using both supplied constructs dealing with sex and elicited constructs which were a mixture of those elicited from each partner separately. Each partner rank-ordered ten photographs of strangers on all constructs. Then, all the constructs elicited from both partners were pooled and they completed a 'duo grid' together using the same set of elements (actually, it was more of a 'grid duet').

The husband and wife were faced with the same photographs and the same constructs, and were asked to argue out each decision between them so that the final rank-ordering consisted of their agreed placings. The specific purpose of the duo grid was to try to see whose construct system was, in this rather mechanical sense, 'dominant', and to see how the issue of dominance related to the level of sexual activity between the couple. (p. 169)

They assessed the relationship between this duo grid and the individual grids of both partners first by rank-ordering the correlations between constructs in each grid separately from highest positive to highest negative, and then by computing the Spearman rank-order correlation between these rankings in the duo grid and those in each of the individual grids. This procedure was repeated four times during the course of psychotherapy, and dominance was found to relate to level of sexual activity. As the data summarized in Table 3 show, when the husband was dominant there was little sexual contact; whereas when the wife was dominant sexual activity increased.

There was no attempt to have one partner predict the specific grid test responses of the other. Bannister and Bott (p. 171) comment that 'if we see sex as

Table 3. Correlations between single grids of a husband and wife with their 'duo' grid and the relation of these to their level of sexual activity

Occasions	Husband	Wife	
1	0.59	0.09	Sexual activity nil
2	0.19	0.64	Sexually active
3	0.33	0.48	Sexual activity decreasing
4	0.63	0.56	Sexual activity almost nil

(Reproduced by permission of Penguin Books Ltd., from Bannister, D., and Fransella, F., *Inquiring Man: The Theory of Personal Constructs*, 1971, p. 154.)

a role relationship and note Kelly's dictum that to the extent that one person construes the construction processes of another he can play a role in a social process involving the other person, then this seems a glaring oversight in the therapists' grid explorations of the partnership'.

Wijesinghe and Wood (1976) have recently devised yet another repertory grid technique for use with couples. Their approach incorporates features of both Ryle and Breen's (1972a,c) double dyad grid and Bannister and Bott's (1973) duo grid. Wijesinghe and Wood's procedure was designed, in part, to assess 'the extent to which a person is able to construe the construction processes of his or her spouse and a comparison of this with the therapist's construing of the particular spouse's construction processes' (p. 287). Their 'pilot study' was based on an out-patient psychotherapy group consisting of four married couples each of whose relationships was considered by the referring psychiatrist to be affecting the psychological health of one of the partners. At the time of the study, the group had already been meeting one hour a week for about a year.

First, a rank-order repertory grid test was individually administered to each client using the the *self* and the other seven members of the group as figures. The same set of four constructs, which represented dimensions which the therapist felt to be particularly relevant to interactions within the group itself, were supplied to all the clients. In addition, another four constructs were elicited individually from each client. After completing an individual grid test, spouses exchanged their lists of elicited constructs, and were instructed to rank-order the same eight elements on each construct 'as you think that your husband/wife has done them' (p. 288). Finally, the therapist himself was asked to fill out a separate grid for each client, using that client's own elicited constructs, 'as he thought that individual had ranked the elements' (p. 288).

It was found that all four husbands were more accurate than their wives in predicting the others' grid responses. This would appear to be inconsistent with Ryle and Breen's (1972a) hypothesis that neurotic men are less accurate and neurotic women more accurate in predicting their spouses grid responses ('accurate empathy'), since in every case the husband was identified as the 'ill' partner on the initial referral form. On the other hand, three out of four wives were found to be more accurate than the therapist in predicting their own husbands' responses; whereas only one husband showed the same degree of accuracy. Wijesinghe and Wood (p. 292) suggest that 'one possible reason for the lack of a clear indication of relative accuracy of perception may have been due to the husbands', though reasonably accurate in their perception of their wives, behaving in a way which made it difficult for others to predict their perceptions accurately'. The fact that clients surpassed the therapist in 70 per cent of the cases in predicting the responses of their own spouses seems consistent with the general assumption that what is being measured is direct familiarity with the others' construction processes, although the therapist in this study also may have been relatively 'unempathic'.

Duck (1977) points out that the probability that one person will be able to understand the construction processes of another person should increase with the degree of similarity between their personal construct systems (i.e. 'commonality'). Kelly himself (1955, p. 99) suggests that 'commonality between construction systems may make it more likely that one construction system can subsume part of another'. Richardson and Weigel (1971) have spelled out some of the specific implications of this model of interpersonal understanding for the marriage relationship. They hypothesize that the crucial factor in any satisfying marriage is the extent to which both partners can effectively grasp each others' personal outlooks; and 'a certain basic commonality between the PC (personal construct) systems of spouses may be necessary in order for mutual understanding to occur' (p. 4).

An experiment designed to test this hypothesis was carried out by Weigel, Weigel, and Richardson (1973). This research involved twenty-four married couples and a control group formed by randomly pairing twenty-four male and twenty-four female subjects. Each subject was presented with the same list of forty bi-polar dimensions, e.g. *calm-quick tempered, mature-immature*, etc., and asked to choose 'the 10 most meaningful and 10 least meaningful in describing others'. The degree of 'congruence' between the personal construct systems of each pair of subjects was assessed in terms of the number of times they included the same dimensions in their personal lists of the ten most meaningful constructs. The *Marital Adjustment Scale* (Locke and Wallace, 1959) was also administered to all forty-eight married subjects.

Weigel *et al.* found no significant differences between the married couples and the randomly assigned pairs with respect to the number of shared constructs. Also, the latter index did not correlate significantly with the scores of the married couples on the *Marital Adjustment Scale*. They conclude that their research 'yields no evidence to support the hypothesis of a positive relationship between the degree of congruence of spouses' personal constructs and the reported success of their marriage' (p. 213). This result may be due in part to the way in which they operationally defined the concept 'personal construct', that is, subjects were simply asked to choose the '10 most meaningful' constructs from the same standard list of forty bi-polar dimensions. Previous research has shown that we can expect to observe only a relatively small degree of overlap between such 'standard' (investigators') lists of dimensions and sets of constructs elicited from subjects individually (e.g. Oswalt, 1974), and that subjects tend to regard constructs elicited from themselves as 'more meaningful for describing persons' than dimensions supplied from a variety of different sources (e.g. Isaacson, 1966; Landfield, 1965; Isaacson and Landfield, 1965). Thus, different results might have been obtained if they had elicited a representative sample of constructs from each of their subjects individually and then measured the degree of similarity between married couples and random pairs with respect to the content of their personal construct systems (cf. Duck, 1973).

Maslow (1953), in discussing similarity of personality between marriage partners, suggests that couples tend to be more alike in terms of 'basic' personality characteristics than in terms of 'superficial' ones. It is possible that there is more congruence between spouses with respect to their 'core role' constructs, that is, those which are most important in defining the 'self-concept' (cf. Lemon and Warren, 1974), than with respect to more 'peripheral' constructs, that is, ones which 'can be altered without serious modification of the core structure' of their systems (Kelly, 1955, p. 565). The procedures employed by Weigel *et al.* seem more likely to have turned up constructs which were relatively peripheral to the individual's personal construct system than those which were central to its core structure (cf. Mair, 1977; Stefan, 1973).

FRIENDS

A series of studies by Duck (1973,1975,1977; Duck and Spencer, 1972) has shown convincingly that commonality between persons with respect to the content of their personal construct systems provides a basis for predicting who will eventually become friends out of a previously unacquainted population. Duck has also demonstrated that it is commonality in terms of those constructs which relate specifically to the psychological description of people that serves to differentiate established friendships from affectively neutral pairs of persons. Finally, he has found that different kinds of constructs—'physical', 'role', 'interaction', 'psychological'—are differentially related to and predictive of friendship choices at different ages. This is consistent with the developmental trends in the nature of interpersonal construing discussed in Chapter 8.

Duck (1973, p. 25) proposes that 'commonality of (constructive) processes is conducive to an increase in the probabilities for construing another's process and thus enhances the likelihood of social communication'. This implies that the more similarity which we observe between a particular individual's personal construct system and that of another person ('commonality'), the greater will be his potential understanding of the other's constructions of events ('sociality'), and hence, the more likely that he will be able to communicate effectively with that person (i.e. establish a 'role relationship'). In this respect, Duck's own model of interpersonal construing differs somewhat from that of Kelly. The latter contends (1955, p. 99) that 'commonality can exist between two people who are in contact with each other without either of them being able to understand the other well enough to engage in a social process with him'. Thus, Duck's assertion (p. 25) that 'it is therefore derivable from the structure of PCT (personal construct theory) that similarity of construing processes will facilitate the formation of friendships . . . (that is) friendship follows from similarity of processes because it eases communication' is not fully consistent with Kelly's (1955, p.99) own assumption that 'commonality may exist without those perceptions of each other which enable the people to understand each other or to subsume each other's mental processes' (cf. Bender, 1968a).

Duck also assumes that it is 'validating' to find that one's own constructions of events are shared by others, becasue this serves as subjective evidence of the accuracy of one's own construing. In short, commonality with others in terms of personal constructs provides each of us with a 'measure of social reality' (a source of consensual validation). In this context, Duck emphasizes similarity in the content of individuals' personal construct systems rather than in the way that they are organized. Landfield, in his studies of effective relationships in psychotherapy (reviewed below), takes both of these variables into account. Duck assumes, however, that it is the surface content and not the underlying structure of a personal construct system which is most available to others in the course of everyday social interaction. Consequently, in most of his own research he has used the 'list form' of Kelly's (1955) *Role Construct Repertory Test* in which a set of personal constructs is elicited individually from each subject by the presentation of successive triads of figures; however, each figure is not categorized in terms of every construct as in the 'grid form' of this test (cf. Bannister and Mair, 1968). Thus, Duck's methodology does not yield data suitable for any kind of 'structural' analysis.

In his first study in this series, he recruited twenty-six subjects, twelve women and fourteen men, from the same senior psychology class at a British university, who had all known one another for three years or more. He employed a sociometric technique to determine the pattern of friendships within this group and then administered his rep test to all the members individually. Each subject first nominated twelve of his own personal associates on the basis of a standard list of 'role titles', and then successive triads of these figures were used to elicit eighteen bi-polar constructs from him. Finally, the *Allport–Vernon Study of Values* was completed by every subject.

The sociometric data were used to identify all established friendships among group members. Only reciprocated choices were used to differentiate between *friendship pairs* and *normal pairs* within the group (resulting in the exclusion of one female subject). Duck hypothesized that 'the Reptest is able to differentiate friendship pairs from nominal pairs by showing that friends have more similar constructs' (p. 60). In order to test this hypothesis, he enumerated the similarities with respect to elicited constructs between all possible pairs of subjects. The only criterion which he used in comparing constructs was 'conceptual similarity', that is, any two constructs 'which expressed the same idea in the same or different words' were classified as similar. For example, 'say what they feel'—'tend to hide emotions' was counted as similar to 'expresses feelings readily'—'reserved in expression of feelings'. As an indication of the inter-judge reliability of this classification of constructs, Kendall's coefficient of concordance among three independent raters was found to be 0.76 ($p < .01$). Duck reports that the mean number of similar constructs was significantly higher for the friendship pairs than for the nominal pairs ($t = 4.73$, 24 df, $p < .001$). No significant differences were observed between friendship and nominal pairs with respect to similarity in their responses on the *Allport–Vernon Study of Values*. In addition, a direct comparison between this instrument and the rep test indicated that (p. 62) 'the Reptest is superior to the attitude test when it comes to differentiating established friendship pairs from nominal pairs in terms of similarity': $z = 2.59$ ($p < .005$).

Duck hypothesizes further in the light of these findings that the discriminant validity of any 'cognitive' test employed in this specific area of research will depend mostly upon its appropriateness to the temporal developments in the relationships under examination. He suggests that the development of interpersonal relationships involves a progression form relatively global to more differentiated cognitive assessments of the other. That is, 'there is a shift from concern with general and undifferentiating characteristics to those which are increasingly peculiar to a particular individual' (p. 62). This implies, according to Duck's analysis, that in established relationships mutual interest will focus more upon specific personality characteristics than on general attitudes. He argues further that, once the relationship has progressed to the stage that the personality of the other is the main concern of each partner, the focus of interest can become refined to the extent that both partners are aware of similarities and differences between themselves in terms of the content of their respective personal construct systems. Duck concludes that his 'filtering hypothesis' implies that 'in established friendships, tests which assess personality in global terms . . . may be less powerful than that which taps personal constructs' (p. 63).

As a further test of this 'filter model' of friendship formation, Duck compared the rep test with the *California Psychological Inventory* (CPI), employing a group of subjects within which many friendships had become well-established. He specifically predicted that the CPI, which is designed to tap several global dimensions of personality, would not differentiate friendship pairs from nominal pairs, whereas the rep test would. First, he administered a sociometric test to forty subjects, twenty-nine female and eleven male student teachers, aged 18 to 23, who had all lived together in the same university hall of residence for one year. Every subject also completed the CPI and the same rep test as that used in Duck's initial study. The sociometric data were again used to identify all reciprocated friendship choices within this group (resulting in the exclusion of two female subjects).

When friendship pairs were compared with the nominal pairs with respect to similarity in terms of each of the eight dimensions of the CPI, only one difference (on *self-acceptance*) reached the .05 fiducial level of statistical significance. Friendship and nominal pairs were also compared with respect to similarities in terms of personal constructs using the same procedures as those employed in the previous study. Once more, there was a significant difference in favour of the friendship pairs ($t = 2.279$, 37 df, $p < .05$). Moreover, a direct comparison between the rep test and the CPI in terms of their discriminatory power in differentiating between friendship and nominal pairs showed that the rep test was significantly ($p < .01$) more accurate. Duck concludes that (p. 68) 'the advantages of the Reptest over the CPI at this stage (of friendship formation) seem to depend on more personality relevant items'.

Duck's third study was concerned with the important question of whether or not people are actually aware of the degree of similarity between themselves and their friends with respect to the content of their personal construct systems. If not, then his 'consensual validation' explanation of construct commonality between friends becomes less tenable. That is, if commonality is not perceived at some level, it can hardly serve as a source of validational evidence for one's own point of view. The third study was carried out contemporaneously with the second one, employing the same subjects. They were instructed to consider each of the personal constructs previously elicited from themselves one at a time and to write down the names of any of their own acquaintances whom they thought would use the 'same way of categorizing people'. They were allowed to put down 'everyone' if they felt that a given construct was used more or less universally, and 'no-one' if they thought that they themselves were the only ones likely to use it. Their responses were classified in terms of four jointly exhaustive and mutually exclusive categories: (1) 'subject named as user of the construct some close friend who did in fact use it'; (2) 'subject alleged the use of a construct which the person indicated that he did not use'; (3) 'subject did not name someone as a user of a particular construct and the person did not use it'; and (4) 'subject omitted the name of someone who did share a common construct with him'.

These data were arranged into a fourfold contingency table separately for each subject, which was then submitted to a Fisher's Exact Probability Test. The largest value of p observed for any particular subject was .02. In general, subjects were found to be approximately twice as likely to be accurate as inaccurate (categories (1) and (3) above). Those errors which did occur tended to fall predominately into category (2), that is, they involved extending the assumption of commonality with respect to personal constructs between themselves and their friends further than was actually warranted on the basis of these data. In summary, the results of this study indicate that subjects are fairly accurate in perceiving whether or not commonality exists between themselves and particular friends, and when they do make errors, they tend to overestimate the degree of commonality involved. Duck interprets the latter finding as suggesting that the perception of similarities with respect to personal constructs has more 'subjective importance' than the perception of differences. He points out that this is what we might expect on the basis of his 'consensual validation' explanation of the role played by construct commonality in the choice of friends.

Duck also reports that a reanalysis of some of the data from his first three studies revealed that female subjects exhibited highly significant differences between nominal and friendship pairings regardless of the sex of the partner; whereas male subjects manifested significant differences only between friendship and nominal pairs of the same sex. In addition, female subjects showed significantly more similarity with their friends of the same sex than with those of the opposite sex, while no significant effect for the sex of the partner was observed for male subjects. Thus, 'while females are similar in construing to friends of either sex, the amounts of similarity are greater for friends who are also female' (p. 73).

In summary, these data indicate that (a) construct similarity distinguishes same-sex friendship pairs from same-sex nominal pairs for both male and female subjects; however, (b) in the case of cross-sex pairings, construct similarity relates to the friendship choices of female subjects only. Duck suggests in the light of these results that 'although both sexes use the same apparent cognitive strategy for choosing their friends of the same sex, when it comes to choosing friends of the opposite sex, males and females use different "filter" strategies.

Females appear to look for similarities of construct systems in both cases, yet males do so only when choosing male friends and look for something else when choosing potential female friends' (p. 73).

Duck has also carried out further research dealing with the development of friendships which shows that similarities between persons in terms of the content of their personal construct systems tend to precede friendship formation. Given the evidence from his previous work that the friendship choice strategies of men and women seem to differ where the opposite sex is concerned, he decided to employ separate samples of male and female subjects in these longitudinal studies. This type of research requires populations within which no friendships have yet been formed, but where they can be expected to occur.

In his first study in the longitudinal series, Duck employed as subjects twelve men and sixteen women living in two different residence halls segregated on the basis of sex on the same British university campus. Construct similarities between subjects were assessed on each of two occasions: initially at the beginning of their mutual interaction within the group, and six months later when their patterns of friendship had become established. In the male group, only four reciprocated friendship choices were identified on the second occasion by means of the usual sociometric technique. Since one particular subject was involved in two of these pairings, the number of subjects available for comparisons in terms of construct similarities was reduced to seven only. Nevertheless, a significant difference between friendship and nominal pairs in terms of construct similarities was observed on the second occasion, while not on the first. Duck argues that 'the finding that conceptual similarity between friends is apparent by the time of the second Reptest is support for the contention . . . that there are changes in the *type* of similarity as a relationship continues' (p. 82).

In the female group, almost all the women formed at least two reciprocated friendships according to the sociometric data. In this group, the pairs who later were to become friends were found to have significantly more similar constructs than the nominal pairs on the first occasion of assessment. This indicates that construct similarities tended to predate friendship choices within this group. On the other hand, it was observed that after six months of acquaintance the degree of commonality between friends was no longer significantly greater than that between nominal pairs *in terms of all the constructs* elicited from these subjects. A further analysis of these data did show, however, that on the second occasion of testing the friendship pairs were significantly more alike than the nominal pairs with respect to 'psychological' constructs (i.e. 'those describing a character, personality or cognitive attribute'). Duck offers the following interpretation of this finding:

These arguments propose an attention to those constructs which describe other people at the level of character, personality and psychological characteristics. Such descriptions were argued in Chapter 1 to be sources of validational doubts and to be especially the kind of description on which a social comparison and social reality grounding would be valuable. However, in view of the complex and personal nature of these constructs one would only wish to compare oneself with, and gain validity from, those with whom one felt some commonality or for whom one felt respect. Thus filter theory would not predict an emphasis upon such constructs until after the development of friendship to the stage beyond the primitive. In other words a concern for psychological construing should be evident (and should be evident only) after friendship had become firmer. In terms of the present measures, this predicts that a concern for psychological construing should manifest itself on the second Reptest and that similarity on this kind of construct should distinguish friendship pairs. (p. 84)

Direct comparison between the two groups showed that (a) the average amount of construct similarity between the male subjects in general was significantly lower than that between female subjects in general ($p < .001$); and (b) the former made fewer friendship choices per subject than the latter ($p < .001$). Thus, in that group in which there was a higher level of commonality with respect to personal constructs across all subjects, a greater number of friendships were established. This is clearly consistent with Duck's general hypothesis that 'similarity of constructs is a precursor of friendship and not simply its product' (p. 89). He speculates further on the basis of this study that there may be two distinct stages through which the development of any friendship progresses. In the initial stage, each partner may be primarily concerned with the non-psychological construing of the other. During the later stages, further interaction between friends might involve mostly communication and understanding of one another's psychological constructions. If so, then commonality with respect to non-psychological constructs may facilitate interactions between new acquaintances, whereas similarity in terms of psychological constructs may become increasingly important as their relationship develops.

ACQUAINTANCES

An important question in the context of Duck's model is whether subjects tend to describe personal associates of long standing and new acquaintances in different terms. His hypothesis that there is a gradual shift in mutual interest from physical characteristics and behaviour to psychological processes as the relationship between two persons develops implies that people use more 'role' and 'physical' constructs than 'psychological' ones in describing persons whom they have just met for the first time as opposed to friends and old acquaintances. In order to test this hypothesis, he employed a sample of thirty-seven first-year students, fourteen women and twenty-three men, attending a British polytechnic. Every subject completed the same form of rep test as that used in all the previous studies. They were then assigned to five different discussion groups consisting of from seven to nine members in such a way that none of the members of any group were previously acquainted with one another. After participating in a forty-minute discussion based on some of Kogan and Wallach's (1964) *Choice-Dilemma* problems, each group was disbanded and every subject completed a second rep test, using the members of the group as elements.

All the constructs elicited from each subject were classified on the basis of three categories—'psychological', 'role', and 'other'—by three independent judges, who achieved an inter-scorer reliability of $z = 9.167$ ($p < .001$) on the Binomial Test. A comparison of the constructs used by subjects on the two versions of the rep test revealed that they used significantly fewer 'psychological' constructs to describe the memebers of their respective discussion groups, whom they had just met (second occasion of testing), than to describe persons whom they had known much longer (first occasion of testing) ($p < .001$). Comparable results were obtained for both male and female subjects. This finding lends support to Duck's general hypothesis that 'in describing new acquaintances subjects would be less prone to particularize them in terms of underlying "motivation" and psychological factors' (p. 98).

All constructs elicited from subjects in this experiment were then reclassified in terms of a fourth category: 'interaction constructs' (see Chapter 8). A reanalysis of the data showed that significantly more 'interaction' constructs were employed to characterize new acquaintances than to describe old ones ($p < .001$). Duck interprets this finding as indicating that people notice one another's style of social interaction well before they begin to perceive those similarities with respect to psychological construing which are 'ultimately discernable between those who enter into friendship with one another' (p. 99). This raises the issue of the extent to which information which is gleaned during the early stages of an acquaintance is used as a basis for formulating specific hypotheses which are then tested at a later stage in the development of the relationship. For instance, the constructs which are typically employed during the initial stages of acquaintance, that is, those referring to physical characteristics, roles, and styles of interaction, may carry a number of implications in terms of superordinate 'psychological' constructs within the same conceptual structure. Duck himself specifically proposes that 'progression through the stages of acquaintance, and the frequency of interaction which it engenders, facilitates the use of more superordinate and more differentiated constructs by allowing the testing of previously derived hypotheses and extrapolations to those superordinate constructs' (p. 102)

He carried out a further study to test the hypothesis that information attended to earlier is used as a basis of further inferences in terms of 'superordinate' constructions. Sixty-two students, forty-nine women and thirteen men, in the same Introductory Psychology course completed a rep test on two occasions. In the first of these tests, well-known public figures were used as elements in eliciting constructs. Subjects were also asked to answer the following question for each of the constructs elicited from themselves: 'if a person has the quality denoted by the positive pole, what other characteristics is he likely to have?' They were limited to a maximum of five 'implied characteristics' for each construct. Following this test, subjects were assigned to nine separate discussion groups of approximately the same size in such a way that they were not previously acquainted with any of the other members of their respective groups. Each group met separately to discuss the same list of public figures as that used in the initial rep test, and to compare their constructions of them. After about twenty minutes of discussion, a second rep test was administered to every subject in which the elements consisted of all the members of his or her group.

All the constructs elicited from subjects on both rep tests were classified in terms of a set of four categories: 'psychological', 'role', 'interaction', and 'other'. When these data were compared with those from the preceding experiment described above, in which a list of figures personally known to each subject was used to elicit constructs from him, the results indicated that 'whether subjects construe those whom they know distantly from the media, or those met and interacted with in task-like situations, a different distribution of constructs is observable from that shown when subjects construe those who are personally well-known' (p. 106). Also, when recently met acquaintances were used as elements to elicit constructs, relatively more 'psychological' and 'interaction', and fewer 'role' and 'other' constructs, were elicited from subjects than when distant public figures were used as elements. Duck argues that 'this clearly indicates differentiation of process as a function of directness of knowledge' (p. 107).

The 'implications' which subjects derived from their own constructions were also classified using the same set of categories as that applied to their original elicited constructs. The results revealed that 'the constructs derived as implications have produced greater amounts of psychological constructs at the expense of role constructs' (p. 107). Duck contends that this particular finding supports his hypothesis that in the early stages of acquaintance subjects are able to elaborate the implications of subordinate, 'non-psychological' constructions in terms of superordinate, 'psychological' constructs. He submits that this 'invites the conjecture that these superordinate constructs give individuals the guidelines to similarities that they may expect to observe later and they thus constitute a powerful filter of acquaintance' (p. 108). He also argues that the superordinate, 'psychological' constructs carry extensive 'superordinate implications' in terms of subordinate, 'non-psychological' constructs, thereby providing a basis for deriving further concrete hypotheses which can be tested in the course of further interactions.

Duck speculates that the 'task-orientation' of the discussion groups in these experiments may have imposed severe constraints upon the patterns of constructions which emerged. He suggests that if the group situation had been structured to resemble a 'true social encounter' more closely, the subjects may have developed more elaborate hypotheses from their original impressions of other members. Therefore in his next experiment some of the groups were allowed to discuss freely whatever topics they wished. He hoped that this would permit their 'filtering' processes to operate more normally.

Two types of group interactions were employed in Duck's next experiment: (a) *social groups* in which subjects were free to discuss any personal information whatsoever, and (b) *casual groups* in which information of a personal nature was elicited from each subject in the presence of other members without any further interaction. He reasoned that any difference between these two groups should primarily be a result of the different kinds of discussion allowed rather than of the type of information available to subjects in forming impressions of other members. The subjects assigned to each group were not previously acquainted with one another. In one group of each type—social and casual—subjects were led to expect that they would participate in further interactions with the other members.

Thus there were actually four different kinds of group structure: (1) 'casual, no expectancy'; (2) 'social, no expectancy'; (3) 'casual, expectancy'; and (4) 'social, expectancy'. The last type of structure was assumed to provide the closest approximation to a 'real-life' social encounter. The first type was seen as representing the situation which was least promising for the formation of friendships. Duck also assumed that a social atmosphere and free discussion are more important than the expectation of future interaction in the operation of 'normal filtering processes'. Therefore he expected the 'social, no expectancy' situation to be more conducive to normal patterns of interaction than the 'casual, expectancy' situation.

Twenty-seven British undergraduates, all previously unacquainted, were assigned to four separate groups of approximately seven members. Each group received one of the four treatments described above. Following the group-interaction phase of the experiment, each subject completed a rep test in which all the members of his or her own group served as elements for eliciting constructs. As in Duck's previous experiments, all the constructs elicited from subjects were classified as either 'psychological', 'interaction', 'role', or 'other'. At first, the data for each kind of construct were analysed separately in order to determine the effects of expectancy and type of interaction. These preliminary results indicated that the amount of psychological construing was significantly affected by the type of interaction—'social' or 'casual'—but not by expectancy. Specifically, more 'psychological' constructs were elicited from those subjects who participated in 'social' interactions than from those who engaged in 'casual' interactions.

There were no significant effects for either expectancy or type of interaction in terms of either 'interaction' or 'other' constructs. Within each level of expectancy, differences between the two types of interactions were observed in terms of the numbers of both 'psychological' and 'role' constructs, with more 'psychological' constructs being used by the members of 'social groups' and more 'role' constructs used by the members of 'casual' groups. Within the 'social' groups, the shift from 'no expectancy' to 'expectancy' resulted in an increase in the number of 'role' constructs at the expense of other constructs. Finally, in the 'casual' groups, a comparable shift in expectancies produced an increase in the numbers of both 'psychological' and 'interaction' constructs at the expense of 'role' constructs.

Duck interprets this complex pattern of results as lending support to his own intuitively arranged 'hierarchy' of experimental treatments. That is 'as individuals become more involved in a situation which resembles real-life acquainting, such information as they have accrued leads them on to higher-level construing and inference' (p. 120). For example, he notes that subjects employed more 'psychological' constructs to describe members of their groups following the 'social' type of interaction, which presumably involves 'real-life' processes to a greater extent than the more artificial 'casual' type of interaction. Moreover, there was a larger difference between the 'casual, no expectancy' group and both of the 'social' groups in terms of the number of 'psychological' constructs elicited than between the 'social' groups and the 'casual, expectancy' group. Presumably, the 'casual, no expectancy' condition least resembled 'real-life'. Nevertheless, as Duck himself points out, the subjects who engaged in 'social' interactions in this particular experiment 'show patterns a long way short of those in the natural situation' (p. 119)—that is, when a sample of subjects' own personal associates are used in eliciting constructs from them.

On the whole, the results of this experiment, and of the previous one, seem to provide extensive support for Duck's 'filter' hypothesis, which specifically implies that as the basis of acquaintance expands there is a progressive shift of interest from 'factual' information about others to more concern with their styles of interaction; and eventually, construing focuses primarily upon psychological processes. These findings also lend considerable support to his notion that information acquired during the early phases of impression formation is used in part to derive hypotheses which are then tested at later stages of the acquaintance. Duck's 'filter' hypothesis is also consistent with the differences observed in earlier studies between successive stages in the development of friendships. In the early stages of friendship formation, overall similarity with respect to personal constructs is found. At later stages, similarity in terms of 'psychological' constructs seems more important.

Men and women would appear to concentrate on the same kind of information during the early stages of acquaintance, and they seem to employ the same general strategies in 'filtering' this information. Also, both men and women tend to select their friends of the same sex partly on the basis of perceived similarity to themselves with respect to personal constructs. On the other hand, there is some evidence from Duck's research that men and women may employ somewhat different strategies in forming relationships with partners of the opposite sex (p. 115 above).

Perhaps the most significant implication of Duck's research from the point of view of Kelly's general model of social cognition is that 'the shift away from a major concern with the construal of another's behaviour (or interaction style) toward construal of his construct system marks an important change in emphasis and is also the stage where the greatest differences are possible between individuals' (p. 138). Duck proposes that the shifts in emphasis from 'behaviour' and 'role' construing to 'psychological' construing observed in his own studies may reflect a general progression from viewing people predominately in terms of 'stereotypes' to a greater 'individuation and differentiation' of them as persons. This assumption implies specifically that the more sensitive an individual is to similarities and differences between other persons with respect to the content of their personal construct systems, the greater the extent to which he should be able to differentiate between them in forming impressions of their 'personalities'. This hypothesis receives direct support from the finding of Adams-Webber *et al.* (1972) that an individual's degree of accuracy in discriminating between new acquaintances in terms of their personal constructs relates to the extent to which he tends to differentiate between persons on the basis of his own constructs. Thus, as Duck (1973, p. 146) himself concludes, it seems that 'psychological construing is associated with greater inferential and social ability both at the stage of behaviour construal and when construal of constructs occurs' (p. 146).

He also suggests that these shifts in social perspective may involve changes in the nature of the 'data' themselves as well as the kind of inferences which are derived from them. For instance, the use of 'psychological' constructs may require attending to a wider and more complex range of cues than is needed in the use of either 'role' or 'interaction' constructs. In addition, the 'evidence' for psychological inferences tends to be more subjective and open to a variety of different interpretations. Thus, consensual validation through comparing one's own constructions with those of others may become increasingly important as psychological construing develops. This consideration serves to underline the importance of the developmental changes in the content of individuals' personal construct systems discussed in Chapter 8 (Barratt, 1977b; Brierley, 1967; Little, 1968), especially the finding that psychological constructs do not become predominant until adolescence. As we shall see in Chapter 8, Duck (1975) also found that 'different levels of constructs were differently related to, and predictive of, relationships and friendship choices discovered at different ages—suggesting, so it was argued, a functional relationship between personality development and friendship choice' (Duck, 1977, p. 18). Thus there seems to be a fairly close parallel between the 'levels of relationship' which occur developmentally and the 'stages of acquaintances' observed in Duck's experiments reviewed above.

THERAPISTS AND CLIENTS

Landfield (1971, p. 17) points out that according to Kelly, 'the critical factor in the development of productive role interaction or sociality lies in the ability of one or both participants in a dyadic relationship to subsume the points of view of the other person'. In short, what Duck terms 'psychological' construing is a necessary condition for any form of role relationship. Landfield (1971, p. 18) specifically hypothesizes that it is the key to successful relationships between therapists and clients, that is, 'the ability of one or both members of a therapy dyad to encompass aspects of the construct system of the other person'. There have been several studies in which repertory grid technique has been used to assess the accuracy of a therapist's inferences about his client's personal construct system and to locate specific areas of misunderstanding.

Cartwright and Lerner (1963) report that clients in 'client-centered' therapy were more likely to improve when their therapists' understanding of them gradually increased during treatment. In this study, the therapist's understanding of the client was assessed in terms of the degree of similarity between the client's construing of himself on the basis of ten elicited constructs and the therapist's use of these same constructs in role-playing the client.

Watson (1970) attempted to predict the repertory grid responses of one of his own clients on four occasions spaced at intervals of two months during the course of psychotherapy. The constructs used by the client in completing the grid were derived from the content of discussions in therapy sessions and the elements were people assumed to be significant figures in the client's life. The results showed some gains in the therapist's understanding of the client's construct system over the period of eight months; however, there was little change in the content of the client's construing during therapy.

Rowe (1971) administered a repertory grid test to a psychiatric patient using a list of his own personal associates as elements. These were judged on the basis of both elicited and supplied constructs. She then asked the treating psychiatrist to predict his client's categorization of these figrues. Although the overall degree of accuracy was quite modest, it was observed that most of the discrepancies between the two grid protocols occurred in relation to one particular construct and a single figure. Rowe (1976) points out that the therapist himself can use the grid to learn the client's own language. In a subsequent study Rowe and Slater (1976) also used grids to assess psychiatrists' understanding of their clients. One psychiatrist was given the constructs and elements from a grid test completed by a client whom he had selected and was asked to fill the grid out as he supposed the client had. As in Rowe's (1971) earlier study, 'though he showed a fair degree of insight on the whole, there was one area where he had misconstrued his patient's views' (Rowe and Slater, 1976, p. 123). A second psychiatrist and his client completed the same grid both before and after a course of psychotherapy. The psychiatrist's attempt to reconstruct the client's grid protocol was more successful following treatment, and again, specific areas of misunderstanding showed up.

A dyad grid was administered by Ryle and Lunghi (1971) to a client who had been in therapy for more than two years with the same therapist. The therapist then attempted to 'predict' his client's responses on this test. Ryle and Lunghi rank-ordered the twenty-four dyad elements (relationships) on the basis of the therapist's accuracy in predicting how they had been rated by the client. They found that the five most accurately predicted elements were as follows: 'self-to-father', 'therapist-to-self', 'mother-to-self', 'father-to-self', and 'self-to-therapist'. These elements represent those relationships which had been discussed most frequently in the course of therapy, and consequently, were 'most immediately accessible' (Ryle, 1975) to the therapist.

The most sophisticated measure of empathy based on repertory grid procedure was developed by Smail (1972) in a small therapeutic group. This measure was validated against clients' and therapists' ratings. The therapy group consisted of a single male therapist and seven neurotic clients, including six women and one man, ranging in age from 22 to 37. At the time of Smail's study, this group had been meeting weekly for seven months. One client left the group before the completion of the research, and was consequently excluded from most of the comparisons summarized below. On the initial occasion of testing, ten constructs were elicited individually from each client, using the members of the group as elements. Then grid procedures were used to assess the degree of relationship between each of these constructs and every other one for that particular client. The construct which exhibited the highest level of overall relationship with the other nine was selected as the single 'most representative' construct for each client.

On the second occasion of testing, less than a week later, every subject judged all members of the group separately on each of the 'representative constructs' identified on the first occasion. The subject was instructed to imagine that he was each of the other five members in turn and to rank-order all the figures on that person's 'most representative construct'. He was asked to try to put himself in the other's place and to imagine how the other would rank the members of the group on that particular construct. Finally, each subject rank-ordered all group members 'according to the degree to which they felt these were able to understand the others or put themselves in their place, in the way the subjects themselves had just been asked to do' (p. 167). The therapist also completed all these procedures on the second occasion of testing.

Each subject was assigned a single 'empathy score' based on the 'average relationship between a subject's prediction of every other's ranking on the other's representative construct and the ranking actually given by every other subject' (p. 167). The therapist himself achieved the highest empathy score on the repertory grid task, and he was also ranked highest on understanding by both the clients and himself. In general, the rank-order correlation between the empathy scores of the group members and their average ranks in terms of 'understanding' as assessed by other members was an impressive 0.99 ($p < .01$). When their empathy scores were compared with the therapist's rankings of them in terms of 'understanding', the rank-order correlation was 0.83 ($p < .05$). Empathy scores were not found to correlate significantly with either IQ, age, Neuroticism or Extroversion. They did, however, relate significantly to 'thinking-introversion' scores from Caine and Smail's (1969a, b) *Direction of Interest Questionnaire*. The latter index has been found to relate to a 'psychotherapeutic' as opposed to an 'organic' orientation to clinical material, and to a generally psychological as opposed to somatic attitude (Smail, 1970). This suggests that accurate empathy as measured by Smail (1972) relates to 'psychological' construing as defined by Duck (1973, 1977).

Smail also hypothesized that an important factor in determining one person's ability to predict successfuly the construction processes of another person will be the extent to which they both share a similar construct system in the first place. In order to test this specific hypothesis, he calculated the correlation of each subject's rankings of group members on a given construct with the rankings of the same figures produced by the subject from whom that particular construct had been elicited. This provided the basis for a 'shared experience' index for each subject which 'expresses the amount of overlap between his own and others' constructs' (p. 168). These 'shared experience' scores were found to correlate 0.84

($p. < 05$), with the 'empathy scores' of the same subjects. Smail (1972, p. 169) concludes on the basis of this finding that 'where two subjects both construe elements in an initially similar way, they are better able to predict the other's performance'. This is clearly consistent with Kelly's (1955, p. 99) own hypothesis that 'commonality between construction systems may make it more likely that one construction system can subsume part of another'. It is congruent also with the finding by Halpern and Lesser (1960; cited in Landfield, 1971) that there is a significant relation between accuracy in predicting an acquaintance's self-ratings and personality similarity between predictor and 'target'.

Smail does not provide evidence bearing on the question of whether empathy relates to improvement in group psychotherapy; however, a study by Fransella and Joyston-Bechal (1971) suggests that there may be some connection. Specifically, they report that the only two clients in a psychotherapeutic group showing significant improvement were the two who were found to be the most accurate in construing how other persons saw them as measured by repertory grid comparisons.

Landfield (1971, p. 13) asserts that 'some commonality is necessary for the development of interpersonal communication between client and therapist'. He contends that 'content congruency', that is, similarity with respect to 'implied meanings' between a client's personal constructs and those of his own therapist is required for the initiation and maintenance of any therapeutic relationship. This line of reasoning leads him to the specific prediction that those clients who terminate psychotherapy prematurely will exhibit significantly less commonality in terms of elicited constructs with their respective therapists than clients who do not drop out early. In the context of this hypothesis, Landfield interprets the premature termination of a psychotherapeutic relationship as indicative of the 'inability to maintain a relationship'. He reports that the results of his own research 'support the relationship between greater client-therapist congruency in the content of their personal constructs and nonpremature termination' (p. 77; cf. Landfield, 1970). This evidence seems to provide a fairly close parallel to Duck's (1973) finding that commonality with respect to personal constructs serves as a basis for predicting the formation of friendships between previously unacquainted persons.

Landfield (1971, p. 75) claims that 'the significance of the relationship between construct congruency and (non) premature termination is increased by focussing on more important content categories'. Specifically, he reports that when comparisons are made on the basis of only those constructs which exhibit the highest degree of overall relationship with the other constructs elicited from the same individual—either client or therapist—a closer relationship can be observed between construct commonality and length of stay in therapy. We noted above that Smail (1972) subsequently found a high correlation between commonality ('shared experience') and empathy in terms of those constructs which showed the highest level of relationship with all the other constructs elicited from the same client. This suggests the possibility that Landfield's own measure of 'construct congruence' may also relate directly to the extent to which a client and therapist are able to understand one another. This in turn is likely to influence how long the client remains in therapy. In short, it would seem that 'productive social interaction, as defined by the sociality corollary, depends on some commonality' (Landfield, p. 17). As Eiser and Stroebe (1972, p. 205) put it, 'the "commonality" and "sociality corollaries", taken together, predict, among other things, that individuals who are cognitively similar (i.e. have similar construct systems) will be able to communicate more effectively with each other'.

Landfield (1971) hypothesizes also that psychotherapy will tend to terminate prematurely whenever the client and therapist regard one another's personal constructs as relatively meaningless. In this context, the meaningfulness of any given construct for a particular subject is operationally defined in terms of how extremely he rates himself and others on it. Thus Landfield predicted specifically that 'clients and therapists in premature dyads, rating one another on the other person's construct dimensions, will have significantly smaller summed extremity ratings at the beginning of therapy than clients and therapists in non-premature dyads' (p. 72). This prediction was confirmed ($t = 2.24$; $p. < .05$); however, when either the client's or therapist's ratings were taken alone, no significant relationship was found. The general assumption that rating extremity reflects 'meaningfulness' was also supported indirectly by the finding that both clients and therapists rated one another less extremely across all constructs when therapy terminated prematurely than when it progressed to 'full maturity'.

Landfield argues on the basis of these results that at least one of the factors contributing to the premature termination of psychotherapy is an inability to subsume the other person's constructs at the outset, that is, to use them 'meaningfully'. This conclusion does not follow strictly from the observed negative relationship between premature termination and rating extremity exhibited by both client and therapist in terms of one another's personal constructs. It does, however, seem to be consistent with other evidence that commonality between persons with respect to the content of their construct systems enhances communication and mutual understanding, that is, 'sociality' (Duck, 1973, 1975, 1977; Smail, 1972). As we shall see in the next chapter, this notion of sociality within the context of a 'role relationship' serves as the conceptual groundwork for Kelly's own distinctive approach to psychotherapy, which has been elaborated by Bonarius, Fransella, Landfield, and others.

6

Conceptual Reorganization and Change

Kelly conceived of the psychological processes which take place in psychotherapy as similar to those which occur in formal scientific enquiry. He saw the therapist as helping his client to formulate 'theories', derive and test specific hypotheses within the framework of these theories, evaluate the results of his own experiments, and revise his theories in the light of events as he himself is able to interpret them. The client himself is viewed as the principal investigator in this enterprise, although the therapist participates as an active collaborator. Thus, as Bannister and Fransella (1971, p. 130) put it, 'in construct theory psychotherapy the model for the relationship between the so-called therapist and the so-called patient is somewhat that of research supervisor to research student'. It is the client's construct system which is being explored and not that of the psychologist; however, the latter can contribute a great deal in the way of what Landfield (1971) terms 'methodological construction', that is, 'to assist a client in the ways of learning, focussing on personal exploration and experimentation' (p. 7). In short, the role of 'therapist' from the standpoint of personal construct theory is to aid the client in experimenting with his own constructions of events, not to represent reality to him (cf. Morris, 1977).

FIXED ROLE THERAPY

As we saw in the preceding chapter, Kelly's (1970) 'sociality corollary' asserts that 'to the extent that one person construes the construction processes of another, he may play a role in a social process involving the other'. We noted also that his definition of role as a course of activity carried out in the light of one's understanding of another's point of view has served as the central focus for research concerned with interpersonal relations within the context of personal construct theory. Kelly's unique notion of role also provides the basis of an experimental procedure which he developed for activating personality change without resorting to applied psychology. This novel form of 'psychotherapy' is called 'fixed role therapy'. Kelly himself views it not as a treatment, but as an investigative project in which the client himself is the chief investigator and is fully aware of this fact.

According to Kelly, an individual enacts a role in the psychological sense of the term only to the extent that his behaviour is guided by his own anticipations of another person's constructions of events. Fixed role therapy requires that both the client and the psychologist understand the meaning of role in precisely these terms.

The client—call him Jim—is first asked to write a brief character sketch of himself from the perspective of a third person who knows him very well. The psychologist studies this sketch and then prepares the 'enactment sketch'. The latter is a sketch that might have been written as a self-characterization by a hypothetical 'Chuck', whose part the client himself will be invited to play for a while.

The client is asked to pretend that he—Jim—has gone away on holiday for a fortnight, and that in his place 'Chuck' materializes. The client is to enact as best he can the part of Chuck—all that he might do, say, think or even dream. The client and the psychologist meet frequently during the period of enactment to plan experiments and evaluate the results. At the end of this period, Jim 'comes back' and is asked to appraise the experience in whatever way makes the most sense to him.

In eliciting the client's original self-characterization, the psychologist instructs him to write a character sketch of himself just as if he were the principal character in a play. This format is used in order to encourage the client to represent his personality as a coherent whole rather than simply supply a list of all his good and bad points. The purpose of the exercise is to find out how the client structures his own self-concept within the context of his personal network of constructs, or 'implicit personality theory'. Prior to preparing the enactment sketch, the psychologist analyses the client's self-characterization in terms of the principal axes of reference which he has used in identifying himself. It is also important to discover how the client uses his own experience in his attempts to validate his conception of himself, and in what ways he sees himself as developing in the future. Finally, it is necessary to determine what the client's own language means to him.

In producing the enactment sketch itself, the psychologist usually attempts to formulate at least one hypothesis to be tested. This hypothesis may either be stated explicitly in the sketch or merely implied. It may also be an alternative to one which the client himself proposes in his own self-characterization. For example, if the client portrays himself as a 'cautious' person, the alternative *from his own point of view* might be to play the role of someone who is 'aggressive'. Kelly (1955) himself recommends casting the enactment in terms of a novel dimension—one which may never have occurred to the client, and which he may find quite difficult to integrate with the current structure of his personal construct system. Nevertheless, he can explore the implications of the new dimension by playing the part depicted in the enactment sketch, that is, by using the new dimension to structure his own behaviour.

Kelly insists that the enactment sketch should present a role in the personal construct sense of the term. That is, the part played by the client should involve his acting in the light of what he understands to be the outlooks of particular persons. His attention needs to be focused not only on the behaviour of others, but also upon their diverse points of view. Kelly (1955) offers an illustration of such an enactment in his summary of the case of 'Ronald Barrett'.

Kelly (1955) asserts that it is also essential for the psychologist to bear in mind that the purpose of the enactment is not to eradicate the personality of 'Jim' and replace it with that of 'Chuck'. The therapist does not directly criticize or question the integrity of Jim as a personality. Jim is at all times treated with respect. The key to the whole experiment is the fact that 'Chuck', by virtue of his contrast to Jim, is so clearly a hypothetical rather than a 'real' person. Thus the enactment of 'Chuck' is explicitly the test of a hypothesis from the standpoint of both client and psychologist. The 'Jim' whom the client has come to know so well is also, according to Kelly, only a hypothesis. However, since the client cannot imagine any substantial alternative to his being 'Jim', he cannot easily grasp the point that his own personality is a hypothetical construction as well. All that he typically experiences are the various consequences of his behaving like 'Jim'. 'Chuck', on the other hand, is so patently a made-up personage that he can be dealt with as a hypothesis far more readily by the client.

During 'rehearsals' the psychologist usually plays the parts of several significant figures in the client's life as 'supporting roles'. Although his initial attempts to portray these roles may not be convincing enough to lend strong support to the client's enactment of his new part, the psychologist's performance can be aided by frequently 'exchanging parts' with the client himself. Kelly regards this exchange as an extremely important feature of the experiment without which the client may come to see one part as dominant over the other. He also contends that this frequent exchange of parts allows the client to attempt a reconstruction of the point of view of the other person, which is necessary in order to enter into a role relationship with him.

In the course of these rehearsals, the psychologist himself concentrates upon showing the client how specific hypotheses can be used as a basis for structuring interactions between himself and others and interpreting the outcome of these interactions after they have taken place. For example, say that the client is an university student. Kelly suggests that he could start out with a brief interview with one of his instructors since relations between students and instructors typically involve relatively few personal constructs, and usually ones which are quite easily verbalized. The psychologist might propose that the client engage one of his instructors in a short after-class discussion on some topic relevant to the course. In this situation, it should be fairly easy for the client to concentrate on understanding the point of view of the instructor. The client can also expect to receive immediate feedback on his own attempts to grasp the instructor's outlook.

Prior to this interaction, the psychologist can assist the client in hypothesizing what the instructor will say to him and how he will say it. In developing this hypothesis, the client may find it helpful to enact the part of the instructor during an exchange of roles with the psychologist. Following the interaction proper, the psychologist and the client can go over what happened together, comparing the actual outcome with the client's original hypothesis. At this stage, a replay of the interaction, including an exchange of parts with the psychologist, may help to clarify several important features of the situation for the client.

Following this evaluation of the client's first experiment, his second enactment can be planned— say one between the client and one of his close friends. Once more, the psychologist collaborates with the client in formulating specific hypotheses and later assessing what actually happened in relation to these hypotheses. Kelly submits that in the course of this ongoing sequence of enactments opposite significant persons in his own life, the client may gradually realize that he can experiment more successfully with his interpersonal relations using his own behaviour as the 'independent variable'. That is, his own behaviour is the one variable in any situation which is potentially under his control and can be manipulated systematically. Eventually, as he becomes a more skilful experimenter, he may discover that he is able to elicit from his social environment fairly definite answers to the questions which he poses through his own behaviour. If we bear in mind that the behaviour of the 'scientist' is ultimately the only independent variable in any experiment, then we can view the client in fixed role therapy as the principal investigator in an open-ended programme of research in which he continues to pose new questions through his own behaviour. Thus, in a sense, fixed role therapy is based on a radical form of 'behaviorism' in which the client is not the protagonist in a drama of which he is not the sole author, but rather a 'scientist' formulating and testing out his own hypotheses.

At the end of the fortnight, when 'Jim' returns, the psychologist invites him to assume responsibility for evaluating what has happened while he was on holiday in the way in which it makes the most sense to him. The psychologist also points out that the client himself will be responsible for whatever he subsequently chooses to undertake in the light of this experience. Kelly feels that it will probably be better in the long run if the client decides to abandon the role of 'Chuck' altogether no matter how much he prizes the experience gained during that particular enactment. His future task will be gradually to construct a personality through a new series of experiments, which could well take the rest of his life.

TWO CLINICAL ILLUSTRATIONS

Bonarius (1967b, 1970b) presents a detailed case history of 'Peter', a Dutchman in his early twenties who was a client in fixed role therapy. Peter originally complained of frequent bouts of depression, profound dissatisfaction with his work, and severe conflicts with his dominating mother and other members of his household. He had established some sort of temporary relationship with a variety of different women, but these had all been of very short duration. He was diagnosed by a psychiatrist as suffering from a character neurosis and latent homosexuality. His IQ was reported to be 125, and he scored highly in terms of both extraversion and neuroticism.

Bonarius (1970b, p. 215) offers the following clinical interpretation of the self-characterization sketch written by this client:

... it appears that he has difficulty in giving structure to his behaviour. He even seems to reject such a structure because, as suggested by the last sentence, this would imply a loss of freedom. Apparently for Peter *being free* implies that neither he himself nor other people can anticipate what he will do the next instant. He construes himself as primarily completely free.

Since freedom in Peter's conception, means living on the impulse of the moment, the world around him, the persons in his environment, must comply with him. Otherwise he would be subjected to utter chaos. So in order to avoid unbearable anxiety, his surroundings should be tied to him, *tied* to his momentary wishes and whims. As long as he can manipulate others, he himself can be *free* ... a lasting relationship would tie him to the other persons. That would threaten the construction of himself as *being free*. (p. 216)

The enactment sketch which Bonarius produced for this client portrayed a hypothetical 'Geert Douwe' whose deepest concern in life was 'understanding people', especially his family, his girl-friends and himself. Other salient axes of reference in this enactment sketch were *listening-persuasion*, *feeling-discussion*, and *forgiving-compulsion*. These three constructs were included to provide a specific context for elaborating the implications of being 'understanding'. It was hoped that the client could experiment with the notion of being an understanding person without relating it to the issue of *being free-being tied*. Peter was asked to enact the role of Geert Douwe for a fortnight, during which six rehearsals were held. In these rehearsals Bonarius and the client frequently exchanged parts involving friends, girls, and members of his family.

Bonarius reports that, at the conclusion of this enactment, the client claimed that he felt much better, his bouts of depression had disappeared, his job situation had improved, and he could relax at home. His psychiatrist conducted an interview with him at the termination of fixed role therapy and also carried out a follow-up three months later. On both occasions he found the client much improved and in no need of further treatment. In his own analysis of this clinical history, Bonarius emphasizes that the aim of fixed role therapy is to initiate and encourage the development of a new set of interrelated constructs which will enable the client to cope not only with his own problems, but also with future situations which can not be specifically anticipated at the time of 'treatment' by either therapist or client. He concludes that 'FRT is fixated on neither the past nor the present, but paradoxically provides the patient with a flexible approach to the future' (Bonarius, 1970b, p. 218).

Fixed role therapy was also employed in the treatment of a nineteen-year-old Englishman admitted to a British psychiatric hospital following his second appearance in court for homosexual acts with adolescent boys (Skene, 1973). He had previously spent nine months in a subnormality hospital after his first appearance in court for a similar offence. Skene describes his client as an only child, who was both over-protected and over-indulged by his mother. The results of psychological testing suggested that he might be considered of 'borderline-subnormal intelligence' (Full Scale WAIS IQ of 77), as well as 'conventional, defensive, and submissive to authority' (*Dynamic Personality Inventory*). Clinically, he impressed Skene as exhibitionistic and extraverted, 'but at the same time felt inadequate sexually'.

A repertory grid test based on the eight photographs from the *Bannister–Fransella Grid Test* (1967), described in Chapter 4, and a set of constructs elicited from the client during a clinical interview was used to assess his attitudes towards sexual relations. His constructs and all the 'significant' ($p < .05$) relationships found between them are listed in Table 4 given on next page. Skene offers the following analysis of these data:

He had some confusion in his sexual roles. He did not differentiate homosexual from heterosexual feelings and he identified with neither. Homosexuality did not therefore exclude being attracted to the opposite sex. Nonetheless, he saw some differences in the two sexual roles; homosexuality implied being quite manly and happy-go-lucky, but getting one into trouble. Being manly was construed with anxiety. On the other hand, being heterosexual was construed with his being taken advantage of financially. He also put the concept of 'money grubbing' at his own door, and this too was construed with anxiety. He felt that he experienced no guilt and would not like to change. He would like to have friends who were socially acceptable and liked by his mother. (p. 289)

In preparing the enactment sketch, Skene made no attempt to focus directly upon the client's homosexual behaviour. He invented the role of 'John Jones' who is a 'bearded, jolly, very happy-go-lucky chap', who is both talkative and a good listener, usually casual in conversation and always agreeing openly with others, interested in current affairs, a good sportsman, organizes games with other patients and enjoys dancing. The client attempted to enact the part of John Jones for a period of six weeks, during which he met with the psychologist twelve times. He also kept a daily diary of his experiences as John Jones. The client did not 'stay in role' on weekend leave with his parents. He did not receive any medication during the enactment period and fixed role therapy was the 'main form of psychological treatment'.

Skene reports that the client encountered few difficulties with this part, becoming an active participant in the activities of the hospital social centre and several sports clubs, and also learning to dance. He made several male friends of his own age, and began to 'go steady' with a woman of about his own age outside the hospital. 'They went out together for several months, each "going Dutch", and he said that he demonstrated his affection toward her' (p. 290). He confided to the psychologist after the enactment, however, that she was married and separated from her husband. At the end of six weeks the client was advised that he might discontinue his enactment of the part of John Jones and assume 'any role he found personally agreeable'. Skene indicates that 'he continued as happy-go-lucky, interested in sports and entertaining, but apart from this abandoned the John Jones character' (p. 290). The client himself described his experience in

Table 4. Before treatment

He construed those people who are most:	as being like those people who are most:
anxious	like I am
	I don't like
	liked by mother
	my ideal self
like me at moment	money-grabbing
	people I most like
	like to be friends with
	liked by people
	manly
money-grabbing	I'd like to be
	guilty
	not good to stay with
	rough types
those liked by mother	liked by people
	most guilty
	not ugly
those most anxious	not ugly
	those I'd like to be friends with
	get me into trouble
my ideal self	I'd like to be friends with
	guilty
I'd like to be friends with	not most manly
not liked by people	guilty
	not kind
	not manly
	not good to stay with
	rough types
	ugly
most guilty	—
most kind	happy-go-lucky
	not rough
	not ugly
most happy-go-lucky	not rough
	liked by people
most manly	not those who would get me into trouble
	not rough
	not ugly
good to stay with	not rough types

Level of significance: $p < 0.05$

(Reproduced by permission of the British Psychological Society from Skene, R. A., 'Construct shift in the treatment of a case homosexuality', *British Journal of Medical Psychology*, (1973), **46**, p. 288, published by Cambridge University Press.)

134

fixed role therapy as 'just like a play that went off well'. After further psychological testing was completed, he was discharged from the hospital.

A second repertory grid was administered to the client six months later using the same elements and constructs. Table 5 summarizes the pattern of 'significant' ($p < .05$) correlations between constructs in the second grid. The two grids were directly compared to ascertain what significant changes in the client's personal construct system might have occurred in the course of fixed role therapy. Skene interprets the results of this comparison in the following terms:

In the grid, however, there was still the association between heterosexuality and homosexuality. In other words his sexual orientation was still undefined, but the patient wished, and was able, to relate better to the opposite sex and felt less anxious in his current construing. The findings therefore indicated that his social anxiety had been alleviated to some extent and he felt more motivated for change. (p. 291)

Skene also reports that retesting with other psychological measures, including the *Dynamic Personality Inventory*, indicated that the client had become more outgoing and sociable, less conventional and submissive to authority, and more

Table 5. After treatment

He construed those people who are most: anxious	as being like those people who are most:
like me at moment	liked by mother
	kind
money-grabbing	I dislike
	not liked by mother
	not like to be friends
I dislike most	get me into most trouble
	rough types
those liked by mother	kind
	happy-go-lucky
my ideal self	kind
	manly
I'd like to be friends with	happy-go-lucky
	good to stay with
not liked by people	not happy-go-lucky
most guilty	get me into trouble
	not good to stay with
most kind	attracted to opposite sex
most happy-go-lucky	—
most manly	—
get me into trouble	not good to stay with
	ugly
good to stay with	—

Level of significance: $p < 0.05$

(Reproduced by permission of the British Psychological Society from Skene, R. A., 'Construct shift in the treatment of a case homosexuality', *British Journal of Medical Psychology* (1973), **46**, p. 290, published by Cambridge University Press.)

flexible. In addition, 'he adopted sexual roles to a greater extent, although these were basically of a feminine identification (as seen from the *Dynamic Personality Inventory*)' (p. 291). A follow-up assessment five months later revealed that he had obtained a job, had a circle of 'mates', and had joined a sports club. His girl-friend had become reconciled with her husband and had broken off with the client, leaving him depressed but 'contemplating courting another girl'.

A third repertory grid test was administered to him as part of this follow-up assessment, using a list of his own personal associates as figures and constructs elicited directly from himself on the basis of these figures. The results suggested that (p. 291) 'he currently construed himself as like people who are attracted to the opposite sex in the usual way'. At the time of this final evaluation there had been no further homosexual behaviour reported and Skene himself felt that 'his adjustment might be considered as of a more improved, heterosexual nature' (p. 291).

Skene concludes that the changes which appeared in grid testing following fixed role therapy reflected an increase in general social competence as well as a reduction in anxiety associated with heterosexuality, resulting in at least a partial resolution of the client's conflict and the appearance of more heterosexual behaviour. He suggests that although similar changes might have been effected by 'behavioural' therapy, the advantages of Kelly's fixed role approach 'would seem to lie in the fact that the patient himself feels that he is embarking on an adventure and he feels that he is in control' (p. 292).

AN EXPERIMENTAL EVALUATION

The two case histories summarized above provide useful illustrations of how specific experimental treatment programmes involving some form of fixed role enactment can be designed, implemented and evaluated in the individual case; however, they cannot serve as hard evidence for assessing the relative effectiveness of this approach in relation to more conventional modes of therapy. Only one experiment has been reported so far in which Kelly's fixed role therapy has been directly compared with another method of treatment.

Karst and Trexler (1970) employed both fixed role therapy and Ellis' (1958) 'rational-emotive' therapy in the treatment of public-speaking anxiety. They point out that each one of these approaches emphasizes change in the client's interpretation of events and his anticipations concerning the consequences of his own actions rather than the client's behaviour as such. On the other hand, they note that 'whereas Ellis proposes a set of fairly fixed "rational" perceptions that he believes most men should accept and use, Kelly prescribes no definite or best way a person should construe a situation' (p. 360). Karst and Trexler did not hypothesize that either one of these approaches to 'cognitive therapy' would be more effective than the other in the specific treatment of public-speaking anxiety. They did predict that both methods would be significantly more effective than no treatment at all.

Twenty-two American undergraduates, fifteen women and seven men, all of whom reported that they experienced relatively high levels of anxiety while speaking in public, participated as volunteer subjects in this experiment. Fixed role therapy was carried out with eight of these subjects, rational-emotive therapy with another eight of them, and the remaining six received no form of treatment. The authors, one of whom had studied fixed role therapy with George Kelly, and the other of whom had studied rational-emotive therapy with Albert Ellis, served as co-therapists in all therapy sessions. Fixed role therapy was implemented by means of the following procedures:

The first session began with an orientation to the rationale of FRT. The subjects were helped to describe what roles they adopted while speaking in public and what alternative roles were available. The homework assignment was to observe other people's responses to public speaking situations, to infer the role this person was adopting, including the underlying thoughts and feelings, and to compare it with their own. In the second session, following a discussion of homework, subjects were given hypothetical situations calling for assertive public-speaking responses and were asked to write down what they would ordinarily think, feel and do. This was followed by discussion from the point of view that alternative roles might help reduce anxiety. Homework was to write a description of an alternative role for public speaking, and try it to the extent possible. In the final session the constructions adopted by each subject were discussed and then tried out before the group. These speeches and roles were briefly discussed, and a summary statement given. (p. 362)

Five self-report measures, which varied widely among themselves in terms of their specificity and relevance to the experimental situation itself, were used to assess the effects of both forms of treatment on public-speaking anxiety: (1) *The Temple University Fear Survey Scale* (Reynolds, 1967), which purports to be a measure of general anxiety; (2) a *Social Fear Scale*; (3) Paul's (1966) shortened form of Gilkenson's *Personal Report of Confidence as a Speaker*; (4) a single item, *No. 4*, from the *Fear Survey Scale* specific to public speaking; and (5) a 10-point *Anxiety Scale*, similar to Walk's (1956) *Fear Thermometer*. Karst and Trexler considered the fifth measure to be the one which was the 'most specific to the experimental situation'. No significant differences were found between groups in terms of any of these five measures at the beginning of treatment.

Following the experimental treatments, a Kruskal–Wallis analysis of variance was calculated separately for each of these measures to determine any significant differences between groups with respect to improvement scores, defined as the difference between subjects' pre- and post-treatment scores. Mann–Whitney U tests were used to make specific comparisons between groups, the results of which are summarized in Table 6. The 'most specific' *Anxiety Scale* showed significant differences ($p < .01$) in the expected direction between groups. Specifically, subjects receiving fixed role therapy exhibited significantly more improvement than either those receiving no treatment ($p < .001$), or those treated with rational-emotive therapy ($p < .05$). Those receiving the latter form of treatment also improved significantly more than untreated control subjects ($p < .03$).

Changes with respect to Item 4 from the *Fear Survey Scale*, which deals specifically with public-speaking anxiety, were also significant ($p < .05$) and in the

Table 6. Mann–Whitney U test p levels for group comparisons with self-report measures

	Comparisons		
Measure	FRT vs. NT[a]	RET vs. NT[a]	FRT vs. RET[b]
AS	.001	.021	.050
Item 4	.010	.245	.102
PRCS	.004	.018	.304
SFS	.157	.157	.459
FSS	.021	.071	.234

[a] p levels taken with $n_1 = 6$; $n_2 = 8$; one-tailed tests.
[b] p levels taken with $n_1 = 8$; $n_2 = 8$; two-tailed tests.
(Table 3, 'Mann–Whitney U test p levels for groups comparisons with self-report measures', from Karst, T. O. and Trexler, L. D., Initial study using fixed-role and rational-emotive therapy in treating public speaking anxiety. *Journal of Consulting and Clinical Psychology* (1970), **34**, p. 363, copyright 1970 by the American Psychological Association. Reprinted by permission.)

same direction. Comparisons between particular groups revealed that subjects participating in fixed role therapy improved significantly more than subjects who did not receive any form of treatment ($p < .01$); however, those involved in rational-emotive therapy did not improve more than the untreated controls ($p = .245$). A direct comparison between the two methods of treatment slightly favoured the fixed role technique ($p = .102$), but this difference was not significant. An analysis of scores on the measure of *Personal Confidence as a Speaker* indicated that subjects receiving the fixed role therapy ($p < .005$) and those receiving the rational-emotive therapy ($p < .02$) improved more than the untreated control subjects; but no significant differences were found between these two methods of therapy ($p = .304$). On the *Fear Survey Scale* subjects engaged in fixed roles improved significantly more than the untreated control subjects ($p < .03$); however, no difference was observed between the latter and subjects involved in rational-emotive therapy ($p = .071$). Finally, no significant differences were found between groups in terms of improvement in their scores on the general *Social Fear Scale*.

Karst and Trexler provide the following summary of their main findings: 'Three of five self-report measures reached or exceeded the 95% level of confidence; one measure, FSS, reached the 90% level. All differences were in the expected direction. Generally, FRT seemed to be slightly more effective than RET' (p. 364). The final statement seems a bit too conservative in the light of the fact that the mean improvement score of those subjects who participated in fixed role therapy exceeded that of subjects in both the rational-emotive therapy group and the untreated control group on all five measures. A 'post-therapy data sheet', consisting of four questions evaluating their experience in therapy, was also completed by all subjects at the conclusion of the experiment. The subjects who received fixed role therapy evaluated their treatment as more helpful than those receiving rational-emotive therapy ($\chi^2 = 4.0$, 1 df, $p < .05$). Finally, the fixed role therapy group showed significantly more improvement than the control group on four out of five measures, whereas the rational-emotive therapy group did so on only two out of five measures.

These preliminary findings seem quite encouraging for fixed role therapy as far as they go. On the other hand, there are no other relevant studies with which to compare Karst and Trexler's results. Therefore, it is impossible at this stage to formulate even the most tentative conclusion about the general efficacy of this form of treatment. From the standpoint of personal construct theory this specific area of research is an extremely important one, since as Pervin (1975, p. 300) notes, fixed role therapy is the method of psychological treatment 'that is particularly associated with personal construct theory, and it does exemplify some of the principles of the personal construct theory of change'. As we have seen, Kelly (1955) derives the rationale of this novel approach to psychotherapy from his 'sociality corollary'. Thus, any experiment which serves to demonstrate the relative efficacy of this form of treatment also lends support to the sociality corollary and the related theoretical assumptions discussed in previous chapters (cf. Stefan, 1973).

FLUENCY THROUGH RECONSTRUCTION

A second approach to psychotherapy which has been derived directly from the principles of personal construct theory is a method for treating stuttering developed by Fransella (1972). The basic assumption of this technique is that 'the path from stuttering to fluency is seen as being a process of reconstruing' (p. 56). Kelly's (1970, p. 15) 'choice corollary' asserts that 'a person chooses for himself that alternative in a dichotomized construct through which he anticipates the greater possibility for the elaboration of his system'. Hinkle (1965, p. 21) submits that this proposition implies that 'a person always chooses in that direction which he anticipates will increase the total meaning and significance of his life'. Fransella (p. 58) has derived from Hinkle's argument the specific hypothesis that 'a person stutters because it is in this way that life is most meaningful to him'. She proposes that the individual who stutters usually construes himself as a 'stutterer' whenever he is in direct verbal communication with adults; and when he enacts the role of stutterer, he finds that he is more or less able accurately to anticipate how they will respond to his utterances and how he, himself is likely to react to their behaviour. Thus, paradoxically, he experiences more of a sense of 'poise' in a social situation when he plays the part of the 'stutterer' than he would if he were to attempt to speak fluently. 'In the world of fluency there may lie many unknown hazards and a vastly decreased ability to predict these pitfalls' (p. 58).

More specifically, Fransella points out that the 'stutterer' tends to be relatively unskilled in the interpretation of typical responses to fluent speech, including non-verbal gestures, eye contact, postures, etc. She suggests that in most social situations his attention is primarily focused upon himself and the difficulty that he experiences in speaking. His usual basis for attempting to establish 'role relationships' with others is his own expectation concerning how they will react to his stuttering, rather than anticipation about how they might interpret the content of his communications.

Fransella posits that the 'stutterer' has developed a specific subsystem of constructs the focus of convenience of which is his own speech. Whenever he enacts the role which he has elaborated for himself within the context of this particular subsystem he can predict what will happen. That is, 'he "knows" that he is unlikely to be interrupted, to be shouted at, even, in many cases, to be disagreed with; he easily holds the listener's attention, albeit unwillingly' (p. 59). Since he tends to enact the role of the 'stutterer' in almost all social interactions, he has little or no opportunity to interpret the responses of others to his speech and behaviour when he is not stuttering. Like everyone else, he feels less anxious in a given situation when he has some basis for anticipating how others will interpret his behaviour and respond to him, and he can predict the reactions of people better from the standpoint of a 'stutterer' than from that of a 'fluent speaker'. Thus, according to Fransella's model, 'where he is unable to construe the construction processes of others, even if only in a stereotyped way, he has to fall back on the one role he knows all too well—that of stutterer' (p. 60).

Why then is stuttering so often a source of anxiety and embarrassment to the individual who stutters? Applying the principle of functional differentiation between subsystem (elaborated in Chapters 3 and 4 above), Fransella reasons that 'a person can maintain a construct subsystem relating to himself as a stuttering speaker which contradicts many ideas he has about himself as a person' (p. 60). The limited focus of convenience of his 'problematic' subsystem is the sphere of face-to-face, verbal communication with others. Fransella argues that the main source of conflict for the person who stutters is that he finds it difficult, if not impossible, to integrate his 'me as a speaker' subsystem with the rest of his personal construct system as it applies to himself. 'If the *me as speaker* subsystem is viewed as one part of the total construct system, then every time he plays the stutterer role he is aware of the relative absence of implications of this role in relation to his total system' (p. 62).

This general hypothesis receives support from Fransella's (1968) finding that when the concepts *me* and *stutterers* were rated on a set of nine *Semantic Differential* scales by a group of 'stutterers' and two groups of 'non-stutterers', (a) the stutterers tended not to associate these two concepts with one another in terms of the first two factors extracted from their ratings; and (b) stutterers and non-stutterers did not differ in the way in which they rated either concept (see Figure 3 below). 'Thus, the stutterer seems to take the same view of other stutterers that non-stutterers take, but this is not the way he sees *himself*' (Bannister and Fransella, 1971, p. 145). In addition, Fransella (1972) indicates that a significant positive relationship between the constructs *like me in character* and *stutterers* is only rarely found in the implication grid data collected from individuals who stutter. This finding contains an interesting parallel to that of an earlier case study in repertory grid assessment reported by Fransella and Adams

140

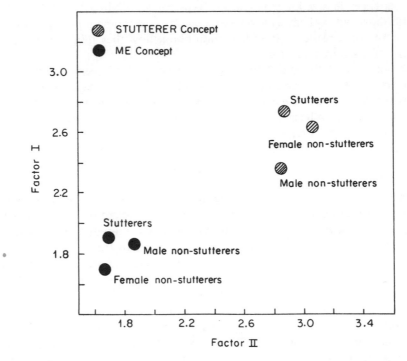

Figure 3. Concepts *Me* and *Stutterers* used by stutterers, male and female non-stutterers on a semantic differential plotted along the first two factors. (Reproduced with permission from Fransella, F., *Personal Change and Reconstruction*, 1972, p. 24. Copyright by Academic Press, Inc. (London Ltd.)

(1966) in which a convicted 'arsonist' characterized himself differently from 'people who commit arson'. Hoy (1973) has also obtained similar results in administering a repertory grid test to 'alcoholics'. He reports that 'alcoholics as a group were found not to construe themselves as alcoholics either denotatively or connotatively' (p. 98).

Fransella (1972, p. 62) suggests that the prospect of fluency is usually anxiety-provoking for the individual who typically stutters: 'To be suddenly fluent instead of stuttering would produce an immediate awareness of the relative lack of implications within the speaking situation'. It follows that a method of treatment which produced immediate changes in the client's pattern of speech would probably increase his anxiety and discomfort. Fransella herself has developed an innovative approach to the treatment of stuttering in which the client is assisted in carrying out a series of experiments in which he enacts the part of a fluent speaker. In these experiments the client himself is again the principal investigator, as he is in Kelly's fixed role therapy; and his own speaking behaviour is viewed as the main 'independent variable' which he manipulates and controls, rather than as the 'dependent variable' as it is seen in conventional modes of speech therapy. The purpose of these experiments is gradually to elaborate the implications of speaking fluently in social situations. That is, the client will have an opportunity to find out what to anticipate from others when he enacts the role of fluent speaker. This should eventually provide a basis for his 'reconstruing' the situations in which he typically stutters.

Fransella (1972) portrays the role of the 'therapist' in this venture as follows:

It is the job of the therapist to take the stutterer along slowly enough so that he can creep up on fluency a glimpse at a time. That he is going to change as he becomes more fluent is undeniable; there will be all sorts of things he will be able to do which were previously unavailable to him, new roles to adopt, new limits to impose on his behaviour. (p. 63)

In summary, this approach focuses upon the person who is speaking rather than on speech as such. It is assumed that an individual stutters because he has never before been in a position to develop the implications of construing himself as a fluent speaker; however, he has conducted all too many experiments in stuttering and has elaborated a whole host of implications of construing himself as a stutter. In these 'experiments' with stuttering he has been so involved in construing his own pattern of speech and noting the reactions of others to it, that he has not found out very much about how people respond to fluent speech. Thus, Fransella hypothesizes that 'if he can build up a system of constructs and implications to make fluency more meaningful, so he will be more likely to gain and maintain that fluency' (p. 69).

Fransella (1972) reports a study in which she treated a group of twenty 'stutterers', three women and seventeen men, all of whom were over the age of seventeen and had no history of psychiatric disorder. Each client had stuttered for as long as he or she could remember. Fransella first administered an 'implication grid' test (Hinkle, 1965, described in Chapter 3) to every client to assess the 'meaningfulness of being fluent' to them personally. This was undertaken on the general assumption that one could 'be more successful in predicting a stutterer's responses or reactions to a situation if one is given some of the constructs the stutterer himself uses to make sense of his world than if one has available only "stereotype" constructs that others use to construe stutterers' (p. 77). This seems an especially important point in the light of her earlier finding that stutterers and non-stutterers tend to characterize 'the stutterer' in the same way (Fransella, 1968). That is, since both stutterers and non-stutterers appear to share the same stereotyped view of stutterers in general, it becomes crucial to assess how each individual who stutters construes himself and his own speech behaviour.

Fransella argues, following Hinkle (1965), that the meaning of a personal construct depends in part on its specific range of both superordinate and subordinate implications in terms of the other constructs within an individual's system. She has simplified Hinkle's original 'implication grid' technique in order to provide a convenient clinical measure of the pattern of relationships of implication which articulate the structure of an individual's personal construct system (Fransella, 1969). Fransella and Bannister (1977) point out that,

Fransella had found with her sample of stutterers that the task Hinkle set the person was too complex. This might be due to cultural differences as well as individual differences in ability to perform the conceptual task. Hinkle's subjects were American college (university) students, while Fransella's were people of wide ranging abilities from several countries. (p. 51)

Fransella's version of this technique is usually referred to as the *Bi-polar Impgrid* because it allows for the implications of both poles of each construct to be elicited. Fransella and Bannister (p. 49) also point out that 'the identification of orthogonal and ambiguous "dilemmas" can only be carried out if the implications of both poles of a construct are noted'.

In general, Fransella's 'bi-polar implications grid' is administered to each subject individually in the following manner. Each of the constructs elicited from the subject is recorded on a separate card in bi-polar form with one pole labelled *a* and the opposite pole labelled *b*. Then all cards bearing constructs are spread out before the subject in a single display. A second set of identical cards is also produced, with each card cut in half so that one pole of the construct appears on each half. The 'half-cards' are then shuffled and dealt to the subject one at a time. As each 'half-card' is presented, the subject is asked to consider the 'trait' inscribed on it, say *aloof*, and asked if 'all you know about a person is that s/he is *aloof*, what from all these other characteristics on the cards in front of you could you expect to find in an *aloof* person?'. The subject then scans all the cards on display and designates those cards which bear the name of another trait she or he would expect to find in an *aloof* person as well as the specific pole (*a* or *b*) of the relevant construct which should apply (cf. Fransella and Bannister, 1977, pp. 48–52).

In administering this test to her sample of 'stutterers', Fransella (1972) asked them to complete two separate grids on each occasion of testing. These tests were based on different sets of elicited constructs, one of which was relevant to 'being a stutterer' (S-grid) and the other of which pertained to 'being a non-stutterer' (NS-grid). In eliciting constructs for both types of grid test, she employed four photographs of strangers of the same sex as the client. Kelly's (1955) 'method of successive triads' (described in Chapter 2) was used, including the client himself in every triad. In the S-grid test, the phrase 'me as others see me when I am stuttering' was used to represent the 'self' figure, and in the NS-grid test, 'me as others see me when I am not stuttering'. In both forms of this test, the emphasis is placed on understanding the constructions of other people in accordance with Kelly's definition of role. Six different triads were used in each grid test to elicit constructs. The client was always asked to 'think of yourself and the two people represented in the photographs as if viewed by a fourth person who might see two of them as being alike in some important way and thereby different from the third' (p. 82). Each client was permitted to supply as many constructs as he wished for a triad, but usually only one was offered. Fransella used a different set of four photographs on each occasion of testing.

The second step in the administration of these implication grids involved the use of two identical decks of cards, prepared individually for each client. On every card in both of these decks a different construct was recorded, with each of its poles designated as either *a* or *b*. Each of the cards in one of these decks was then cut in half so that only one pole of a construct appeared on either half. Call this Deck X. The deck of 'uncut' cards (Deck Y) was spread out on a table in front of the client. Then Deck X was thoroughly shuffled and presented to the client one card at a time. He was asked for each of these 'half-cards' in turn that if all he knew about a given person was the information contained on that card, for example that he was *honest*, which of the other attributes listed on all the 'full-cards' in front of him would he expect that person to exhibit, in addition to honesty. This technique was employed by Fransella to elicit the full range of implications for each pole of every construct in terms of all the other constructs elicited from the same client. The resulting data were arranged in an implication grid format such as that represented in Figure 4, which was taken from Fransella and Bannister (1977, p. 50).

Fransella has developed her own method for the mathematical analysis of this type of data matrix. Her procedure for determining the pattern of significant relationships between each construct and every other is far too complex to summarize here. It is described fully in Appendix 1 of her book (Fransella, 1972, p. 239).

Altogether, a total of ninety-three implication grids were completed by her twenty clients in the course of treatment. The most grids completed by any one client was ten, and the least was two. She also elicited several self-characterization sketches from each of her clients, using the format designed by Kelly (1955). This was undertaken in order to provide additional information about the client's own view of his world, and also to encourage him to verbalize whatever changes were taking place in his own personal constructions during treatment.

Fransella also frequently obtained tape-recorded samples of the speech of each of her clients. The intervals between these recordings were usually about six weeks. The speech samples consisted of two minutes of spontaneous speech and the reading of a prose passage. These speaking and reading tests were systematically alternated from one session to the next. All speech samples were analysed at the conclusion of the entire treatment programme. Three separate measures of stuttering were used in scoring these protocols: (1) *total disfluencies*, including interjections of sounds, syllables, words, phrases, part-word repetitions, word repetitions, revisions, incomplete phrases, broken words, and prolonged sounds (Johnson, Dailey, and Spriestsbach, 1963); (2) the number of different words in which these disfluencies appeared (Sander, 1961); and (3) the rate of utterance.

A detailed individual treatment history is presented by Fransella (1972) for each one of her twenty clients. She herself was the therapist in evey case. She has also provided extensive extracts from eighty-two separate interviews with one particular client. The basic hypothesis was the same in every case, that is, stuttering will not diminish until the person construes himself, to some extent at least, as a fluent speaker' (p. 160).

Figure 4. A completed bi-polar implications grid. (Reproduced with permission from Fransella, F., and Bannister, D., *A Manual for Repertory Grid Technique*, 1977, p. 50. Copyright by Academic Press Inc. (London) Ltd.)

Bannister and Fransella (1971, pp. 135–6) offer the following broad summary of this treatment programme:

In a study of twenty stutterers, this was achieved by concentrating on the construing of fluency. The vast majority of stutterers, no matter how severe their disability, have moments of fluency. It was these that formed the basis of construct change and elaboration. Each fluent episode was discussed in great detail—*the stutterer was made to construe it.* Only too often one finds that the stutterer has not done this when fluent. He has construed it globally as 'I was not stuttering'. He had not looked to see what difference this made to how he felt and behaved, how the listener reacted and what aspects of the situation might have led to his being fluent. The focus is on the *joint* search for common denominators in such situations.

Fransella (1972, p. 226) also points out that 'this form of treatment goes far beyond the reduction of the speech defect itself. It is seen as having to continue until the fluent person has sufficient ways of interpreting himself and others to make reasonably accurate predictions possible'.

It was found that, at the beginning of this treatment programme, clients in general produced significantly more relationships of 'implication' between constructs in their S-grids than in their NS-grids ($p < .01$). Fransella interprets this result as indicating that 'at the start of treatment the stutterers were better able to construe themselves as stutterers than as non-stutterers' (p. 115). She argues that, if we are willing to assume that the total number of implications in each grid protocol is an index of 'meaningfulness', then 'being a stutterer was significantly more meaningful' for her clients at the beginning than being a non-stutterer.

Following treatment, on the other hand, significantly more relationships of implication were found between constructs in the clients' NS-grids than in their S-grids ($p < .05$). Fransella suggests that following treatment 'they were better able to construe themselves as non-stutterers than as stutterers, representing a highly significant reversal from their construing at the start of treatment' (p. 116). Further support for this interpretation of her results is provided by the finding that the total number of implications in the NS-grids increased significantly from the first to the last occasion of testing ($p < .005$). There was no significant decrease, however, in the total number of implications in the S-grids during the same period. Another relevant finding was that, on the first occasion of testing the S-grids contained a 'higher ratio of implications for superordinate constructs' than the NS-grids. Fransella interprets this outcome as 'indicating that the stutterer has a more workable and flexible as well as a more extensive sub-system to do with himself as a stutterer than as a fluent speaker at the start of treatment' (p. 117).

One problem with this set of measurements is that the total number of implications which appear in any one grid protocol, which is Fransella's operational definition of 'meaningfulness', will depend in part on the number of constructs elicited from the subject at the outset; and this was allowed to vary freely from one subject to another; and, even more importantly, from one type of grid test to the other. Fransella herself admits that 'it was possible that the total number of implications in a grid might be a simple function of the number of constructs elicited' (p. 114). She argues, however, that this seems unlikely because the Spearman rank-order correlation between the total number of implications and the average number per construct was 0.85 for the S-grids and 0.91 for the NS-grids. Nonetheless, it does not strictly follow from this that she would have found any significant differences between S-grids and NS-grids on either the first or last occasion of testing, or between grids of the same type of construction across occasions, in terms of the *average number of implications per construct*. Unfortunately, no analysis based on this score is reported.

This seems to be a very important consideration, because it leaves open the possibility that the findings summarized above do not represent changes in the clients' construct systems with respect to the number of relationships of implication between their constructs ('meaningfulness') so much as changes in terms of the number of constructs elicited from them ('differentiation'—Crockett, 1965—see Chapter 3). We cannot determine on the basis of the information supplied by Fransella how many constructs were elicited from each client on each type of grid on each occasion of testing. It would be interesting to ascertain whether clients tended to use relatively more constructs to characterize themselves as 'stutterers' at the beginning of treatment (i.e. high differentiation on S-grids) than as 'non-stutterers' (low differentiation on NS-grids); and during treatment increased with respect to the number of constructs which they used to characterize themselves as 'non-stutterers' (high differentiation on NS grids). It does seem possible that the kind of treatment programme described by Fransella could have resulted in her clients' becoming gradually more 'cognitively complex' (i.e. 'differentiated') in terms of construing fluent speech as opposed to stuttering. That is, they may have acquired a larger repertory of personal constructs which could be used to anticipate how others might respond to them in the role of 'fluent speaker', while not changing much in terms of the number of constructs which they apply to their stuttering. Unfortunately, the data needed to test this hypothesis have not yet been published.

The results that are reported by Fransella do suggest that, if there were a systematic increase during treatment in terms of the number of constructs which her clients used to characterize themselves as fluent speakers, then this increase in 'differentiation' would have been accompanied by a corresponding increase in the level of 'integration' as represented by her index of the total number of implicative relationships among constructs. This is what we might expect to occur on the basis of Kelly's (1955) own model of the development of conceptual structures, which is summarized in Chapter 3. This hypothesis also seems consistent with the results of Fransella's analysis of her data in terms of 'implication saturation', which is defined as 'a simple count of implications in relation to the total number possible' (Fransella and Bannister, 1977, p. 52).

The number of possible implications in any grid is determined directly by the number of constructs contained in that grid. Although Fransella (1972) does not supply a formula for computing her 'implication saturation' scores, the example given (p. 115) suggests that it is obtained simply by dividing the total number of implications observed in a grid by the total number possible. This would yield a measure of 'meaningfulness' which is not contaminated with the number of constructs elicited from the subject. The analysis based on this index revealed that there were no significant differences between the two types of grid tests, S and NS, on any occasion of testing; and no significant changes during treatment in terms of either type of grid test for the group as a whole. Given that treatment produced systematic changes in the total number of implicative relationships between constructs, but not in the number of implications per construct, in the NS-grids; it seems likely that there were increases both in the number of constructs elicited and in the number of relationships between them in the NS-grid during treatment. This would suggest that what takes place in therapy is a gradual differentiation and reintegration of the structure of that subsystem used to construe fluent speech. In short, the underlying process is one of cognitive development as defined in Chapter 3.

Fransella also reports that the rates of speaking and reading increased significantly during the treatment programme. In addition, the number of disfluent words and the total number of disfluencies were reduced significantly. She hypothesized that these improvements in her clients' speech would be related to increases in the 'meaningfulness of being a non-stutterer', operationally defined as the total number of implications in the NS-grids. According to Fransella, this hypothesis 'was supported, both in the case of reduction in disfluent words and in total disfluencies (Sign Test, $p < .002$, in both cases)'. There was also a significant correlation between the total number of implications in the NS-grid on the first occasion of testing and the degree of the reduction in the number of disfluent words in the spontaneous speech samples as a result of treatment ($r = 0.61$; $p < .01$). Fransella argues on the basis of the latter finding that 'the more the "nonstutterer" construing system was elaborated before the start of treatment, the greater was the chance of a reduction in speech errors' (p. 134).

Once more, it might be useful to have a record of the number of constructs elicited from each client on both the S and NS-grids on all occasions of assessment to compare with indices of increased fluency during treatment. This is because it is not clear from the data presented by Fransella whether improvement in the speech samples relates to the degree of 'integration' of the non-stuttering subsystem ('meaningfulness'), the degree of 'differentiation' ('cognitive complexity'), or perhaps both.

In further analysing the results of treatment, Fransella divided her total sample into two groups: (1) those clients who had shown more than a 50 per cent improvement on either measure of fluency derived from their speech samples; and (2) those who either exhibited less improvement or terminated treatment prematurely, regardless of their level of improvement before discontinuing therapy. These two groups were then compared with each other in terms of their mean 'implication saturation' scores. The results indicated that the 'improvers' obtained significantly lower saturation scores on the S-grids on the first occasion of testing than either the 'non-improvers' or the 'drop-outs' (Mann–Whitney U test; $p < .001$). In other words, 'those who had a higher ratio of ticks (implications) were less likely to improve—they had a more tightly-knit system about themselves as stutterers' (Fransella and Bannister, 1977, p. 52). Fransella (1972) does not indicate, however, how many (if any) of those clients who terminated treatment prematurely may have met her criterion of improvement at the time when they dropped out. In any event, this particular finding provides the clearest evidence that there is a negative relationship between the level of 'integration' of a client's 'stutterer' subsystem at the beginning of treatment and subsequent improvements in the fluency of his speech. This is because, as we noted above, the 'implication saturation' score as a measure of integration is not confounded with the number of constructs elicited from the client (i.e. 'differentiation'), as is the total number of implications.

Thus Fransella's results seem consistent with previous findings that persons who exhibit relatively high levels of interrelationship among a set of constructs as assessed by means of implication grid technique exhibit greater resistance to changing anticipations based specifically on those constructs than persons who evidence lower levels of relationship (Crockett and Miesel, 1974; Hinkle, 1965). Bannister (in Fransella, 1972, p. 226) describes Fransella's treatment programme in the following terms:

The continual focus on the content and meaning of the stuttering situation seems to rule out very effectively the use of vague notions such as 'anxiety' and 'depression' . . . It seems to force the patient into looking for meaning, looking for significance in his stuttering or not stuttering, so that he is never allowed to get away with the idea of a sort of 'free floating' stuttering . . . He is allowed to follow the line out from stuttering very extensively but it is a line from stuttering and returns to it and resettles as its focus on stuttering again every time.

It seems quite plausible that those clients who have developed a highly integrated subsystem of personal constructs whose focus of convenience is their own stuttering might benefit least from the type of treatment developed by Fransella. In the next section, we shall see that the level of integration of the client's construct system may also interact with that of the therapist's own system in determining the outcome of psychotherapy.

DIFFERENCES IN CONCEPTUAL STRUCTURE
BETWEEN CLIENT AND THERAPIST

Landfield (1971) has carried out an extensive programme of research concerned with the conceptual changes which occur in psychotherapy within the general framework of personal construct theory. Some of this work has been discussed in preceding chapters. We shall be concerned here with his examination of specific changes in the construction processes of clients undergoing psychotherapy which can be related to structural properties of the personal construct systems of their particular therapists.

In this research, Landfield employed a form of repertory grid technique to measure what he terms 'functionally independent construction' (FIC), which is operationally defined as 'the number of functionally different dimensional units of meaning inferred from a Rep Test grid' (p. 14). A relatively low FIC score is interpreted as indicating that 'a person's construct dimensions are highly integrated and organized'; and a relatively high FIC score that 'his construct dimensions are used more independently of one another and may not have implications for one another' (pp. 14–15). Landfield suggests also that relatively moderate FIC scores may relate to 'more effective functioning' than either very high scores, which tend to reflect 'confusion' (see Chapter 4), or very low scores, which are seen as indicating 'simplicity' (see Chapter 3).

Landfield points out that he has 'carefully avoided designating our organizational score as a measure of cognitive complexity, a term which might carry the erroneous implications that a high FIC score denotes the ability to encompass complexity and a low FIC score denotes an inability to encompass complexity' (p. 15). The specific procedure for computing the FIC score from repertory grid data is far too complicated to describe here. It is explained fully in Landfield's book, together with a summary of a computer program written in Fortran IV, and evidence bearing on its test-retest reliability.

He hypothesizes that 'the therapist's capacity to provide his client with problem-solving stimulation' is enhanced whenever there is a difference between the therapist and the client with respect to the degree of organization of their respective personal construct systems. He argues specifically that 'a client-therapist difference in FIC scoring, at the beginning of therapy, provides an important context of relationship within which the client may reconstrue or reinterpret events of importance to him' (p. 20). It was predicted that (a) 'a client whose constructs are tightly interrelated (low FIC) will profit most from interaction with a therapist whose own constructions are less well organized (high FIC)', and conversely, (b) 'a client whose constructs are loosely interrelated (high FIC) will profit most from interaction with a therapist whose own constructions are more tightly systematized (low FIC)' (p. 20).

The clients in this research project were all undergraduates seen in the student health service of an American university, typically for one session per week. The therapist involved in this project were either faculty members in the Department of Psychology of the same university or advanced graduate students in a Ph. D. programme in clinical psychology with at least one year's full-time experience as psychotherapists. In all, there were seven male and one female therapists, each of whom saw three different clients. The twenty-four clients, eleven women and thirteen men, each completed twelve sessions of psychotherapy over a period of thirteen weeks. Another thirteen clients, eight women and five men, started therapy; but they terminated before their seventh interview.

The twenty-four clients who completed therapy were divided into the twelve who improved most and the twelve who improved least by three independent judges, who agreed amongst themselves on twenty cases (83 per cent). These judges also agreed with the therapists' evaluations of improvement in their own clients in twenty cases. The judges' assessments of improvement were based on comparisons between the typescripts of pre- and post-therapy interviews with each client conducted by a trained interviewer who was not the client's own therapist. Landfield found that, as he had predicted, the differences between the therapists and clients with respect to FIC scores at the beginning of treatment were significantly higher for the twelve most improved clients than for the twelve least improved ones ($p < .01$).

Landfiled also hypothesized that improvement in psychotherapy would be accompanied by increased covergence between clients and therapists with respect to the level of organization of their personal construct systems. He operationally defined convergence as a decrease in the difference between the FIC scores of a client and his therapist from the beginning of treatment to the thirteenth week. As predicted, a significantly higher degree of convergence was observed in the most improved group than in the least improved group. It was also found that the FIC scores of the clients showed significantly more change than those of their respective therapists during the course of treatment ($p < .02$). Landfield concludes on the basis of the latter finding that 'therapists did contribute to the convergence or divergence scores, but not to the extent of their clients' (p. 84).

In summary, divergence with respect to FIC scores between client and therapist at the beginning of treatment seems to relate to the client's improvement; and improvement during treatment appears to be accompanied by a convergence between client and therapist in terms of their FIC scores, the scores of the former exhibiting more change than those of the latter. Landfield does not indicate, however, whether the *direction* of the difference between their FIC scores at the beginning of therapy, that is, whether a particular client's FIC score is originally higher or lower than that of his own therapist, makes any difference in terms of subsequent improvement on the part of the client. It is also not possible on the basis of the information provided by Landfield to estimate the extent to which the observed convergence between the average FIC scores of clients and therapists in the twelve cases showing the most improvement could have been the result of simple regression towards the mean in the clients' FIC scores.

The test-retest reliabilities for the FIC score reported for all clients are fairly low (0.44, 0.48, 0.51). As much as 75 per cent of the variance in these scores could be due to measurement error. This would allow considerable room for random variations in a client's FIC score from one occasion of testing to the next. Since it was the most improved clients who showed the largest differences between their own FIC scores and those of their respective therapists at the beginning of therapy, we could expect these clients to show more regression toward the mean in difference scores over a thirteen-week period.

Landfield himself does not advance a specific hypothesis to explain how improvement on the part of the client may lead to greater congruence between client and therapist with respect to their FIC scores. However, an explanation of this finding can be put together on the basis of some of the general assumptions of his model. First, he proposes that (p. 15) 'a moderate FIC score may be related to more effective functioning' than either a very high score or a very low one. If we were willing to assume that, on average, the personal construct system of a therapist was functioning more effectively than that of his client at the beginning of therapy, we could expect the FIC score of the client to be appreciably higher or lower at first than the relatively 'moderate' score of his therapist. In so far as therapy 'works', in the sense that the personal construct system of the client is in fact functioning more effectively at the conclusion of treatment than at the beginning, this outcome could be reflected in the client's obtaining a more 'moderate' FIC score after completing therapy. Therefore, we might expect the client's score to deviate less from the relatively 'moderate' score of his therapist at the end of therapy than at the start of it.

There is also evidence that the FIC scores of those clients who were judged to have shown the most improvement in therapy deviated further, in one direction or the other, from those of their respective therapists at the outset than did the FIC scores of those clients who were judged to have improved least. This finding is also consistent with the hypothesis that the FIC scores of clients can be expected to become more 'moderate' as they improve in the course of therapy. Since the clients who showed the greatest divergence, either up or down, from the relatively moderate scores of their therapists at the beginning of therapy were those who were found to be the most improved at the end, the hypothesis implies that these same clients will show the most convergence with their therapists at the conclusion of therapy where convergence is defined as *the amount of decrease* in the difference between the scores of the client and therapist. In short, we can expect those with the highest difference scores at the beginning to realize the greatest decreases in difference scores, given that these are the clients who showed the most movement. This, of course, is exactly what Landfield found. The finding that the FIC scores of clients showed significantly more change during treatment than did those of their therapists is also consistent with this line of reasoning.

The main problem with this interpretation of Landfield's results is that it implies that it is the client who is functioning least effectively at the beginning of therapy, that is, the client whose FIC score shows the greatest divergence from the relatively moderate score of his therapist, who is likely to improve the most during therapy. This could indicate a simple 'starting position effect'. In short, those who have the 'most room for improvement', do in fact show the most improvement. Unfortunately, the means and standard deviations of FIC scores for clients and therapists at the beginning of therapy are not reported, and consequently we cannot evaluate this hypothesis directly against the data themselves.

Landfield offers the following hypothetical example of the effects of 'organizational incongruence' between therapist and client at the beginning of therapy on the pattern of communication and mutual understanding which may develop between them throughout the course of treatment:

The significance of organizational incongruence can be illustrated. A therapist can assist his client in placing a particular experience within a broader framework or within a more restricted framework of meaning. And this can be done without drastically changing or invalidating the experience of the client. A client's complaint about a friend's cruel behaviour can be accepted by the therapist as having validity but only in the context of time, situation and people. A client's report of an unexplainable kindness by another person can be tentatively reflected by the therapist as having larger or more profound implications. (p. 20)

He suggests that now he has shown the importance of 'organizational incongruence' in the therapist-client relationship, the therapist 'might deliberately and helpfully vary his role along the axis of functionally independent construction', or if he cannot systematically vary the level of organization of his own personal construct system, he can at least assess that of his prospective clients and select only those with whom he is somewhat 'organizationally incongruent'.

On the other hand, Landfield also reports that there is a significant relationship between 'organizational incongruence' between therapist and client and premature termination of therapy by the client. Specifically, the FIC scores of clients who left therapy early were found to deviate from those of their respective therapists to a greater extent than those of clients who remained in therapy for at least the prescribed thirteen weeks ($p < .01$). We saw in the preceding chapter that those clients who drop out of therapy early also tend to enjoy less 'congruence' with their therapists with respect to the content of their personal construct systems. In short, Landfield's research suggests that 'premature termination may be related to lower client-therapist congruence in both the content and organization of their personal construct systems' (p. 79).

Landfield does not indicate, however, whether clients who exhibit incongruence with respect to their therapist in terms of both content and organization are more likely to drop out of therapy early than are clients who are incongruent with their therapists in terms of only one of these facets of their construct systems. He also provides no information about the extent to which these two conditions were associated with one another in his own sample of therapists and clients. Thus, it is difficult to evaluate the significance of his findings for predicting and explaining premature termination of therapy.

In general, clients who completed the entire thirteen-week programme exhibited relatively higher levels of 'content and organizational congruence' with their therapists at the outset than did those who quit early. Of those who remained in therapy at least thirteen weeks, the clients who showed the most improvement at the end evidenced less 'organizational congruence' with their therapists at the beginning; however, as they improved, the level of organization of their personal construct systems began to approach that of their therapists. Thus, although a client who exhibits a relatively low level of organizational congruence with his therapist at the start of therapy is more likely to drop out of treatment prematurely, he is also more likely to benefit from it if he sticks with it. In short, a therapist who follows Landfield's suggestion of selecting his clients on the basis of 'organizational incongruence' with himself will have a higher rate of success with his clients, and may also have more free time. Landfield (p. 82) speculates that it is 'a moderate amount of client-therapist organizational incongruency, found in the context of content congruency, that appears to facilitate improvement'. Nevertheless, he does not report any data which bear directly on the important question of whether or not 'organizational in-congruence' is a better predictor of eventual improvement when client and therapist are relatively congruent with respect to the content of their personal construct systems.

Another of Landfield's hypotheses is that 'improvement in therapy is accompanied by a shift in the present-self of the client toward the ideal of the therapist as described within the client's language dimensions, i.e. personal constructs of the client rather than those of the therapist' (p. 23). This hypothesis was tested in the context of 'variable term' psychotherapy with thirty-six clients, nineteen women and seventeen men, seen once a week by one of six therapists. Personal constructs were elicited from both therapists and clients at the beginning of therapy. These constructs formed the basis of a set of 13-point scales on which both clients and therapists were asked once a month to (1) 'rate yourself as you see yourself now in the present'; (2) 'rate your ideal'; and (3) 'rate the other person as you see him now' (i.e. the clients rated their therapists, and *vice versa*). The therapists rated their ideals only on the first occasion. Then, three 'highly experienced external judges' divided the total sample of clients into those who had 'improved most' and those who had 'improved least' on the basis of a comparison between verbatim transcripts of pre- and post-treatment interviews. These clients were seen by their own therapists for an average of six or seven interviews, and only six of them were seen for more than twelve sessions. None of the clients was considered to have been severely disturbed at the beginning of therapy.

Each client's ratings of his 'present-self' on the first and last occasions of testing were compared with his therapist's ratings of his (therapist's) 'ideal' on both the therapist's and the client's personal constructs. On the basis of these com-parisons, every client was categorized as either 'moving toward' or 'moving away from' the ideal-self of the therapist, according to whether the number of overall discrepancies between his own self-ratings and the ideal-self ratings of his therapist increased or decreased from the beginning to the conclusion of treatment. This analysis was done twice—once for ratings based on constructs elicited from the clients and once for those based on constructs elicited from the therapists.

Landfield found that, as he had predicted, those clients who were judged to be 'most improved' at the end of therapy 'moved toward' the ideal-selves of their respective therapists on the basis of their own (clients') personal constructs significantly more than those clients who were judged to be 'least improved' ($p < .01$). On the other hand, no significant relationship was observed between improvement and movement toward the therapists' ideal-selves on the basis of constructs elicited from the therapists themselves. Landfield interprets these results as suggesting that 'since most therapy is of shorter duration and since many therapists presumably do try to communicate with their clients in a language which the clients will best understand, it is more likely that the improved client will move toward the therapist's values which are plotted within the client's own language framework—or personal construct system' (p. 89). He points out also that his own results are consistent with Rosenthal's (1955) earlier finding that those clients who improve in psychotherapy tend to identify more closely with the values of their therapists at the conclusion of treatment. Landfield adds that his own data indicate that this may occur 'only in the construct dimensions or social language dimensions of the client' (p. 90).

Landfield himself provides the following summary of what he believes to be the main implications of his research concerning the psychological interaction between therapist and client:

The finding that content congruency (commonality) has particular relevance to premature termination suggests that the communication process is facilitated by some commonality of social interest, values and language. However, the finding that improvement in longer-term therapy clients is associated with some incongruency in client-therapist conceptual structures suggests the importance of complimentary roles in which shared content allows for communication and certain organizational differences maximize the constructiveness of the relationship. These results strongly suggest that a psychotherapist should not only become aware of his client's personal construct system, but he should also try to understand his client's system in relation to his own personal construct system (p. 154) . . . Finally, improvement in therapy was associated with a shift in the present self of the client toward the ideal of the therapist. However, this shift occurred within the dimensional language of the client and not within that of the therapist. One implication of this finding is that to the extent that a therapist may plot his personal ideal in a meaningful way within the framework of his client, his client may improve. (p. 157).

Much of the research which has been discussed in this and previous chapters has been concerned with the structural analysis of the personal construct systems of individuals in assessing different levels of cognitive development, forms of psychopathology, and changes in the context of psychotherapy. On the other hand, it is not only construct systems, but also individual constructs which have varying structural properties. In the next chapter we shall consider the way in which people organize their personal judgements in terms of the contrasting poles of dichotomous personal constructs.

7

Assimilation and Contrast

In discussing the implications of his controversial 'dichotomy corollary', Kelly (1955, 1969) argues that the contrast pole of a personal construct is as necessary as the similarity pole in defining its meaning. He submits that the underlying relation between the alternative poles of each construct is essentially one of binary opposition. That is, every construct involves a single bi-polar distinction, and it is meaningful in so far as it serves as the basis of perceived similarity and contrast among the elements to which it is applied. Within the 'minimal context' of any construct, one of its poles represents a likeness between at least two elements, and its opposite pole represents their contrast to at least one other element (cf. Epting, *et al*, 1971). Kelly assumes that the dichotomous nature of personal constructs is an essential feature of our thinking, and that no construct can be understood fully without encompassing both of its poles. Thus, 'the Dichotomy Corollary assumes a structure of psychological processes which lends itself to binary mathematical analysis' (Kelly, 1955, p. 63).

It is possible that a clearer understanding of the way in which people typically distribute their judgements with respect to the alternative poles of their constructs could facilitate the evaluation of more comprehensive levels of organization within their personal construct systems. For instance, Reid (1975) contends that the majority of statistical procedures currently used for analysing repertory grid data are based on certain *a priori* assumptions concerning the distribution of elements in terms of each construct; and that such assumptions are often made implicitly, and therefore remain unexamined. On the other hand, some investigators have resorted to the practice of imposing a known distribution with invariant properties directly upon the subject's responses; for example, he may be required to rank-order the elements on the basis of the constructs (cf. Bannister and Mair, 1968). Reid (p. 1) points out that,

Psychologically, the use of constrained scales presents many problems (e.g. unknown rank intervals; ambiguous scaler placement on bipolar scales; the meaning and number of ties; and the consequent reduction in the sum of squares; the nonequality in the direction of ranking on bipolar scales, etc.). On the other hand, alternative scaler methods (e.g. 'free' rating scales and alternative statistics (e.g. matching scores, Pearson r, etc.) yield bogus measures of similarity if the assumption of interval equality is not met. The problem for rep grid users in this respect is *construct 'lopsidedness'*, and the confounding of similarity measures this produces. (italics mine)

CONSTRUCT LOPSIDEDNESS

Until just recently, construct lopsidedness (or 'maldistribution'—Bannister and Mair, 1968), that is, the tendency of subjects to allot more elements to one pole of a construct than to its opposite, has been treated primarily as a methodological issue in repertory grid assessment. For example, Bannister (1959, cited in Fransella, 1972) points out that 'meaningless correlations' between constructs can arise whenever the ticks (1s) and blanks (0s) in the grid have a lopsided distribution. Cochran (1976a) has shown that as the distribution of a subject's judgements on each construct becomes increasingly lopsided, the relationships between his constructs are gradually inflated: 'for instance, if the majority of people were viewed as insincere and deliberate, these two attributes would necessarily co-occur in a large portion of cases, and co-occurrence is the present index of relationship' (p. 277).

Some related effects of construct lopsidedness upon grid measures have been demonstrated by Bavelas *et al.* (1976). They randomly generated by computer seventy-six binary grid matrices with nineteen figures and nineteen constructs. These sets of grids were varied systematically with respect to the relative proportion of ticks and blanks (i.e. 1s and 0s): 10/90, 20/80 . . . 90/10. Several indices of mathematical structure were derived separately from each grid matrix, including the explanatory power of the first factor and the number of factors. The results indicated that 'the number of incidents (1s) may be a major determinant of scores for real subjects' (p. 34). They also determined the total number of 1s and 0s in the repertory grid protocols of seventy six normal subjects judging personal acquaintances on elicited constructs and discovered a significant U-shaped relationship between construct lopsidedness and both the average degree of relationship between constructs and the average distance between figures (cf. Benjafield and Adams-Webber, 1975). Bavelas *et al.* suggest on the basis of these findings that 'the number of incidents (1s) for the entire grid should be held to around 50% for maximum independence of scoring' (p. 36).

The trouble with this specific recommendation is the same as that with several earlier 'solutions' to the problem, that is, it relegates that interesting phenomenon of construct asymmetry to the status of a mere methodological issue which needs to be eliminated rather than understood. Perhaps because of Kelly's (1955) own emphasis upon relationships between constructs in repertory grid evaluation, that is, 'the way in which constructs are linked by virtue of their being applied to the same persons' (p. 268), most researchers have tended to regard construct 'maldistribution' as only a source of potential measurement error, and have either attempted to 'control it out' of their experiments or simply ignored it in the hope that its effects would be more or less random. For example, Bannister

(1962b) introduced a 'split-half' format for grid tests in which the subject is required to allocate exactly half of the elements to each pole of a given construct. Thus, it is not surprising that we have learned very little about the phenomenon of construct lopsidedness in more than twenty-five years of repertory grid research.

In Kelly's (1955) original repertory grid test no restrictions were imposed on subjects with respect to the number of elements which they could allot to either pole of a construct. Kelly did assume, however, that the *a priori* probability that a subject will allot a given element to one pole of a construct (p) is, on average, the same as the probability that he will allot it to the opposite pole (q), that is, $p = q = 1/2$ (cf. Bonarius, 1965, pp. 10–13). The implications of this assumption can easily be understood in terms of the elementary principles of information theory (cf. Bieri *et al.* 1966).

Information can be defined as that which removes or reduces uncertainty (Attneave, 1959). It follows that uncertainty is simply potential information (Garner, 1962). Thus, the same basic unit—the binary digit (or bit)—is used in measuring both concepts. For example, given an event E which has m possible outcomes, each with the same probability of occurring, the amount of uncertainty associated with that event in bits—that is, the minimum number of binary digit (1s and 0s) into which that event can be encoded—will be equal to the logarithm (to the base 2) of the number of possible outcomes (i.e. m). Thus, we can calculate the amount of uncertainty (i.e. potential information) associated with that event by means of the following formula: $H = \log m$ (where H represents the amount of uncertainty expressed in bits, and m the number of equiprobable outcomes).

Whenever the m alternative outcomes are, as in this example, equally likely, p—the probability of any one category of outcome—will be equal to the reciprocal of m, the number of equiprobable outcomes, i.e. $p = 1/m$. It follows that $m = 1/p$. Therefore $H = \log 1/p$. Thus, when all outcomes are equally likely, it is unnecessary for us to distinguish between the amount of uncertainty associated with any given outcome and the average uncertainty of all outcomes. If Kelly's assumption that the probability that a subject will allocate a given element to one pole of a construct is equal to the probability that he will allocate it to the opposite pole were correct, then the contribution of each of these two categories of response to average information would be the same, that is, one bit ($H = \log 1/.500 = 1.00$). As Garner (1962) notes, this is the maximum (or *nominal*) value of H for any dichotomous distribution; whereas probabilities as discrepant as 60–40 will show some loss. Bonarius (1965, p. 12) points out, however, that 'if the proportion of check marks (1s) in one of the two rows (constructs being compared) lies between 33% and 67%, the chance values in Kelly's table (Kelly, 1955, p. 286) remain substantially the same'.

As Brody (1971) explains, H provides an index of the variability of a set of nominally scaled data which is analogous to the variance as a measure of variability when all the requirements of an interval scale have been met. For instance, suppose we have a set of nominal data such as a binary grid matrix and ask someone to select one row-column intersect at random and make a blind guess concerning whether it contains a 1 or 0. On average, his accuracy will be a function of the value of H which can be derived from these data. Thus, when a subject sorts a group of elements on the basis of bi-polar constructs, H provides an appropriate measure of intra-subject variability (cf. Attneave, 1959). Benjafield and Adams-Webber (1975), Clyne (1975), and McCloskey (1974) have shown that individual differences in terms of H scores derived from repertory grids are highly reliabile.

There is now considerable evidence that the distribution of elements with respect to the alternative poles of a given construct which we can expect on empirical grounds is not 50/50, as Kelly originally assumed, but rather closer to 62/38. It has been found in each of five independent experiments, summarized in Table 7, that subjects tend to allot figures to the positive poles of supplied constructs approximately 62 per cent of the time, and to their negative opposites 38 per cent of the time (Adams-Webber and Benjafield, 1972, 1973, 1974; Benjafield and Adams-Webber, 1972, 1975, 1976).

In the first of these experiments, a repertory grid test was administered individually to each of thirty Canadian undergraduates (fifteen women, fifteen men). Kelly's (1955, p. 221) original list of 'role titles' was used to elicit the names of nineteen figures from each subject. The name of each figure so nominated was recorded on a separate card. All nineteen cards were then shuffled thoroughly and given to the subject, who was asked to sort them into two piles according to which figures could be described more accurately, as for example, *excitable*, and which figures were better described as *calm*. No limits were imposed with respect to the number of figures which could be placed in either pile. The cards were then reshuffled and sorted again into two piles on the basis of a second construct, for example, *energetic-lethargic*. This entire procedure was repeated until the subject had sorted the same nineteen figures successively on the basis of each of twelve provided constructs (listed on page 159 below).

For each one of these sorting sequences, the experimenter simply recorded how many figures had been allotted to the positive pole of the construct. The grand mean across all subjects, expressed as the proportion of positive judgements to total judgements, was 0.62 (SD = 0.07).

In the second experiment, eighteen figures were used. Twelve of these figures were selected from the original nineteen so as to include approximately six figures

Table 7. Proportion of positive judgements from five independent experiments reported by Benjafield and Adams-Webber (1976).

Exprt.	N	# Fig.	# Con.	% Pos.	% Neg.	SD
1.	30	19	12	62	38	.07
2a.	30	12	12	62	38	.07
2b.	30	6	12	62	38	.07
3.	30	12	12	61	39	.08
4.	20	12	12	63	37	.08
5.	62	12	12	63	37	.06

with predominantly positive valences, for example, 'a person you have met recently whom you would like to get to know better', and six figures with negative valences, for example, 'the person with whom you feel least comfortable'. An additional six figures were used specifically to represent the contrasting poles of the three major *Semantic Differential* components—'the warmest person you know' and the 'coldest' (evaluation); the 'most active' and 'most passive' (activity); and the 'strongest' and 'weakest' (potency). Again fifteen female and fifteen male Canadian university students were employed as subjects. They categorized all the persons whom they had nominated on the basis of the same twelve constructs supplied to subjects in the first experiment. The mean proportion of positive judgements for the first twelve figures was once more 0.62 (SD = 0.07). It was also 0.62 (SD = 0.07) for the six new figures.

A sample of thirty Canadian high-school pupils (fifteen boys, fifteen girls) was recruited for the third experiment in this series. They each completed a repertory grid test using the same twelve constructs and only the first twelve figures from the second experiment. The mean proportion of figures which they allotted to the positive poles of constructs was 0.61 (SD = 0.08). In the fourth experiment, exactly the same grid test was administered individually to twenty Canadian undergraduates (ten women, ten men). This time, the mean proportion of positive judgements was 0.63 (SD = 0.08). Finally, the same test was administered during regular class-time to sixty-two students enrolled in an Introductory Psychology course at a Canadian university. These students allotted a mean proportion of 0.63 (SD = 0.06) of their judgements to the positive poles of constructs.

Each of these five experiments was carried out by a different research assistant who did not know the results of any other experiment. The same list of twelve constructs was supplied to subjects in all of these experiments: (1) *generous-stingy*, (2) *pleasant-unpleasant*, (3) *true-false*, (4) *fair-unfair*, (5) *active-passive*, (6) *energetic-lethargic*, (7) *sharp-dull*, (8) *excitable-calm*, (9) *strong-weak*, (10) *bold-timid*, (11) *hard-soft*, (12) *rugged-delicate*. These are the same constructs as those employed by Warr and Coffman (1970; discussed in Chapter 2). Each of the three major *Semantic Differential* components of connotative meaning was represented by four constructs in this list: evaluation (1–4), activity (5–8), and potency (9–12). The positive and negative poles of the constructs were identified in terms of the direction of their loadings on these three components.

In a sixth experiment, only three constructs were provided to subjects: *kind-cruel, bold-timid,* and *strong-weak*. They were selected from the list compiled by Kirby and Gardner (1972) to represent evaluation, activity, and potency respectively. Ten male and ten female Canadian undergraduates categorized the first twelve figures from the second experiment on the basis of each of these constructs. The mean proportion of figures which they allotted to the positive poles was 0.61 (SD = 0.16). Thus when only three constructs were employed, the minimum number required to represent the three major *Semantic Differential* components, the mean proportion of positive responses was still quite close to 0.62, which is the grand mean for all 192 subjects. Each of the six sample means lies within 0.01 of this value. No significant differences between female and male subjects were found in any of these experiments.

A study by McCloskey (1974) showed that this proportion is also quite stable over time. He twice administered the same repertory grid test as that used in experiments 3–5 to twenty Canadian high-school pupils—ten boys and ten girls—all of whom had applied successfully for admission to the same university. When he first tested them in August, before they had entered the university, the average proportion of figures which they allotted to the positive poles of constructs was 0.61 (SD = 0.08). McCloskey retested them approximately three months later, after about a month of university life. On the second occasion, the average proportion of figures allotted to the positive poles was still 0.61 (SD = 0.10).

THE GOLDEN SECTION HYPOTHESIS

Pythagoras, the presocratic philosopher and geometer, developed a complex system of numbers and geometrical shapes to which he and his followers attributed great moral significance (Wheelwright, 1966). A central concept in this system was the 'golden section' of a line segment, which can be constructed by dividing a line AB by a point C in such a way that the ratio AC:CB = CB:AB (see Figure 5).

If we assume that the entire line segment AB is of unit length, and let CB = ϕ, then AC = $1 - \phi$. Therefore, $(1 - \phi)/\phi = \phi/1$, or $\phi^2 + \phi - 1 = 0$. If we disregard the negative root (which is extraneous since this ratio is always positive) and solve for ϕ, we find that $\phi = (\sqrt{5} - 1)/2 = 0.61803$. Berlyne (1971) notes that this proportion has had an ubiquitous influence on Western culture, and at least since Fechner (1876), psychologists have been interested in its aesthetic properties. For instance, it has been demonstrated that the rectangle which many people find most pleasing is the 'golden rectangle', which is a rectangle whose sides are in the ratio $1:\phi$ (e.g. Benjafield, 1976). Berlyne also suggests that a possible explanation of the extraordinary appeal of this proportion may lie in its relationship to the concept of *average information* and Frank's (1959, 1964) index of 'strikingness'.

Whenever the alternative categories of response available to subjects have, as in the series of experiments summarized above, different relative frequencies of occurrence, we must distinguish between the amount of uncertainty associated with any one response category and average uncertainty (cf. Garner, 1962). In this situation, we can determine the amount of uncertainty associated with each response category separately, and then obtain a weighted average of these two values. More precisely, the Shannon–Wiener measure of average information is based on the sum of the separate estimates of uncertainty, each multiplied by its

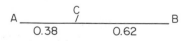

Figure 5. The golden section of a line segment

associated probability as a weighting factor, that is, $H = \sum p \log 1/p$ (Attneave, 1959, p. 8).

Frank (1959, 1964), summarized by Berlyne (1971), proposes that the 'strikingness' of an event depends on two of its properties: (1) its informational content, defined as $\log 1/p$, and (2) its relative frequency of occurrence, defined as p. His specific measure of strikingness is obtained by multiplying these two values together, that is, $p \log 1/p$. It follows that the strikingness of a given event, as operationally defined by Frank, is equivalent to its contribution to average information (H) in the Shannon–Wiener formula. Berlyne points out further that $p \log 1/p$ as a function of p reaches its maximum value when $p = 1/e$, which works out to approximately 0.368 (cf. Attneave, 1959, p. 117). This value is quite close to the minor element in the golden section ratio, that is $1 - \phi = 0.382$. Benjafield and Adams-Webber (1976, p. 14) suggest, in the light of this relationship, that by allotting figures to the negative poles of constructs approximately 38 per cent of the time, we render our negative judgements, taken as a whole, maximally striking as 'figure' against a general background of positive judgements.

This 'golden section hypothesis' can be related to recent work in the psychology of language. Zajonc (1968) found that there is a general tendency to use positive words more frequently than their negative counterparts. Jaspars, Feldbreigger, and Bongaerts (1968) suggest that this 'positivity bias' can be explained in terms of their hypothesis that the concept of *positivity* is a primary cognitive structure, whereas the concept of *negativity* consists of exactly the same structure plus some transformational rule (cf. Clark, 1969; Hamilton and Deese, 1971). As Peeters (1971) points out, this hypothesis implies that (a) positivity represents a simpler concept than negativity, and (b) the former underlies the latter. He pursues this line of inference to the notion that a relatively simple concept of positivity underlies a more differentiated concept of negativity in a figure-ground relationship with the latter serving as the figure and the former as the ground.

Kanouse and Hanson (1972) propose a similar hypothesis to explain why negative impressions are, in general, more salient than positive ones (cf. Warr, 1974). They suggest that positive information, because it is so common, acts as the perceptual ground against which negative information stands out as figure. Benjafield and Adams-Webber's (1976) golden section hypothesis lends precise quantitative form to this general 'figure-ground' explanation by specifying that subjects will allot approximately that proportion of elements to the negative poles of constructs which can be expected to make their negative judgements, considered as a whole, stand out as maximally 'striking' (salient), that is, 37–38 per cent.

The results of an experiment by Eiser and Mower White (1973) provide further support for the golden section hypothesis. Sixty British school children judged twenty nonsense words (e.g. *JOHZAN*) as if they were the names of real people on the basis of twenty bi-polar constructs. These 'names' were constructed by combining pairs of CVCs from Noble's (1961) list with m' scores between 1.70

and 1.91. Each of the constructs consisted of a single trait adjective (positive response category) and the same adjective preceded by *not* (negative response category). Every child judged ten 'names' on constructs containing positive poles which were evaluatively positive (E+) and negative poles which were evaluatively negative (E−), for example, *happy-not happy*. The other ten 'names' were judged on constructs containing positive poles which were E− and negative poles which were E+, for example, *rude-not rude*. Each 'name' was judged on only one construct, and each construct was applied to only one 'name' by any one child, whereas in repertory grid procedure each figure is judged on the basis of every construct.

This experiment was designed in part to test Boucher and Osgood's (1969) 'Pollyanna hypothesis', which asserts that 'There is a universal human tendency to use evaluatively positive words more frequently, diversely and facilely than evaluatively negative words'. This hypothesis clearly predicts that subjects will allot more figures to the E+ poles of constructs than to their E− poles. Contrary to this expectation, Eiser and Mower White report that there was a marginal tendency for the children to make fewer E+ then E− responses. On the other hand, our own reanalysis of their data revealed that the children allotted exactly 38 per cent of the 'names' to the negative poles of constructs irrespective of whether they were E+ or E−. Although this is, at best, a *post hoc* explanation of Eiser and Mower White's results, the observed proportion of negative responses is exactly what we should expect on the basis of the golden section hypothesis.

Adams-Webber (in press) replicated this experiment with sixty Canadian undergraduates (thirty women, thirty men) with comparable results. The overall proportion of negative responses was observed to be 37 per cent. There was no significant difference between male and female subjects. Table 8 provides a detailed comparison of the results of both experiments. The difference between the total number of positive and negative responses was highly significant in the second study ($z = 7.90$; $p < .001$), as it had been in the first ($z = 5.59$; $p < .001$). In neither experiment did the observed proportion of negative responses differ significantly from the value of p defined by max ($p \log 1/p$), which is $1/e$ (approximately 0.368). The distribution of E+ and E− responses was approximately 53/47 in both sets of data. There were more E+ responses than E− ones in the second study ($z = 1.76$; n.s.); whereas there had been more E− than E+ responses in the first one ($z = 1.78$; n.s.). Thus, the overall proportion of E+ responses did not differ significantly from 50 per cent in either set of data. Finally, there were no significant differences among the 'names' in terms of the number of times which they had been allotted to the negative poles of constructs in either the first experiment ($Q = 13.79$; 19 df; n.s.), or the second one ($Q = 13.73$; 19 df; n.s.).

These data furnish strong support for the golden section hypothesis. The fact that comparable results have been obtained with both Kelly's repertory grid procedure and Eiser and Mower White's questionnaire format, in which each figure is judged on one construct only and each construct is applied to one figure only, seems to rule out the possibility that earlier findings could have been merely

Table 8.   Comparisons between the results of Adams-Webber
(in press) and those of Eiser & Mower White (1973).

	Adams-Webber		Eiser and Mower White	
	%	X̄	%	X̄
Response category				
PE +	33	6.65	30	5.93
PE −	30	6.02	32	6.47
NE +	20	3.93	18	3.53
NE −	17	3.40	20	4.07
Total P	63	12.67	62	12.40
Total N	37	7.33	38	7.60
Total E +	53	10.58	47	9.46
Total E −	47	9.42	53	10.54

(Reproduced by permission of the British Psychological Society from Adams-Webber, J., 'A further test of the golden section hypothesis', *British Journal of Psychology* (1978), **69**, published by Cambridge University Press.)

artefacts of repertory grid technique. It is also important that the golden section hypothesis holds when constructs have been completely counterbalanced in terms of connotative meaning, thereby isolating it from the Pollyanna hypothesis. Since only imaginary figures were used in both experiments, and no significant differences were found among these figures with respect to the number of times which subjects allocated them to the negative poles of constructs, it can be argued that the golden section hypothesis applies to the way in which subjects use bi-polar dimensions in general, and not just to how they construe their own personal acquaintances. Finally, the generality of the golden section hypothesis is enhanced by the fact that comparable results have now been obtained using different measurement procedures and different sets of constructs with both schoolchildren and university students in each of two countries, Canada and England.

Benjafield and Adams-Webber (1976) point out that their golden section hypothesis goes considerably beyond Boucher and Osgood's (1969) Pollyanna hypothesis. The latter implies that 'there is a universal human tendency to communicate about the positive aspects of life' (Osgood and Richards, 1973, p. 410). This suggests, as Deese (1973) notes, that 'we are all natural optimists'. Thus, the Pollyanna hypothesis generally predicts that subjects will apply the positive poles of constructs to people more frequently than the negative poles (Warr, 1971); whereas the golden section hypothesis predicts, more specifically, that they will tend to allocate approximately 38 per cent of their personal judgements to the negative poles. Furthermore, Osgood and Richards submit that the *positive-negative* distinction may be more basic than any one of the three *Semantic Differential* components (cf. Benjafield and Green, 1978). They (Osgood and Richards, 1973, p. 381) specifically point out that '*strong* and *active*, as well as *good*, are somehow psychologically positive as compared to their opposites'. This assumption is consistent with Adams-Webber's (in press) finding that the golden section hypothesis holds when constructs have been counterbalanced in terms of connotative meaning.

Further support for the golden section hypothesis is provided by Osgood and Richard's own data (cf. Benjafield and Adams-Webber, 1976). Children were asked to complete a series of sentences of the form 'X is (adjective)———(adjective)': for example, 'X is dangerous———empty'. The task was to decide whether *and* or *but* should be used to fill the blank. Since *and* is positive, and *but* is negative (Osgood and Richards, 1973, p. 377), the golden section hypothesis predicts that *and* should be used in approximately 62 per cent of the sentences, and *but* in about 38 per cent of them. Osgood and Richards report that *and* was used in 62.5 per cent of the sentences, and *but* in 37.5 per cent of them.

The finding that subjects tend to apply the negative poles of constructs to people approximately 38 per cent of the time also seems consistent with Adams-Webber and Benjafield's (1973, p. 235) hypothesis that the positive poles of constructs are used in a rather global way to refer to commonplace or 'normal' characteristics which one expects most of one's acquaintances to exhibit to some extent, and the negative poles to mark deviations from these 'norms', which occur relatively infrequently. Thus, our negative judgements should convey more specific information about persons than our positive judgements, because the former refer to events which are more 'atypical' than those designated by the latter. As Hamilton and Gifford (1976, p. 394) put it, 'since for most varieties of behaviour the norm is positive in value, undesirable (non-normative) behavior is statistically less frequent than desirable behavior and can be considered distinctive'. A general strategy of encoding information which serves to render our negative judgements more 'striking' (salient) than our positive ones should be quite useful in adapting to an environment in which it is the 'deviant' event which is more likely to pose a specific threat than the typical state of affairs. Indeed, there is considerable evidence that the behaviour which we label with negative descriptors is more salient than that which we label with positive descriptors (Kanouse and Hanson, 1972; Warr, 1974).

Benjafield and Green (1978) conducted a further repertory grid experiment in which forty British undergraduates (twenty women and twenty men) categorized twelve figures, six at a time, on the same twelve constructs seven times in succession. Exactly half of the figures sorted across all seven trials were positive in valence (e.g. 'the most ethical person you know') and the other half were negative in valence (e.g. 'the least ethical person you know'); however, on any given trial anywhere from one to six of the figures could have been positive for a particular subject. As expected, they found that the number of positive judgements varied as a function of the number of positive figures categorized. On the other hand, the mean proportion of positive judgements across all seven trials was 0.62 (SD = 0.11). Moreover, on the fourth trial, when every subject sorted three positive and three negative figures, the grand mean was also 0.62 (SD = 0.08). The lowest overall mean for any given trial was 0.60 (SD = 0.13); and the highest was 0.63 (SD = 0.15).

They also observed that approximately 63 per cent of all figures had a majority of positive adjectives assigned to them. They offer the following explanation of this finding:

The golden section hypothesis holds that 'whenever people differentiate one thing into two, they tend to do so in a way that approximates the golden section'. Benjafield and Adams-Webber (1976) presented data supporting this hypothesis based on only the adjectives people used to describe their acquaintances. However, the golden section hypothesis should also apply to the acquaintances described, as well as to the adjectives used to describe them. That is, people should tend to divide their acquaintances into a class of 'typical' acquaintances and a class of 'atypical' acquaintances. A 'typical' acquaintance is here defined as an acquaintance to whom a person assigns a majority of positive adjectives. The reason for so defining them is as follows: since most things are described positively most of the time (Benjafield and Adams-Webber, 1975; Osgood and Richards, 1973), most acquaintances will be assigned a majority of positive adjectives. All acquaintances not assigned a majority of positive adjectives, including those who receive equal numbers of positive and negative adjectives, are here described as *atypical*. One hypothesis to be tested in the present study is that 61.8% of a person's acquaintances will be typical acquaintances.

It is important to bear in mind in relation to this hypothesis that subjects also tend to allot imaginary figures as well as personal acquaintances to the positive poles of constructs approximately 62 per cent of the time; and when imaginary figures are used no significant differences among figures are found in terms of the number of times that they are allotted to the positive poles of constructs (Adams-Webber, in press; Eiser and Mower White, 1973). This indicates that the golden section hypothesis applies generally to the way in which subjects employ bi-polar dimensions and not only to how they characterize their personal acquaintances. It would also be interesting to see whether 62 per cent of one's acquaintances are allocated to the positive poles of constructs more than 50 per cent of the time when each figure is judged on the basis of only one construct, or whether this effect is specific to the repertory grid.

All the evidence in support of the golden section hypothesis that we have considered so far derives from experiments in which the same 'standard' list of constructs was supplied to all subjects alike rather than a different set of personal constructs being elicited from each subject individually, as in Kelly's (1955) original repertory grid test. We saw in Chapter 2 that subjects tend to differentiate more among persons when they characterize them on the basis of elicited constructs than when constructs are provided to them. Unfortunately, it would be difficult, if not impossible, to identify reliably the 'positive' poles of many of the personal constructs elicited directly from subjects themselves (e.g. *dishonest-cruel*). Fransella and Bannister (1977, p. 105) furnish an excellent illustration of this problem:

We may assume that *charitable* to you means the same as *charitable* to me. But for you the opposite pole might be *intolerant* and for me *hold strong opinions*. For you to be *charitable* is good and for me undesirable.

Thus, it is not at all clear how the golden section hypothesis applies to judgements involving elicited constructs. One possibility is to approach this problem indirectly *via* the 'self-concept'.

THE STRUCTURE OF THE SELF-CONCEPT

Kelly (1955, p. 131) proposes that

. . . the *self* is, when considered in the appropriate context, a proper concept or construct. It refers to a group of events which are alike in a certain way and, in that same way, necessarily different from other events. The way in which the events are alike is the self. That also makes the self an individual, differentiated from other individuals. The self, having been thus conceptualized, can now be used as a thing, a datum, or an item in the context of a superordinate construct. The self can become one of the three or more things—or persons—at least two of which are alike and are different from at least one of the others . . . It is, of course, the comparison *he* sees or construes which affects his behavior. Thus, much of his social life is controlled by the comparisons he has come to see between himself and others.

We can determine the extent to which subjects differentiate between themselves and others just as readily in terms of elicited constructs as in terms of supplied ones. That is, whenever the *self* is included in the list of figures categorized in terms of a given construct, each of the subject's judgements can be classified in terms of the dichotomy *like-self/unlike-self*. We noted in Chapter 2 that the overall proportion of other figures assigned to the same category as the *self* across a set of bi-polar constructs is one of the most stable of repertory grid indices. Jones (1954) originally reported a two-week, test-retest reliability of 0.86 for a sample of American undergraduates. More recently, Sperlinger (1976), employing a sample of normal adults in the UK, found an eight-month, test-retest reliability of 0.95. It has also been found that more than half of the variance in several other 'structural' indices derived from repertory grids—including the average correlation between constructs, the number of significant correlations between constructs, the average distance between figures, and the explanatory power of the first factor—can be accounted for in terms of their relationship with this one variable (Adams-Webber, 1969, 1970b).

Lemon and Warren (1974, p. 123) hypothesize that a person's judgements of others 'automatically involve a kind of self-comparison process . . . (in which) the self-construct will act as an anchoring point to produce the effects of assimilation and contrast familiar in psychophysics and from Hovland and Sherif (1952)'. If so, we might expect the distribution of subjects' *like-self/unlike-self* judgements also to approximate the golden section. There is some evidence that this is the case.

Adams-Webber and Benjafield (1974) administered a repertory grid test to thirty Canadian high-school pupils (fifteen boys and fifteen girls) in which they categorized themselves and eleven associates on each of twelve supplied constructs. The proportion of *like-self* judgements, averaged across all subjects, was 0.61 (SD = 0.06). Adams-Webber (1976) administered the same test to sixty Canadian undergraduates (thirty women and thirty men), and found that the average proportion of *like-self* judgements was 0.62 (SD = .08). No significant differences between male and female subjects were found in either experiment. Clyne (1975) also administered this test to seventy-five women attending another Canadian university. She reports that 0.61 (SD = 0.07) of all their judgements fell into the *like-self* category.

Comparable results have been obtained when constructs were elicited from subjects themselves. Adams-Webber and Benjafield (1976) administered a repertory grid test to thirty Canadian undergraduates (fifteen women and fifteen men) in which they categorized themselves and six personal acquaintances on the basis of the same twelve constructs as those supplied to subjects in the three experiments summarized above and an additional twelve constructs elicited from each subject individually. The average proportion of *like-self* judgements across all twenty-four constructs was found to be 0.63 (SD = 0.14). Also, Benjafield *et al.* (1976) administered a repertory grid test to twelve Canadian adults (six men and six women) participating in a group therapist training project. These subjects categorized themselves and twenty-one acquaintances, including the other members of the group, on the same set of twelve constructs supplied to subjects in all the previous experiments, three additional supplied constructs, and seven constructs individually elicited from themselves. The overall proportion of *like-self* judgements across all twenty-two constructs was 0.64 (SD = 0.12)

The reanalysis of the data from three earlier repertory grid experiments yielded similar findings. Morse (1965) administered a grid test to 139 American undergraduates in which they categorized themselves, their parents and two siblings on a set of twenty-two constructs elicited from themselves (subjects). The mean proportion of like-self judgements was 0.62 (SD = 0.15). The same grid test was administered by Adams-Webber (1968) to thirty American undergraduates (fifteen women and fifteen men) and the average proportion of *like-self* judgements was observed to be 0.61 (SD = 0.09). Finally, when Adams-Webber *et al.* (1972) administered this test to twenty-four Canadian undergraduates (twelve men and twelve women), the mean proportion of judgements falling into the *like-self* category was 0.62 (SD = 0.10). No significant sex differences were found in any of the five experiments involving elicited constructs.

The evidence indicates that the golden section does in some way underlie the structure of our 'self-concepts'. When the data are viewed in the light of Berlyne's (1971) suggestion that the golden section ratio allows the minor element to occupy that proportion of the whole which makes it maximally striking, it seems possible that people tend to organize their impressions of their social environment in such a way that perceived differences between themselves and others will stand out maximally as 'figure' against a general background of similarities. Bannister and Agnew (1977) contend that, within the framework of personal construct theory, 'the ways in which we elaborate the construing of the self must be essentially those ways in which we elaborate our construing of others for we have not a concept of self but a bipolar construct of *self-not self*'. This implies that we each have a clear and distinct notion of our own identity in relation to the identities of others only to the extent to which we can discern a specific pattern of similarities and differences between ourselves and others. The evidence considered above suggests that it is the differences which define the contours of the *self* as figure against a diffuse background of similarities.

It was predicted on the basis of this hypothesis that when people are asked to form impressions of someone whom they have just met for the first time, they will tend to assimilate information about this new figure in such a way that the overall proportion of perceived differences between the *self* and other will be approximately 37/38 per cent (Adams-Webber, 1977b). A reanalysis of data from an experiment by Morse (1965) yielded support for this prediction. He asked thirty-six American university students (eighteen women and eighteen men) to categorize successively three new acquaintances whom they had not met previously on the basis of fifteen elicited constructs following a brief interaction with each of them in turn. The subjects also categorized themselves (several weeks earlier) in terms of the same constructs. The proportion of *unlike-self* judgements, averaged over the three 'targets', was 0.362 (SD = 0.15).

Morse's experiment was replicated with minor modifications by Adams-Webber (1977b) with another sample of American university students (fifteen women and fifteen men). It was found that when these subjects were asked to categorize a single new acquaintance following a brief conversation with him on a set of twenty-two personal constructs previously elicited from themselves, the mean proportion of *unlike-self* judgements was 0.364 (SD = 0.17). The subjects were then given some additional information about the 'target' (specifically, how he had characterized himself in terms of his own personal constructs), and allowed to revise as many of their original impressions as they wished in the light of these new data. All but five subjects made some changes in their initial judgements, the average number of revisions being 1.9. Nonetheless, the average proportion of *unlike-self* judgements remained 0.364 (SD = 0.17) after all changes had been recorded. There was no significant difference between male and female subjects. The observed value (0.364) is quite close to that derived from Morse's data (0.362), and both results lie within .01 of the value of p defined by max ($p \log 1/p$), which is $1/e$, or approximately 0.368. These two sets of data are clearly consistent with the hypothesis that people assimilate new figures into their personal construct systems in such a way that perceived differences between those figures and the *self* stand out as maximally salient.

On the other hand, an alternative approach to the interpretation of 'construct maldistribution' recently developed by Cochran (1976a, b) suggests that people tend, on average, to be relatively insensitive to differences between themselves and others in construing behaviour. Cochran (1976a, p. 281) points out that whenever a subject sorts a given set of figures dichotomously on the basis of any bi-polar dimension, for example, *agreeable-argumentative*, his judgements can be 'transformed into a symmetric matrix with the stimulus persons along the top and down the sides' such as that represented in Figure 6.

Cochran (p. 281) explains that the entries in this matrix all represent implied

Elements	1	2	3	4	5	6	7	8	9	10
1	X	S	S	S	S	D	D	D	D	D
2		X	S	S	S	D	D	D	D	D
3			X	S	S	D	D	D	D	D
4				X	S	D	D	D	D	D
5					X	D	D	D	D	D
6						X	S	S	S	S
7							X	S	S	S
8								X	S	S
9									X	S
10										X

Note. Element Comparisons: S = Similarity Judgement
D = Difference Judgement

Figure 6. Similarity and difference matrix. (Figure by Larry Cochran, 1974)

'similarities' and 'differences' arising from all possible paired comparisons between figures:

Entries within the matrix are either S (for similarity judgment) or D (for difference judgment). Enter an S if a pair of stimulus persons are within the same group (i.e. both are considered agreeable) or a D if a pair of stimulus persons are in contrasting groups (i.e. one agreeable and one argumentative) . . . if a matrix were developed for each construct, then maldistribution may be found by simply counting the number of S entries which exceed that which would be obtained if all bipolar allocations were equal.

Suppose, for example, that a particular subject sorts ten figures in terms of a bipolar dimension as follows:

$$+ + - + - - + - + -$$

This specific sequence of positive and negative judgements, or any other in which there are exactly five positive and five negative outcomes, will yield the distribution of Ss and Ds represented in Figure 6. That is, this matrix summarizes the results of all possible comparisons between figures, of which there are forty-five, including twenty-five potential judgements of difference and twenty potential judgements of similarity. Whenever the number of positive judgements is equal to the number of negative ones, as in this example, the number of implied differences (Ds) is maximized. This is consistent with the fact, noted earlier, that H as an index of overall intra-subject variability in a grid matrix reaches its maximum value (i.e. one bit) when exactly 50 per cent of the figures are assigned to the positive poles of constructs. Cochran (1976a) shows that, as construct lopsidedness increases (in favour of either pole), the number of implied differences (Ds) is thereby decreased while the number of implied similarities (Ss) is correspondingly increased. Thus, he interprets construct lopsidedness as a 'measure of a person's similarity/difference orientation toward the stimulus persons' (p. 280).

Cochran's model implies specifically that subjects with relatively low lopsidedness scores on the repertory grid are potentially aware of more differences between people, including themselves, than are those subjects with relatively high lopsidedness scores. Cochran (1976b) characterizes the latter as generally 'oriented toward similarities' (p. 38). He further suggests that such a general orientation towards similarities could reflect, among other possibilities, an 'impoverished set of criteria for applying constructs to people' (p. 38). In the light of this hypothesis, the finding that subjects typically allocate the majority (62/63 per cent) of their acquaintances to the same poles of their constructs as they use to characterize themselves implies that they tend to overlook differences between themselves and others in interpreting their interpersonal experience. This would also support Jones' (1954, p. 49) hypothesis that 'there is a general tendency for a person to identify with others in the sense of seeing himself more like than different from most Rep Test Figures'. The finding that the greater the extent to which an individual categorizes himself as similar to others on his own constructs, the easier it is for others to anticipate his self-characterizations (Adams-Webber, 1973), also raises the possibility that, on the whole, we receive more 'validation' from others for noticing similarities between them and ourselves than for noticing differences.

On the other hand, subjects have been shown to encode information about new acquaintances in such a way that differences between the *self* and others occupy that proportion of total impressions which should render them maximally 'striking' (about 37 per cent), at least according to Frank's (1959, 1964) operational definition of this concept (Adams-Webber, 1977b; Morse, 1965). This suggests that, in a more fundamental sense, we emphasize differences between ourselves and others in forming impressions of people. Although this could be simply an illustration of Bartlett's (1958, p. 94) principle that 'to untutored observation differences make far more immediate impression than likeness', other studies indicate that subjects also tend to allot their close personal associates, such as parents and siblings, to the same categories as the *self* between 62 and 63 per cent of the time in terms of personal constructs (Adams-Webber, 1968; Adams-Webber *et al.*, 1972; Morse, 1965). Thus, we seem to emphasize differences between ourselves and those whom we have known the longest as well as those whom we have just met for the first time.

It is, of course, possible that the tendency to allocate others to the same categories as the *self* approximately 62 per cent of the time is merely a 'side-effect' of a more general propensity to distribute positive and negative judgements in the golden section ratio. Perhaps we assimilate our impressions of both the *self* and others to the same general stereotype of 'normality', defined primarily in terms of the positive poles of constructs. That is, the *self* and most of one's associates might be seen as sharing to some extent the same undifferentiated 'halo' of positive traits. For example, the majority of one's acquaintances may be construed as more or less *kind*—no doubt, some will be perceived as kinder than others—but relatively few people will be regarded as actually *cruel*. Against such a global background of positive 'normality', those behaviours which we designate with the negative poles of our constructs (about 38 per cent) could stand out as figure (cf. Kanouse and Hanson, 1972).

ANXIETY

Another hypothesis concerning construct lopsidedness has been developed by Radley (1974). We have seen that H provides a measure of variability in repertory grid data. Erickson and Wechsler (1955) found that experimentally induced anxiety led to reduced values of H in a laboratory discrimination task. This is consistent with the general notion that individual response variability declines with increasing anxiety (cf. Maher, 1966). There is also evidence that construct lopsidedness in the grid, upon which H depends, correlates with anxiety. Fransella and Bannister (1977, p. 84) report that 'anxious people (i.e. high scores on the Taylor Manifest Anxiety Scale) tended to put most of their elements into one pole of each construct and leave the other one fairly empty ($p < .05$)'. Radley argues in the light of this finding that lopsided construing provides a strategy for preserving the linkages between an individual's constructs in the face of contradictory or ambiguous feedback from the environment. That is, by forcing the majority of figures to 'fit' the same pole of every construct, he is able artificially to maintain the level of relationship between his constructs even when confronted with events which are inconsistent with those relationships. Since, from the standpoint of personal construct theory, anxiety is defined in terms of impending loss of conceptual structure (Kelly, 1955), lopsided construing may provide a defense against it in so far as it preserves structural relations, that is, prevents their 'loosening' (Bannister, 1960).

Davidson (1977) examined the implications of the hypothesized correlation between lopsided construing and anxiety in terms of Leary's (1957) suggestion that rigidly defended persons, lacking interpersonal resilience, should show less differentiation with respect to interpersonal themes which they attribute to the protagonist and other figures in TAT stories. Davidson predicted specifically that 'if then maldistribution (lopsidedness) scores on the Kelly repertory grid reflect a defense against anxiety (Radley, 1974) and if a positive correlation between the interpersonal themes attributed to the TATH (TAT Hero) and the TATO (TAT Others) also reflects anxiety (Leary, 1957), these two measures ought to correlate positively' (p. 2). As predicted, a significant correlation ($r = 0.52$; 21 df; $p < .01$) was found between these two indices. Also, Radley's hypothesis that 'inconsistency' in one's interpersonal experience relates to lopsided categorization of people receives support from the finding that lopsidedness in repertory grids correlates negatively with stability over time in subjects' characterizations of particular acquaintances (Benjafield and Adams-Webber, 1975; Clyne, 1975; Cochran, 1976b).

An experiment specifically designed 'to test the effect of lopsided categorization in preserving construct relatedness' was carried out by Cochran (1976a, p. 276). Thirty-four Canadian undergraduates 'were required to form impressions of inconsistent stimulus persons in order to disrupt conceptualization' (p. 275). It was found that those subjects who 'emphasized similarities' among these inconsistent figures in a repertory grid test (i.e. categorized them lopsidedly) maintained or increased the degree of interrelationship between constructs to a significantly greater extent than did those subjects who emphasized differences. Cochran (1976a, p. 283) concludes that this finding 'provides clear empirical support for the (i.e. Radley's) hypothesis that lopsided categorization functions to preserve conceptual relatedness in the face of inconsistent and invalidating stimulus combinations'.

A problem in interpreting the results of this experiment from the point of view of personal construct theory is that 'an inconsistent stimulus person' was operationally defined in normative terms, that is, in terms of supplied constructs. Delia *et al.* (1970; cited in Chapter 2) have shown that 'inconsistent' combinations of normative constructs have significantly fewer implications within an individual's personal construct system than inconsistent combinations of constructs elicited directly from himself. Cochran simply assumed that, in general, 'inconsistent attributes (e.g. *warmth* and *selfishness*) are by definition incompatible with construct organization and cannot be readily integrated within one's established frame of reference' (p. 277). It is not clear, however, why the particular 'inconsistent stimulus persons' used in this experiment should be especially conceptually disruptive for any particular individual. For instance, Fransella and Bannister (1977, p. 97) point out that

Mair (1966) found that the relationship between constructs averaged from subjects' grids and the relationships that would have been predicted between the verbal labels used in terms of dictionary meaning were closely associated, that is, synonyms were highly positively related, antonyms were highly negatively related and so forth. Equally of note is the fact that the relationships for an individual between their constructs were not *precisely* those which a dictionary would have predicted. This is an expected finding in that both common sense and construct theory (the commonality corollary) would predict that a substantial part of the relationship between our constructs reflects cultural teaching, but also that each of us develops idiosyncratic meanings (the individuality corollary) for words derived from our unique personal experience.

Bannister and Mair (1968, p. 211) define an 'inconsistent figure' as one whose profile in terms of a specific set of related constructs used by a particular subject is not consistent with the pattern of linkages between those constructs *within that subject's own personal construct system*. They explicitly formulate the hypothesis that the attempt to understand such 'inconsistent figures' may initiate the elaboration of new constructs and construct relations. Also, Adams-Webber (1970a, p. 39) argues that new structure evolves within a personal construct system to accommodate events which are ambiguous within the context of existing structure. An excellent illustration of this process is provided by Arthur Koestler's (1954) description of his reaction to his first chaotic impressions of Russia in 1932:

Only slowly does the newcomer learn to think in contradictions; to distinguish underneath a chaotic surface, the shape of things to come ... I learnt to classify automatically everything that shocked me as the 'heritage of the past' and everything that I liked as 'seeds of the future'. By setting up this automatic sorting machine in his mind, it was still possible in 1932 for a European to live in Russia and yet remain a communist. (p. 53)

In Kellian terms, when Koestler, who by his own account of these events arrived in Russia an enthusiastic member of the Party expecting to enter the '21st Century', had many of his specific anticipations invalidated, he was able to avoid loss of conceptual structure ('anxiety') by employing a new superordinate construct—*heritage of the past-seeds of the future*—to reorganize his expectations and minimize inconsistencies among them. On the other hand, another person might have adopted the alternative strategy proposed by Radley (1974), that is, used lopsided categorization of events to maintain the current level of relatedness among his constructs without making any changes in the structure or content of his system.

Benjafield and Adams-Webber (1975) suggest that subjects with relatively low lopsidedness scores in the repertory grid show more consistency over time in their characterizations of themselves and their associates (cf. Clyne, 1975; Cochran, 1976b) because they are able to achieve more stable interpersonal judgements by simultaneously integrating multiple perspectives on the same events. This mode of organizing information is typical of developmentally mature cognitive structures (Adams-Webber, 1970a; Feffer, 1970). Further support for this hypothesis comes from a recent study by Barratt (1977a). He reports that construct lopsidedness significantly decreases between ages 8 and 12, and correlates negatively with teachers' ratings of children's general level of social maturity. Applebee (1976) also found that construct lopsidedness decreases significantly as children grow older. He interprets this finding as evidence that there is a somewhat more equal elaboration of both poles of constructs by older children. In this same general vein, Widom's (1976) finding that 'primary psychopaths' exhibit significantly more construct lopsidedness in the repertory grid than normal controls could also reflect differences in terms of cognitive development in the social sphere with psychopaths exhibiting relatively immature conceptual structures for construing people and interpersonal situations.

NOMINAL VERSUS CONTRASTIVE POLES

Deese (1973) relates the tendency of subjects to use the positive poles of bipolar dimensions more frequently than their negative counterparts to the phenomenon of 'linguistic marking' (cf. Bierwisch, 1967; Greenberg, 1966). He notes that pairs of asymmetric, transitive, adjectival opposites, such as *long-short* usually have one member which (a) came into the language at an earlier date, (b) occurs more frequently, and (c) is the first to be used correctly by children. An adjective which has all of these characteristics (e.g. *long*) is termed *unmarked*, and its opposite is said to be *marked*.

Clark (1969) contends that each unmarked adjective has two senses, whereas its marked counterpart has only one sense. The former usually provides the name of the underlying distinction represented by the pair (e.g. *length*), and can be neutralized in certain contexts. For example, the question, 'How long was the meeting?', can be understood as a straightforward request for an estimate of the length of the meeting in question. On the other hand, the question, 'How short was the meeting?', implies something more. The questioner has already assumed that for some reason it was a short meeting, and is merely enquiring about the extent of its 'shortness'. Furthermore, it would make sense to ask 'How long was the short meeting?', but it would sound very strange if someone were to ask us 'How short was the long meeting?'.

Clark maintains that the unmarked member of each pair of contrasting adjectives (with some exceptions) can be neutralized in this way because it serves both a nominal function, that is, it provides the name of the dimension as a whole (*length*), and a contrastive function, that is, it designates one specific pole of that dimension. Its marked opposite, on the other hand, is presumed to serve only the contrastive function of designating the other pole of the dimension. This 'linguistic' distinction between marked and unmarked adjectives, as elaborated by Clark, closely parallels Kelly's (1955) own distinction between the *nominal* and *contrastive* poles of a personal construct.

As we saw in Chapter 1, Kelly (1955) assumes that the minimum context of a construct consists of 'at least two things which have a likeness and one thing which is, by the same token, different (p. 111). He posits further that 'any one of the like elements in the context of a construct may give the construct its name . . . [and] 'the symbol [name] of a construct is usually one of the like elements' (p. 149). Thus, the 'nominal pole' of each construct is presumed to subsume the name of the construct itself as well as a group of elements which are similar to one another in some respect; while the 'contrast pole' subsumes only elements which are different in the same respect from those subsumed under the nominal pole.

There is ample evidence that comparative sentences of the type 'Mary is happier than John' are easier to recall when they contain 'unmarked' adjectives than when they contain 'marked' ones. For example, it is easier to remember that 'Mary is happier than John' than that 'John is sadder than Mary' (Clark and Card, 1969; Benjafield and Giesbrecht, 1973). This suggests, in the light of the analogy between the concept of linguistic marking and Kelly's own distinction between the nominal and contrastive poles of constructs, that judgements involving the nominal poles of constructs might be easier to recall than those involving the contrastive poles (cf. Adams-Webber, 1977c). Adams-Webber, Benjafield, Doan, and Giesbrecht (1975) hypothesized that the difference between the nominal and contrastive poles of constructs in terms of ease of recall would be greater for relatively lopsided constructs than for relatively balanced ones.

It was assumed that unmarked adjectives are typically positive and marked adjectives negative in terms of the Semantic Differential components (Deese, 1973); and that positive adjectives usually refer to the nominal poles of constructs while negative adjectives usually refer to the contrastive poles. This is consistent with the fact that positive adjectives are used more frequently than negative ones, and unmarked adjectives are used more frequently than marked ones, and the former usually provide the names of the dimensions which they represent. It was reasoned that since frequency of usage relates directly to response availability, the verbal responses which are used most often by a subject as labels for his own experience will be more available to him in recall than those labels which he uses relatively infrequently (cf. Benjafield and Doan, 1971). Since the degree of lopsidedness of a given construct is based on the relative frequency of usage (and, by implication, the availability) of each of its two poles by a particular individual, the difference in availability between the alternative poles of a construct can be expected to vary as a function of its degree of lopsidedness. Therefore it was predicted specifically that, while positive (unmarked) adjectives in general would be recalled more easily than their negative opposites, as in previous experiments (across subjects), the difference between positive and negative adjectives with respect to ease of recall would be more pronounced for those constructs which were relatively lopsided in favour of their positive poles than for relatively balanced constructs (within subjects).

A repertory grid test was used to determine the relative degree of lopsidedness of each of eight supplied constructs, represented by pairs of antonymous adjectives, individually for each of thirteen Canadian undergraduates. Each subject then completed a memory task involving eight comparative sentences including either the positive or negative poles of these constructs (cf. Benjafield and Giesbrecht, 1973). As in previous studies (Clark and Card, 1969; Benjafield and Giesbrecht, 1973), more sentences containing the positive (unmarked) adjectives were correctly recalled *verbatim* than sentences containing their negative (marked) opposites. On the other hand, there was a significant interaction between linguistic marking and individual differences with respect to construct lopsidedness such that, as expected, the greatest difference between the numbers of positive and negative adjectives correctly recalled by a particular subject occurred for the constructs which were the most lopsided in his own repertory grid protocol. It had also been found in previous research that subjects recall positive adjectives incorrectly in the place of their negative opposites (Clark and Card, 1969; Benjafield and Giesbrecht, 1973). That is, they tend to remember 'John is happier than Mary' although they were originally told that 'John is sadder than Mary'. Adams-Webber *et al.* (1975) found that such 'transformations' from negative to positive adjectives occurred significantly more often for relatively lopsided constructs than for relatively balanced ones.

The results of this experiment suggest clearly that individual differences with respect to the relative frequency of usage of the nominal (positive) and contrastive (negative) poles of a given construct can influence memory for specific information encoded in terms of that construct. The more 'balanced' the distribution of an individual's judgements between the alternative poles of a particular construct, the less the difference between these poles in terms of ease of recall. Conversely, the more lopsided the distribution of an individual's judgements in favour of the nominal pole of a construct, the greater the extent to which his memory for information encoded in terms of the nominal pole will exceed that for information encoded in terms of the contrastive pole.

This relationship may help to explain, at least in part, why the more lopsided the distribution of an individual's personal judgements between the alternative poles of his constructs, the less consistent he tends to be in his characterizations of himself and others from one situation to another (Adams-Webber and Benjafield, 1974; Benjafield and Adams-Webber, 1975; Clyne, 1975; Cochran, 1976b). Since each judgement of a difference between two persons (including the *self*) entails that one of them must be allotted to the contrastive pole of a construct (Cochran, 1976a), the person with relatively lopsided constructs may be more likely to forget such 'contrastive' (marked) information or distort it by transforming it into its opposite. Thus, we might expect the individual with a relatively 'balanced' view of his social environment to remember specific differences between persons more accurately than the individual with a more 'lopsided' perspective. This relationship seems to take on added significance in the light of the findings that the more lopsided the distribution of an individual's judgements on a particular construct in favour of the nominal pole, the more useful he tends to regard that construct for characterizing people in general, and the more definitely (extremely) he judges his acquaintances on it (Adams-Webber and Benjafield, 1973).

The recent finding that children's usage of the alternative poles of constructs becomes progressively less lopsided as they grow older, and presumably gain in social experience (Applebee, 1975, 1976; Barratt, 1977), suggests that their memory for information encoded in terms of the negative poles of constructs and, by implication, their recall of specific differences between persons, might improve as they mature. This hypothesis raises the question of whether there may be some 'optimal' level of construct balance. Obviously, a construct in terms of which all figures are assigned to a single pole (either one) would have no discriminatory power at all. On the other hand, as we have seen, a construct which is perfectly symmetrical will have maximal discriminatory power. This is perhaps why many users of grid procedures directly impose such a distribution upon their subjects' responses. The golden section hypothesis implies, however, that the distribution which is theoretically optimal from the standpoint of noting differences between people is approximately 62/38. That is, this is the distribution which permits one's contrastive (negative) judgements to stand out maximally and to make the largest contribution to average information. Also, the finding that the lopsidedness scores of normal adults tend to converge upon the golden section suggests the possibility that those of children may move progressively from more lopsided distributions toward the golden section as they mature. Adams-Webber and Davidson (1978) found that fifteen-year-old subjects distributed their positive and negative judgements in the golden section ratio.

Fransella and Bannister (1977, p. 98) point out that

One of the puzzling gaps in the use of grids has been, in fact, in the area of psycholinguistics. Language is so dense and rich that it presents extreme problems for anyone attempting a systematic analysis. It is therefore strange that among the many studies in the formal field of psycholinguistics virtually none have made use of what is clearly one of the most flexible forms of systematic attack on the nature of language—the repertory grid . . . equally they have ignored the degree to which personal construct theory provides a framework for the study of 'language' which did not divorce it from 'behaviour' and 'perception'.

Kelly's (1955) assumption that it is the similarity (nominal) pole which subsumes the name of the distinction represented by the construct as a whole does seem to have some specific 'psycholinguistic' implications which can be examined by means of repertory grid procedures. If the nominal (positive) pole provides the name of the construct, then the meaning of the nominal pole should be more 'fixed' in terms of common usage than is that of the contrast (negative) pole. This suggests that people may enjoy more 'degrees of freedom' in employing the contrast poles of constructs. Thus, it can be hypothesized that, if positive adjectives usually serve the nominal function of providing the names of bi-polar dimensions (Clark, 1969; Deese, 1973), then we might expect subjects to keep their usage of positive adjectives as consistent as possible with what they understand to be their commonly accepted 'lexical' meanings (commonality), while using their negative counterparts more idiosyncratically in the light of personal experience (individuality).

For instance, Mair (1967, p. 226) notes that 'the contrasts between poles of constructs often differ considerably from those which seem to be dictated by the logic of the public language . . . studies seem to demonstrate enough variety in pole contrasts to encourage more attention to this problem in psychological measurement generally and grid measurement in particular'. By employing the negative pole of a given construct more idiosyncratically than its positive pole, we may be able to 'rotate' the meaning of the dimension in terms of its axis of reference slightly away from what Mair calls the 'logic of public language' so that it 'fits' more closely into the structure of our own personal construct systems. In Piaget's (1960) terms, we may 'accommodate' to the dictates of public usage more in our deployment of the positive poles of constructs, and 'assimilate' their meanings to the structure of our individual conceptual structures more in deploying their negative poles. In the language of personal construct theory, we may observe more commonality in the use of the nominal (positive) poles of constructs, and more individuality in the use of their contrast (negative) poles. In this way, each individual can try to bridge the gap between the common language system and his own private world of experience.

The general model of construct usage outlined above implies that we can expect to find a higher degree of intersubject agreement concerning the meanings of positive adjectives than concerning those of their negative counterparts. We noted in Chapter 2 that when Bannister (1962a) asked subjects to categorize a set of passport-type photographs of people on the basis of seven adjectives, he observed a significant level of agreement among subjects concerning the specific pattern of interrelationship between the different adjectives; however, there was no significant agreement among them concerning the way in which particular photographs were categorized. The hypothesis, formulated above, that people attempt to keep their usage of the nominal (positive) poles of constructs as consistent as possible with what they understand to be their commonly accepted 'lexical' meanings, while employing their contrast (negative) poles more idiosyncratically predicts specifically that we should find a higher level of consensus regarding the pattern of interrelationship between positive adjectives than with respect to that between their negative opposites. A preliminary test of this prediction has been carried out by Adams-Webber (1977c).

Thirty Canadian undergraduates, fifteen women and fifteen men, were assigned randomly to three groups of approximately ten subjects. All subjects rank-ordered the same set of eight passport-type photographs of strangers (four men and four women) successively on the basis of six adjectives on two occasions approximately one week apart. On one occasion they ranked the photographs on the basis of positive adjectives only, and on the other occasion on the basis of their negative opposites. Approximately half the subjects in each group used the positive adjectives first, and the other half used the negative adjectives first. Three sets of eight photographs were used in each group, being randomly assigned to subjects. Also, a different set of six adjectives was used in each group. Thus, for each of these groups there was an average of twenty separate repertory grid matrices—sixty in all—each representing a single subject's rankings of the same eight photographs on six different adjectives.

For each grid protocol, the rank-order correlations between each set of rankings (construct) and every other were calculated, yielding fifteen correlation coefficients for every grid. Thus for each subject there were two separate matrices of correlations, one based exclusively on positive adjectives and the other on their negative opposites. Next, the fifteen correlations in each of these sixty matrices were separately rank-ordered from the largest positive one to the largest negative one. This procedure produced a 'map' of the pattern of interrelationship among the six adjectives in each matrix. Gathercole et al. (1970) report a median test-retest reliability of 0.72 ($N = 53$) for such sets of rankings. Finally, Kendall's coefficient of concordance was used to determine independently the extent of the agreement among the subjects in each group concerning the pattern of intercorrelation between positive adjectives and that between negative ones.

The data summarized in Table 9 indicate that, as hypothesized, there was more agreement among the subjects in each group concerning the pattern of interrelationship between positive adjectives than that between their negative counterparts. Overall, the average rank-order correlation between subjects within the same groups with respect to the specific pattern of interrelationship between six adjectives was approximately $r = 0.30$ for the positive adjectives and 0.08 for their negative opposites. An analysis of variance indicated that the observed differences in degree of consensus between positive and negative adjectives was significant ($F (1, 2) = 278.587$; $p < .01$).

Differences between positive and negative adjectives accounted for approximately 72 per cent of the total variation in the levels of agreement found in this

Table 9. The average Spearman rank-order correlations
between subjects within groups for positive and negative
adjectives

Group	N	+ Adjectives	− Adjectives
I	11	$r = 0.28^*$	$r = 0.10$
II	10	$r = 0.38^*$	$r = 0.15$
III	9	$r = 0.20^*$	$r = 0.00$

$^* p < .001$
(From data reported by Adams-Webber, 1977c)

experiment. Differences between the three lists of constructs accounted for approximately 27 per cent of the total variance in agreement scores (F (1, 2) = 52.067; $p < .05$). The interaction between these two factors accounted for less than 1 per cent the total variance, indicating that differences between positive and negative adjectives with respect to levels of agreement were almost the same for all three sets of constructs.

In so far as the meaning of a construct is reflected in its specific relationships with other constructs (cf. Lemon and Warren, 1974), these results suggest that there is a higher level of consensus (commonality) concerning the meanings of the nominal poles of constructs than those of their contrast poles. This seems consistent with the hypothesis that people try to keep their usage of the nominal poles aligned as closely as possible with what Mair calls 'the logic of the public language', while using the negative poles more 'idiographically' to represent their own personal experience (individuality). This hypothesis may also have developmental implications.

Applebee (1975, 1976) administered repertory grid tests to children aged 6, 9, 13, and 17, and found that there is an increase with age in the degree of social consensus concerning the pattern of interrelationship between constructs. As in Bannister's (1962a) earlier study, Applebee observed that there was more agreement about the relationships between constructs than about the ratings of particular elements on each construct. In the absence of further evidence, it is tempting to speculate that the development of individual cognitive structures (discussed in Chapter 3) involves both the progressive integration of sets of concepts defined in terms of more or less agreed-on public meanings, for example, *length, health, sincerity,* which can be referred to through the nominal function of the positive (similarity) poles of our constructs, and the increasing differentiation of one's personal world of experience in terms of specific contrasts represented by the negative poles. This suggests that commonality and individuality may be complementary aspects of the same process of development. As Mischel (1974, p. 89) puts it,

No doubt within these public forms of life we develop our own criteria of importance, our personal constructs, if you like. But these arise as personal emphases out of a public stock, and they are made in situations that are intelligible to us only because we have developed a shared system of concepts and ways of behaviour.

In Kellian terms, the nominal function of the positive pole of each construct may serve to anchor its meaning with respect to a public system of concepts. On the other hand, the individual employs the negative pole in such a way that the construct as a whole adequately represents a bi-polar distinction, that is, a contrast, which he has elaborated in the idiographic context of his own personal experience.

Although this hypothesis is purely speculative, it could eventually help to explain why people adopt a strategy of organizing information on the basis of bi-polar constructs in such a way that their 'more idiosyncratic' negative judgements constitute that proportion of all impressions whereby they will contribute maximally to total variability in their constructions of events. Also, the possibility that our personal construct systems are held together primarily in terms of a network of 'normative' relationships, concerning which there is a fairly high degree of public consensus (commonality), may explain not only why there is more evidence of agreement concerning the pattern of relationships between the positive poles of constructs (Adams-Webber, 1977c), but also, why there seems to be a higher level of interrelationship *per se* between the positive poles of constructs (Adams-Webber, 1977a). Finally, the notion that people use the contrast poles of constructs primarily to represent specific contrasts between events in their own personal experience seems consistent with the finding that people tend to judge both themselves and others more definitely (extremely) on the contrast poles than on the nominal poles (Adams-Webber and Benjafield, 1973).

8

New Directions

The research with which we have been concerned so far in this volume falls roughly into a number of major categories which correspond to the series of topic headings from Chapters 2 to 7. In the last few years, however, several new lines of enquiry have emerged within the framework of personal construct theory which do not fit into any of these broad areas of investigation. These new currents have extended the range of convenience of the theory and related measurement techniques far beyond its original province, that is, personality and clinical psychology; and occasionally, outside the field of psychology itself as it has been traditionally defined.

Some of these new directions have been initiated by architects, city planners and urban geographers and include such diverse subjects as preferences for different styles of living-rooms, choice of university and forming impressions of neighbours. In short, this work deals broadly with different facets of our perception of the environment. Psychologists concerned with problems in experimental aesthetics and dramatic art have also applied construct theory and grid techniques in highly innovative ways. Other psychologists and psychiatrists have turned to the same theory and methodology in their attempts to evaluate the specific effects of professional training programmes: do they make any difference? A few have ventured boldly into the arena of current political affairs and tried to make some sense of routine patterns of voting and parliamentary debate from the standpoint of construct theory. There have even emerged some new approaches to the old problem of predicting behaviour.

It will not be possible in this final chapter to offer a comprehensive survey of new lines of investigation within the context of personal construct psychology; however, we can consider in some detail a few representative areas of enquiry which look especially promising in their early stages. Whenever possible we shall consider also how these new threads are linked to the major strands of ongoing research discussed in previous chapters. This is as far as we shall be able to go at present towards anticipating the future development of theory and research in the psychology of personal constructs.

ENVIRONMENTAL IMAGES

Perhaps the most rapidly emerging new area within personal construct research deals with conceptions of the environment. Harrison and Sarre (1971, p. 365) point out that 'Kelly's model, and the empirical methods associated with it, were developed in the field of interpersonal psychology but come very close to being a ready-made approach to the study of environmental images'. Stringer (1976a, p. 183) notes that 'studies of how people view their environment are needed to help solve problems that arise in architecture and urban design'. Therefore perhaps it is not really surprising that much of the initiative in this area has been seized by architects and geographers, rather than psychologists. A considerable portion of their work has been reported in unpublished master's and doctoral theses, many of which have been reviewed by Stringer (1976a, b) and Honikman (1976a). This body of work deals with a wide range of topics including choice of university (Rowles, 1972; Reid and Holley, 1972); housing preferences (Rawson, 1973; Betak, 1977); housewives' impressions of municipal areas (Sarre, 1973); shopkeepers' perceptions of their retailing environments (Harrison, 1973); and attitudes toward seaside resorts (Riley and Palmer, 1976).

Hudson (1974) employed repertory grid technique to assess images of the retailing environment developed by student 'migrants' in Bristol. He requested twenty-six first-term students at Bristol University to record when and where they purchased food during their first ten weeks of residence in the city. A repertory grid test was then administered individually to each student in which the elements were selected from among the most frequently visited stores listed in his or her own personal shopping diary. Particular grocery shops rather than shopping centres were used because the latter tend to be perceived in terms of a few frequently visited shops located therein (Downs, 1970). The entire set of elements included eleven shops common to all students, and a few additional shops visited by the particular student. Personal constructs were first elicited using randomly selected triads of shops, and then each student rated all shops from 1 to 11 on the basis of each of his own constructs.

The variation in terms of the number of constructs elicited from students indicated a considerable range of individual differences with respect to the complexity of their systems of cognitive dimensions for construing their 'retailing environment'. The results of a principal component analysis carried out on the grids of individual students revealed that the number of components with eigenvalues equal to or greater than unity varied from 2 to 6 per student, with a median of 3. The proportion of the total variance that could be accounted for by the first component varied from 30 to 70 per cent, with a median of 44 per cent. Hudson (p. 478) suggests that 'both of these measures again point to a marked degree of interpersonal variation in the complexity of the cognitive models used to interpret reality'. It would be interesting to compare this set of grids with ones elicited from a sample of students who had lived in Bristol for a longer period, or with those elicited from the same group of students after they had acquired a year or so of shopping experience in that city. We might expect that as they acquired greater familiarity with the shops of Bristol, they would be able to apply a wider range of constructs to them and to make more discriminations among them.

Zalot and Adams-Webber (1977) compared residents of high-rise apartments (HR) and single-family homes (SF) in terms of the complexity of their impressions of their immediate neighbours. McGahan (1972) indicates that SF residents interact with their neighbours more frequently than HR residents do. Crockett (1965, p. 62) hypothesizes that 'an individual's constructs relative to others with whom he interacts frequently and intimately will be more complex than his constructs relevant to categories of people with whom he interacts less frequently'. This implies that SF residents should provide more complex characterizations of their neighbours than HR residents.

As expected on the basis of McGahan's findings, SF residents were found to interact with their neighbours more than HR residents. There was a positive correlation between frequency of interaction with neighbours and the number of constructs used to describe them, which is Crockett's (1965; see Chapter 3) operational definition of cognitive complexity ($r = 0.46$; $N = 87$; $p < .01$). Also, as predicted, cognitive complexity related directly to the type of housing (F (1, 83) $= 5.95$; $p < .05$). Thus, specific conditions of housing can influence both the pattern of interaction among people who live in close proximity and the level of cognitive complexity exhibited by an individual in forming impressions of his or her neighbours. Interestingly, across both housing conditions, women interacted more frequently with neighbours and characterized them more complexly than men did.

Honikman, an architect, has applied personal construct theory and repertory grid methodology to the problem of how architects can understand and respond to the needs of their clients. He carried out a novel study designed to identify the superordinate constructs used by people to evaluate specific areas of their houses such as the living-room, as well as the subordinate constructs used to elaborate the implications of their superordinate constructions in terms of the physical features of the areas. Honikman (1976a, p. 177) states that his strategy is 'to trace the development of a meaning pattern from the physical characteristic, e.g. "fireplace" through increasing levels of ordinancy, e.g. "centrality of focus", "friendly" to the superordinate area of evaluation, e.g. "sense of home, security and family"'. He used a set of seventeen colour photographs of different living-rooms to elicit 'superordinate constructs' which represent the 'important ideas with which the informant evaluated living-rooms' (p. 173), for example, *formal-informal*. Then Hinkle's (1965) 'laddering technique' (described in Chapter 3) was used to identify a 'subordinate network of constructs' referring to specific physical features of the rooms. Finally, each respondent completed a repertory grid in which ten of the photographs were rated on 7-point scales based on their own 'superordinate constructs'.

The resulting grid matrices were subjected to principal component analysis with the aim of identifying 'links' between the superordinate constructs representing major areas of meaning, such as *homely*, and subordinate constructs representing physical characteristics, such as *rough bricks*. One particular photograph was selected as a focal point in reference to which three types of 'linkage' were elaborated: (a) 'link by component loading', defined in terms of the extent to which particular constructs and elements can be linked to the same components; (b) 'link by eliciting' which stems from the original elicitation procedure 'since the eliciting of a construct can be traced directly to one of the elements' (p. 176); and (c) 'link by laddering', which indicates increasing levels of ordination across a chain of interrelated constructs. From the results of this analysis the architect attempts to infer what major areas of meaning are important to the client and what specific physical features can be used to translate the client's ideas into an actual living-room design.

Although Honikman (1976a, b) provides a number of case illustrations of this technique, there is not yet any systematic evidence in terms of which we can begin to assess its validity. Stringer (1976b) points out that 'on the practical side we have had no demonstration yet that doing a grid with a client actually does help the process of design' (p. 102). He suggests that it could be useful to compare architectural designs produced with and without the information derived from clients' repertory grids in terms of client satisfcation.

Stringer (1974, 1976a) developed a repertory grid procedure for investigating attitudes concerning alternative schemes for the redevelopment of a shopping centre. He used a series of seven maps representing the current situation and six alternative plans for redevelopment as elements for eliciting relevant constructs from a sample of 196 British housewives living in the area of the proposed site. An average of fifteen constructs were elicited from each respondent, who then rank-ordered the seven maps on the basis of all of her own constructs and a single supplied one, 'the proposal I would most like to see put into effect'. A number of structural indices derived from each grid by means of a principal component analysis were used to assess the extent to which the seven plans could be discriminated. For example, 'a relatively large first component was taken as an indication of lack of discrimination in the construct system' (Stringer, 1976a, p. 194).

It was found that certain cartographic variables influenced the degree of differentiation between the proposals represented by different maps. For example, subjects who were shown coloured maps exhibited significantly more differentiation in terms of all structural indices than those who saw only black-and-white maps. Moreover, certain 'background variables' such as age, educational level, socio-economic status, as well as their specific relation to the project, including length of residence in the area, frequency and purpose of visits to the proposed site and distance from it, and prior knowledge of planning proposals, were found to relate significantly to the degree to which particular subjects differentiated between certain proposals. Stringer (1976a, p. 196) concludes that these preliminary results are 'encouraging evidence for the validity of the technique ... [but] do not go so far as to establish relations between construct systems and overt behaviour in the way that the geographical studies intend to move'. As we shall see in a later section of this chapter, very few studies to date have come to grips with the difficult problem of establishing a link between how individuals construe events and specific behavioural outcomes.

Downs (1976, p. 73), himself a geographer, poses an important question for those interested in the future of personal construct theory: 'although the number of applications of grid methods has not yet reached crisis proportions, elements such as rooms, houses, shopping centres, neighbourhoods, cities, and states have all been run through the mill of grid method . . . why is the methodology so popular?'. Part of the answer may lie in the idiographic emphasis of repertory grid technique (cf. Allport, 1958). Several investigators seem to have first turned to the repertory grid out of their dissatisfaction with the more nomothetic *Semantic Differential*. For instance, Honikman (1976b, p. 89) stresses this aspect of grid procedure: 'it requires that the study recognize the individuality or personal nature with which events are experienced . . . it was this criterion that called into question most of the semantic differential and rating scale studies which were published under the banner of architectural psychology'. As Downs (p. 74) puts it, 'we are growing out of the semantic differential'. On the other hand, the idiographic emphasis of repertory grid technique is itself dictated by the basic assumptions of the psychology of personal constructs.

Many grid researchers have tried to take advantage of the close relationship between measurement operations and theoretical constructs which characterizes Kelly's approach (cf. Bannister and Mair, 1968). Downs argues that 'it is *impossible* to separate the *theory* of personal constructs from its operational procedures' (p. 75); although some have tried to isolate grid methology from the assumptions which originally gave rise to it (cf. Bieri *et al.*, 1966). Downs maintains further that 'it is important that we can interpret our concerns within the framework of the theory's structure, since this enables us to generate research topics' (p. 86). In a similar vein, Stringer (1976b, p. 102) submits that 'for the psychologist and the theoretician, there is little of interest in being shown *tout court* that people can construe pictures of living-rooms . . . something more pointed should come from the intermeshing of PCT with a particular field of application'. In far more personal and subjective terms, Honikman (1976, p. 88) makes a somewhat similar case:

When first I understood the scope of personal construct theory and its location within the overall body of psychology, I enjoyed an almost 'eureka'-like experience. A whole series of mental switches clicked into phase. I could see structures of communication between people and buildings being identified in a way that I as an architect could use as a guide.

Of course, such testimonials cannot constitute evidence for evaluating the validity, or even the utility, of a theoretical model in any field of research. The essential point is that it would seem to be the theoretical implications of Kelly's basic assumptions which have led so many investigators in areas as diverse as architecture, market research and geography to adopt grid methodology. This is indeed in sharp contrast to the numerous psychologists who have attempted to employ grid procedures to measure traditional concepts such as the 'self-concept' without relating their work in any way to the principles of construct theory. In answer to his own question Downs (p. 86) goes so far as to claim that 'the advantages of a unified theory and methodology cannot be overemphasized'.

DIMENSIONS OF AESTHETIC EXPERIENCE

O'Hare and Gordon (1976) applied repertory grid technique to assess people's responses to paintings. Eighteen British undergraduates, nine women and nine men, completed a grid test in which a series of twelve slides of different paintings were rated successively on 7-point scales based on one supplied construct—*like-dislike*—and several elicited ones. A week later they were randomly divided into three equal groups. One experimental group listened to an 'information tape' which contained a detailed description of six of the paintings culled from a variety of art books while the slides of the paintings themselves were projected on a screen in front of them. The second experimental group viewed the same six slides while listening to a 'biographical tape' containing information about the lives of each of the relevant painters. The third group listened to a 'control tape' containing a general discussion of prehistoric art. Following the tape, a new set of constructs was elicited from each subject using all twelve paintings as elements. Finally, subjects rated every painting on both the new constructs and those which had been elicited from them on the first occasion.

Several structural measures were derived from each subject's grid by means of principal component analysis, including the number of components with latent roots greater than unity, the proportion of the total variation accounted for by each of the three major components, and the ratio of the largest latent root to the total variation. They also employed the total number of constructs elicited as an measure of differentiation (Crockett, 1965). In addition, they sorted the constructs elicited from subjects in terms of their content into three separate categories: *stylistic, painterly*, and *impact* (roughly style, composition, and subjective impression). Every subject was assigned three scores indicating the frequency with which they used each category of constructs. The interjudge reliability of this classification was satisfactory (85 per cent).

In contrast to Stringer's (1974, 1976a) findings involving different map formats, discussed in the previous section, there was little relationship between individual differences in terms of the structural measures summarized above and 'background variables' such as previous familiarity with the paintings, degree of specific interest in art and knowledge about painting. However, the results did show that 'indices of greater differentiation are consistently associated with a higher percentage of constructs in the painterly category and a lower percentage in the impact category' (p. 1188), which O'Hare and Gordon interpret as supporting their own hypothesis that 'a more "sophisticated" view of art (defined as a more differentiated one) would be associated with a tendency to use more terms referring to the aspects of pictures and fewer terms referring to their subjective effects' (p. 1186).

Also specific knowledge of the paintings viewed and interest in art in general were both found to correlate with the tendency to use more 'painterly' constructs and fewer 'impact' ones. As expected, only the group who listened to the 'information tape' significantly increased their percentage of 'painterly constructs' from the first to the second occasion. On the other hand, the type of tape to which subjects listened produced no effects in terms of any of the structural indices. O'Hare and Gordon conclude in the light of these results that 'there were no differential changes in the structures of subjects' perceptions of the pictures following exposure to relevant or irrelevant information' (p. 1190). This could have been due to the lack of reliability of the indices of differentiation which they employed, a problem discussed in Chapters 2 and 3. Finally, the 'salience' of the six experimental paintings, defined as the mean percentage of total grid variation which they accounted for across all subjects, increased following the taped presentations significantly more than did that of the six control paintings, suggesting that 'the information provided was attended to and influenced subsequent responding' (p. 1191).

On the whole, this study represents a very promising beginning in the use of repertory grid procedures to study the responses of individuals to aesthetic objects. The importance of eliciting a sample of personal constructs from each subject in this area of research is also indicated by the findings of Bonarius (1970a), discussed in Chapter 2. He found that subjects rated those paintings which they found to be 'most moving' among a series of ten slides more extremely ('more meaningfully') on 7-point scales based on constructs previously elicited from themselves than on constructs elicited from their peers.

Repertory grid technique also lends itself to the measurement of individual aesthetic preferences. Benjafield (1976) developed a form of grid procedure to test the specific hypothesis that the 'golden recetangle', that is, the rectangle whose sides are in the 'golden section' proportion (see Chapter 7), is generally more aesthetically pleasing to people than rectangles in other proportions (cf. Fechner, 1876). Benjafield provides the following explanation of the rationale of his measurement operations:

From the point of view of many cognitive theories judgment is the outcome of a process that develops over time, being at first global and gradually becoming more differentiated and precise. It would be useful to have a scaled preference that reflects this process and takes into account global preferences as well as more articulate preferences for specific rectangles. Consequently, a method for eliciting preferences was derived from Kelly's repertory grid technique, a method which not only allows the subject to gradually articulate his judgments but also yields such a scale. (p. 738)

Benjafield asked 180 subjects, recruited in the Sheffield City Museum and at Sheffield University, to inspect a set of nine rectangles, one of which was a 'golden rectangle', drawn on cards which were laid out in parallel rows on a table, and to 'divide the cards into 2 groups—those you like and those you dislike'. Next, those cards which the subject had indicated that he liked were presented to him again and he was asked to sort them once more into two piles: 'those you like most and those you like least'. Finally, the subject was presented with only those cards which he had allocated to the 'most liked' group and asked to pick the 'one you like best'. As Benjafield points out, this procedure permits an ordinal measure of the extent to which a subject prefers each rectangle. All rectangles allotted to the disliked category on the first sort were scored 0; those allocated to the 'liked' category initially, but not subsequently designated as 'most liked' were scored 1; those assigned to the 'liked most' group on the second sort, but not 'liked best' received a score of 2; and finally, the rectangle chosen as 'liked best' was assigned a score of 3.

Benjafield's analysis of these data revealed that, for rectangles with the same area, the degree of subjects' preferences generally tended to increase as the ratio of their sides approached the 'golden section'. He suggests in the light of these results that the golden section may play an important role in aesthetic preference, just as it does in interpersonal judgement (see Chapter 7).

Personal construct theory has also been applied recently to the study of dramatic art by Moss (1974a, b), who has conducted an analysis of several of Shakespeare's tragedies in terms of Kelly's definition of role. He points out that there is a fundamental analogy between the critic's analysis of a role or scene and the psychologist's analysis of a person or social episode. For example, Moss (1974b, p. 236) suggests that 'Hamlet's famous "to be or not to be" soliloquy is an example of personal construing in terms of discrepant roles, and the fundamental rhythm of the play can be seen as a dialectic movement between role-playing and person construing' (cf. Kelly, 1955, pp. 516–7). Moss hypothesizes that the study of the way in which Shakespeare has portrayed the 'problems' of Hamlet, Lear, Macbeth, Othello, and the protagonists of his other tragedies will contribute to the verification and elaboration of important concepts in the psychology of personal constructs.

Rosenberg (1977; Rosenberg and Jones, 1972) has carried out extensive analyses of the writings of Theodore Drieser in terms of dimensions which were central to his life and personality. He has 'demonstrated, with the analysis of a sample of Drieser's short stories, the feasibility of extracting a person's view of people from completely naturalistic materials' (Rosenberg, 1977, p. 183). (cf. Allport, 1965). Rosenberg (personal communication) is currently undertaking studies of Thomas Wolfe's *Look Homeward Angel*. Rosenberg (1977) notes that 'our interest in the detailed study of an individual has thus brought us very close to the long-standing concerns of personal construct theorists' (p. 185). Although this approach is not limited to the analysis of literary material, it has been extremely fruitful when applied to the characterizations of Drieser.

PROFESSIONAL ROLES: DOES TRAINING MAKE A DIFFERENCE?

During the past few years there has been some research concerned with the effects of professional training on the structure and content of the personal construct system of the individual trainee. Ryle and Breen (1974a) investigated how British social-work students construed their roles and how their constructs changed in the course of a two-year training programme providing both seminar instruction and field-work experience. They designed a 'dyad grid' (see Chapter 5) in which the elements consisted of relationships between the trainees and their clients, tutors, supervisors, and parents. These elements were rated on 7-point scales based on sixteen uni-polar constructs selected to represent a range of judgements relevant to the particular roles being construed, for example, *behaves professionally towards*. Each of twelve social-work students completed this grid test within three months of starting the training programme, and repeated it on two subsequent occasions before completing their training.

It was found that the percentage of the total variation in their grids accounted for by the first two components was significantly smaller on the third occasion of testing than on the first. Ryle and Breen interpret this result as 'indicating an increase in complexity' during training. This interpretation seems problematic in the light of the fact that no control procedures were used, and also the total amount of variation in the grids fell significantly from the first to the last occasion. It could be argued that the latter reflects a general decrease in the extent to which the elements were differentiated from one another on each construct, which would suggest some decline in at least one aspect of 'cognitive complexity' during this period. Finally, as hypothesized, the distance between the *self-to-client* and *ideal self-to-client* relationship decreased significantly during training 'indicating greater confidence in the social-work role' (p. 146). Ryle and Breen conclude that 'the evidence of, in general, greater role confidence and the evidence of greater complexity of construing without greater conformity after the course experience are both encouraging' (p. 146); however, the evidence concerning an increase in complexity is ambiguous.

In a follow-up study, Ryle and Breen (1974b) employed a 'standard' repertory grid test to assess the tutors' judgements of the same twelve students. At the end of the programme, each of the three tutors involved with these students individually completed a grid test in which they rated the original twelve students, plus two others, on 5-point scales based on twenty supplied constructs. They were allowed to throw out or modify any of these constructs and add new ones. Nine of the original pool of twenty constructs were used by all three tutors, for example, *had major personal difficulty in adaptation to the course*. An analysis of ratings based on these nine dimensions indicated that the 'similarity between the construct systems of these tutors was relatively high' (p. 151). On the other hand, these grid data did not prove useful, as had been hoped, for predicting specific problems which arose between particular tutors and trainees.

Another study of changes taking place in students' construct systems during social-work training was carried out in Israel by Liftshitz (1974). She employed a shortened group form of the repertory grid to compare the personal perceptions and attitudes of a group of social-work students with those of their more experienced supervisors. Twelve figures selected from Kelly's (1955) original list of nineteen role titles were used to elicit twelve bi-polar constructs from each subject individually. Each of these figures was then rated dichotomously on every construct.

No difference was found between the students and their supervisors in terms of the percentage of total variation in these grids accounted for by the first factor ('complexity'). Liftshitz identified that construct which was most saturated with the first factor in each subject's grid and assigned it to one of seven possible categories: (1) *task orientation,* (2) *a description of concrete situations,* (3) *abstract intrapsychic characterizations,* (4) *abstract interpersonal characteristics,* (5) *abstract social values,* (6) *intellectual characteristics,* and (7) *affective-egocentric approach.* She also identified which figures were most representative of the positive and negative poles of the subject's 'superordinate construct' (i.e. that with the highest loading on the first component).

Liftshitz provides the following summary of her results:

The student group used the most concrete descriptive categories such as age, sex and profession. Primary figures, such as father, mate or same-sex friend, were the most influential in their construing process. The constructs of their supervisors showed more abstract ability of concern with themselves, others and their task. Their concepts centred on the professional ideal and revealed an internationalization of cherished values. (p. 193)

She poses the question, 'does training make a difference?', and answers it in the affirmative on the basis of these findings. She concludes specifically that training produces an increase in the level of abstraction of interpersonal construing and a change in 'personal models' used in validating constructs.

Adams-Webber and Mirc (1976a, b, c) used repertory grid procedures to assess the development of student teachers' conceptions of their future professional roles during their first six weeks of practice-teaching experience. The basic assumption of this reserarch was that individual teachers evolve specific subsystems of interrelated constructs in terms of which they define their own pattern of involvement in routine activities such as instruction, testing, and counselling, etc. Their role subsystems can be viewed as also having implications for how the various functions of the teacher role are co-ordinated with those of related roles (e.g. pupil, principal, school librarian) within the school system. It was hypothesized that there would be gradual increases in the level of integration of student teachers' role subsystems as they gained classroom experience. Also, Kelly's (1955) assumption that there is a high degree of specialization among subsystems within an individual's personal construct system (cf. Adams-Webber, 1970a) implies that these changes should be specific to their teacher role subsystems and not generalize to other sectors of their construct systems.

The principals of seven schools—randomly selected from all primary schools in the same Canadian city (pop. 120,000)—individually completed the following repertory grid task. Each principal was shown a list of ten 'role titles' (e.g. *teacher, principal, pupil,* etc.) and asked to nominate one individual who occupied each of these positions in his own school. Their names were recorded on separate cards, which were scattered on a table in front of the principal, and he was asked to indicate which figure was most involved in, say, 'handling discipline problems'. The card which he selected was removed from the display, and he was asked to designate which one of the remaining nine figures was most involved in the same function. This procedure was repeated until he had rank-ordered all ten figures from most to least involved in this function. Next, he ranked the same figures in terms of their degree of involvement in a second function, say pupil promotion—and so on—until he had successively ranked them on the basis of their degree of participation in the nineteen different functions (constructs) listed in Table 10.

The data elicited from each principal were arranged in a separate ten-column (roles) by nineteen-row (constructs) matrix. Table 10 reports the mean Spearman rank-order correlation between the principals' rankings of the nine figures on each construct and its level of significance. These data indicate a fairly high level of interjudge agreement considering that each principal rank-ordered a different set of individuals. This suggests that they shared similar conceptions of the function of each role within their schools.

Next, sixty-four regular classroom teachers, recruited from the same schools, individually completed the same repertory grid task. A single coefficient of concordance was computed independently for each teacher's grid. This index, referred to from here on as the *integration score*, provided an estimate of the overall degree of intercorrelation among the nineteen constructs. Following Bannister and Mair (1968, p. 57), it was assumed that the correlations among sets of rankings of the same elements on different constructs reflects the extent to which those constructs are related psychologically for the subject. A single integration score was also computed for each principal. A positive correlation

Table 10.   Average Spearman rank-order correlations between principals' rankings of role figures on 19 activity constructs

Construct	$r_{av.}$	P
1. Defining teaching objectives	.73	.001
2. Designing tests	.64	.001
3. Marking tests	.63	.001
4. Handling discipline problems	.70	.001
5. Pupil promotion	.62	.001
6. Budget spending	.74	.001
7. Referral to other staff	.61	.001
8. Writing reports on pupils	.40	.001
9. Organization of timetable	.59	.001
10. Assessing effectiveness of learning programme	.68	.001
11. Assessing effectiveness of teachers	.62	.001
12. Controlling use of learning materials	.53	.001
13. Determining teachers' workloads	.65	.001
14. Determining what is to be learned	.61	.001
15. Participation in classroom learning	.51	.001
16. Participation in out-of-school learning	.55	.001
17. Deciding where learning occurs	.45	.001
18. Determining emphasis on reading, writing, maths, etc.	.54	.001
19. Determining emphasis on dance, singing, art, etc.	.53	.001

(From Adams-Webber & Mirc, 1976a; p. 339)

was found between the integration score of each principal and the median integration score of the teachers in his own school (Spearman $r = 0.75$; $p < .05$). This suggests a fairly high degree of interaction between the role subsystems of principals and teachers working under them. There were, however, no significant differences between schools in terms of teachers' integration scores.

Finally, twenty-nine student teachers, enrolled in a practice-teaching course in the College of Education, Brock University—none of whom had previous teaching experience and all of whom planned to become teachers—individually completed the same repertory grid task during the first week of the course prior to any practice teaching and on three subsequent occasions, following each of three fortnightly sessions during which they were engaged on a daily basis in supervized teaching in local schools. Each of these sessions was spent in a different school. As a control for the possible effects of repeating the same repertory grid format, an additional grid task was completed on each occasion. In this 'control' grid the same ten role figures were rank-ordered successively on fifteen personal constructs previously elicited from the student using Kelly's (1955) method of triads. The order of the two grid tasks—experimental and control—was counterbalanced across the four occasions.

These data showed, as was predicted, significant increases in the students' integration scores across the four experimental grids ($\chi^2 = 15.44$; 3 df; $p < .01$) and no significant changes across the four control grids ($\chi^2 = 1.10$; 3 df; NS). This result is consistent with the hypothesis that there would be gradual increases in the level of integration of the students' role subsystems as they acquired classroom experience. The fact that there were no systematic changes in the control grids rules out the possibility that the increases observed in the experimental grids were due to the mere repetition of the same grid format; and it also lends support to the second hypothesis that the expected increases in integration would be specific to those constructs which are directly relevant to structuring the teacher role and would not generalize to other sectors of their personal construct systems.

Comparisons between the students' grids and those of the regular classroom teachers indicated that before engaging in any practice teaching the students' integration scores were significantly lower than those of the teachers ($z = -2.97$; $p < .01$); however, after only six weeks in the classroom they had developed role subsystems which did not differ in terms of their overall level of integration from those of experienced teachers (see Figure 7).

The results of this research, and that of Ryle and Breen (1974a, b) and Liftshitz (1974), provide evidence of the construct validity of the repertory grid as a method of measuring progressive changes in the structure and content of the construct systems of individuals undergoing professional training and field experience. A recent study by Bodden and James (1976), discussed in Chapter 3, also showed that supplying specific information to students about various occupations leads to an increase in the level of interrelationship (integration) between constructs which are directly relevant to vocational choice. On the other hand, an earlier study by Agnew and Bannister (1973) suggests that training and

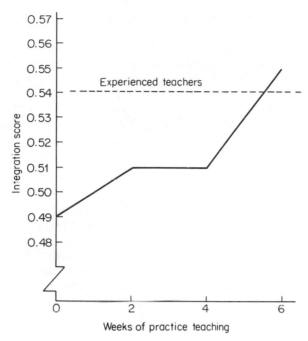

Figure 7. Student teachers' median integration scores as a
function of amount of practice teaching experience. (Figure by
Cameron Adams-Webber, 1978)

experience do not always produce changes in construing. They argue that 'a
specialist language may be regarded as a well defined and publicly agreed network
of terms uncontaminated by lay language with clear implications for work in a
professional field' (p. 69). They then pose the question of whether the diagnostic
concept system currently used in psychiatry meets these requirements, that is,
does it exhibit 'the degree of structure, independence, stability and interjudge
agreement' which characterize the specialist languages employed in other
professions such as engineering, pharmacy, banking, etc.?

Eight consultant psychiatrists recruited from two major psychiatric hospitals
in the UK participated in this experiment. Each selected twenty of his own
patients whom he felt he knew well and 'about whom he had confidence in his
judgement'. These twenty patients were allocated randomly to two lists of ten
patients each. Each psychiatrist then rank-ordered one of these lists of patients
on eight 'lay psychological constructs', for example *generous, reserved*, etc. For
each patient in the second list, the psychiatrists were asked to rank in order of
importance eight diagnostic terms, for example *anxiety state, neurotic depression*,
etc. Agnew and Bannister point out that 'this accords with clinical practice since
psychiatrists naturally think of a single patient and then make a decision as to
which of a number of diagnostic labels is most appropriate, rather than rank
patients under particular diagnostic labels' (p. 70). This entire procedure was
repeated one month later; but this time, the first set of patients was judged on the

basis of the 'psychiatric constructs' and the second set on the basis of the 'lay constructs'.

An analysis of these grids indicated that there was a higher level of interjudge agreement concerning the meaning of lay constructs (average Spearman $r = 0.40$) than concerning those of the psychiatric constructs (average Spearman $r = 0.26$). On the other hand, given the finding that there is generally more consensus concerning the meanings of E+ words than those of E− ones, using the same operations as those employed by Agnew and Bannister (Adams-Webber, 1977c), it is possible that the observed difference is in part the result of the fact that while all of the diagnostic terms have negative connotations, for example, *hysteria*, about half of the lay constructs have positive connotations for most people, for example *considerate*. Nonetheless, these data provide no support for the notion that psychiatrists are able to agree with one another more in terms of their own so-called 'specialist language' than in terms of 'ordinary language'.

Furthermore, no significant difference was found between the lay constructs and the psychiatric ones in terms of stability from one occasion to the next. Agnew and Bannister note that 'an interesting feature of the level of stability found in the lay constructs is that it is unusually low by normative standards... it may be that the psychiatrists, accustomed to viewing these particular people as "patients", have become confused and inconsistent in trying to view them as people' (p. 71).

Finally, they found a significant level of intercorrelation ('contamination') between lay and diagnostic constructs (average Spearman $r = 0.38$), which was approximately the same as the overall level of intercorrelation between the diagnostic categories themselves (see Table 11). The intercorrelations between the lay constructs were considerably higher (average Spearman $r = 0.48$). Again, this outcome may be at least in part a result of the fact that about half of the lay constructs and probably none of the diagnostic constructs had positive connotations, since the average level of intercorrelation between E+ constructs tends to be higher than that between E− ones in the repertory grid (Adams-Webber, 1977a). Agnew and Bannister conclude in the light of their findings that ordinary lay language provides 'at least as structured, as reliable and as public a set of terms for describing human behaviour and psychological characteristics' (p. 73) as does the 'specialist language' used by psychiatrists. These results are in sharp contrast to those of Adams-Webber and Mirc (1976a, b, c) who found that student teachers, after several weeks in the classroom, evidenced a much higher level of intercorrelation (integration) among constructs representing specific curricular functions in the school than among 'lay' constructs in judging themselves and professional colleagues.

Friendly and Glucksberg (1970) investigated the effects of what might be called 'implicit training' (or perhaps 'socialization') in terms of the gradual acquisition of 'subcultural lexicons' by undergraduates at an American university. The purpose of their research was to demonstrate 'differences in the multidimensional structure of social and personality trait words as a function of experience within a

Table 11. Construct pairings (relationships shown as average Spearman rho)

Psychiatrist	Lay-lay	Diag-diag.	Lay-diag.
1	0.40	0.30	0.36
2	0.49	0.28	0.28
3	0.55	0.37	0.26
4	0.66	0.36	0.48
5	0.37	0.37	0.35
6	0.50	0.27	0.27
7	0.34	0.30	0.25
8	0.49	0.48	0.48
Average	0.48	0.34	0.34

(Reproduced by permission of the British Psychological Society from Agnew, J. and Bannister, D., 'Psychiatric diagnosis as a pseudo specialist language', *British Journal of Medical Psychology* (1973), **46**, page 71, published by Cambridge University Press.)

specific subculture' (p. 55). They recruited fifteen first-year and fifteen fourth-year students at the same private university and asked them to ascribe a list of sixty trait adjectives to individuals whom they knew personally. A third of these terms were selected from the student slang lexicon, for example, *wonk*—'an introverted student who studies all the time; generally considered to be physically unattractive' (p. 57).

Measures of disassociation between pairs of traits were used to construct a multidimensional scaling solution for these data (cf. Rosenberg, 1977). A two-dimensional solution provided a satisfactory fit for the data elicited from the first-year students; however, a three-dimensional solution was required for those elicited from the fourth-year students. This outcome was interpreted as reflecting 'real differences in understanding of the words' (p. 59) between freshmen and seniors, indicating that 'not only are new words acquired and fit into a semantic space (or construct system), but also the dimensions of that space itself are altered' (p. 65). Specifically, for the fourth-year data a new axis of reference—'Princeton Social Desirability'—was necessary. Although Friendly and Glucksberg do not attempt to relate the significance of their work directly to the principles of personal construct theory, their findings are clearly consistent with Kelly's (1955) basic assumption that the development of conceptual structures within a specific domain of experience involves the evolution of new subsystems of constructs with specialized ranges of convenience (cf. Crockett, 1965).

ANTICIPATING POLITICAL EVENTS

Du Preez (1972, 1975, 1977) has undertaken a series of studies in which he has systematically applied personal construct theory in a highly innovative way to the analysis of political debates on internal African affairs. First, he carefully compiled a dictionary of bipolar constructs which he abstracted from a review of every debate in the South African House of Assembly on Native, Bantu, or African affairs in the years 1948, 1958, and 1968. Du Preez (1975, p. 267) points out that 'the advantage of such a dictionary is that one gets a clear idea not only of the course of action favoured, but of the alternative rejected'. As Kelly (1955, p. 62) notes, 'much of our language, as well as our every day thinking, implies contrast which it does not explicitly state'. Du Preez's research focuses primarily upon those constructs which are used most commonly by members of the South African House of Assembly, and consequently are those most 'likely to make a political impact'. He found specifically that a list of only forty-six constructs was sufficient to account for 90 per cent of the content of the 685 speeches which he has analysed. He observed also that the frequency of usage of particular constructs varies, as we might expect, from party to party. For example, the construct employed most often by speakers representing the National Party Government was *white survival-loss of autonomy, culture and even life*; whereas the construct used most frequently by the opposition spokesman of the United Party was *economic efficiency-impractical ideology*.

Du Preez has also developed an index of 'awareness of change' based on the average number of reasons offered for opinions and policy statements during the three time periods sampled. He hypothesizes that 'any changes in the frequency of argument for policy would indicate that policy is becoming more or less problematic and is no longer a reiteration of self-evident truths' (1975, p. 269). In addition, 'argument depth' was scored by dividing the total number of tokens in a given speech into the number of 'connections' between these tokens. This index is illustrated using the following argument:

Recognizing nationalism (implies) creating separate homelands erosion in the reserves (implies)? (p. 269)

In his analysis of this argument Du Preez notes that 'three tokens are scored, but only one connection: the implication in the first line'. The final 'argument depth' score is calculated by means of the following formula: number of connections (1) divided by the number of tokens (3); which yields a score of 0.33.

The data summarized in Table 12 are interpreted as indicating that 'government speakers produced more connected arguments in recent than in former years; and the opposition parties all produced more connected arguments than the governing National Party' (p. 269). This seems to suggest that the government tends to regard its own policies as requiring less justification than the opposition; however this difference is becoming less pronounced over time.

Du Preez provides us also with an excellent intuitive analysis of how the introduction of a new superordinate construct into a tightly organized system can help resolve ambiguities within existing structure in the face of events which do not conform to the 'logical' constraints of current construct relationships:

What has changed is the government's model of political relations in South Africa. The

Table 12. Mean depth of argument

Year	National Party	United Party	Native Representatives[a]	Progressive Party[b]
1948	.17	.36	.44	—
1958	.22	.34	.36	—
1968	.32	.37	—	.41
Mean	.24	.36	.40	.41

[a] Three members of the House of Assembly represented the interests of native blacks. (These 'native representatives' were abolished in 1959.)
[b] The Progressive Party was established in 1959.
(Reproduced by permission of P. D. Du Preez from 'The application of Kelly's personal construct theory to the analysis of political debates', *Journal of Social Psychology* (1975), **95**, p. 269, published by The Journal Press.)

units are no longer races, they are nations, and South Africa is multinational rather than multiracial for the purposes of political decision. A problem from the government point of view is that this introduces contradictions; racialism justifies compulsory social segregation, whereas multinationalism does not. To cope with this, a new superordinate construct has been introduced: *international-intranational*. When an event is international, limited forms of social mixing are permitted and racial distinctions are temporarily allowed to lapse. Black competitors in an international event are allowed to live in white areas and mix with white persons on terms of equality, for the duration of the event. Similarly, approved black dignitaries from other countries including the black homelands in South Africa are accorded white privileges for limited periods of time. Racial inequality may now be applied at a domestic level without contradicting a policy of co-operating on equal terms with blacks from other countries. including the 'homelands' of South Africa which are being prepared for self-government by blacks. (p. 268)

Du Preez (1977) has also carried out a study of debates in the Coloured Persons' Representative Council in South Africa, which is an advisory body constituted in 1964 with limited legislative powers in the fields of finance, local government, education, community welfare, pensions, and coloured rural settlements. It currently consists of forty elected and twenty nominated members. Du Preez informs us that a major issue confronting members of this body is one of 'identity':

First, are they Coloured people? Or are they 'so-called Coloured'? Are they Black? The dilemma is that accepting a name embodied in the legislation of the dominant White group is tantamount to accepting White specialist ideology.

He has examined the content of speeches given during specific series of debates in this body—8–10, 13 September, 1975 and 22–24 September, 1976 (following the riots)—in terms of the relationships between alternative 'constructs of identity', for example *Coloured identity, Black identity, Common identity*, etc. and five specific cognitive models of 'possible systems of power'. This study assumes at the outset that 'constructs of identity are dependent upon hypotheses about preferred and possible systems of power . . . (for example) someone who *accepts* Model 1 (White domination) will construe his identity as Coloured, and will reject Black identity'. Interestingly, 17 per cent of the speakers were accepting of Black identity in 1976 after the riots, whereas only 7 per cent had been so in the 1975 debates. In general, the models of power accepted by individual speakers were found to be closely associated to their constructions of identity during both series of debates. Du Preez concludes that 'it is probable that some of these are not deep or permanent commitments. What is clear, though, is that while the model is accepted, the associated identity construct is prominent'.

In an early study of 'political construing' in the UK Fransella and Bannister (1967) used a repertory grid to 'predict' voting behaviour. They administered a grid test to seventy-four eligible voters a fortnight before the British General Election of 1964. Each subject rank-ordered ten personal acquaintances on the following set of nine supplied constructs: *sincere, likely to vote Conservative, proud of being British, like I'd like to be in character, likely to vote Labour, prejudiced, believe in equality, like me in character, likely to vote Liberal.* One week following the election the same subjects reported either how they had voted or would have voted, and indicated also their second and third choices. It was found that their 'voting behaviour' was predictable on the basis of the observed correlations between evaluative constructs such as *sincere* and political party constructs. Although this study was one of the first to come to grips with the difficult problem of relating aspects of subjects' use of constructs in repertory grid tests to their actual behaviour in so-called 'real-life' situations, which is the topic of the next section of this chapter, it falls somewhat short of its objective in that there is an important difference between predicting an observable behaviour and predicting the subject's subsequent report of his behaviour or 'intentions'. The latter has always proved to be the easier task in the framework of personal construct theory and the main focus of attack by its critics (cf. Mischel, 1964).

Bannister and Fransella also devised an operational definition of 'political brand image' in terms of grid measurement: 'A "brand image" might be defined as a construct whose applicability to a particular element is generally accepted, there also being public agreement as to which pole of the construct the element occupies' (Bannister and Mair, 1968, p. 194). For example, both Labour and Conservative Party supporters saw a positive relationship between the constructs *proud of being British* and *likely to vote Conservative*; however, for the Labour Party supporters *proud of being British* related positively to *prejudiced*, whereas for Tory Party supporters it tended to relate negatively to *prejudiced*. Thus, as Bannister and Mair (1968, p. 194) point out, 'the position of the bipolar construct *within the rest of the construct system* may vary considerably where "brand image" (and political image) constructs are concerned'. In this sense, *Coloured identity, Black identity*, etc. can be viewed as having associated 'brand images' in the context of the debates in the so-called Coloured Persons' Representative Council in South Africa (Du Preez, 1977)

NEW APPROACHES TO AN OLD PROBLEM:
PREDICTING BEHAVIOUR

In his analysis of the nature of the predictions which can be derived from personal construct theory, Mischel (1964, p. 190; see Chapter 1) argues that

If we understand the way someone construes then we can predict, e.g. that he is likely to classify another person as being of type X and so to anticipate X-ish behaviour from him; and that, since he construes Y as the right thing to do about X-ish behaviour, he is likely to relate himself to this person by doing Y. So if someone follows certain rules then we can expect certain regularities in his behaviour and thus make predictions.

Unfortunately, there have been very few studies which have attempted to establish a direct link between how an individual characterizes others in terms of his own personal constructs and how he actually behaves toward them. Two experiments of this type have been carried out by Bender (1968b, 1976). In an earlier study, Shoemaker (1955) hypothesized that we tend to expect that people whom we construe as similar will behave in similar ways. Bender (1968b) extended the logic of this proposition along the lines suggested by Mischel above and arrived at the plausible hypothesis that we ourselves will tend to behave in a similar way towards those persons whom we construe as being alike.

He tested this hypothesis by presenting subjects with the names of three personal acquaintances and simply asking them to indicate the two persons towards whom they behaved most similarly. It was predicted that the subjects would select the pair of figures whose matching scores in their own repertory grids was highest. Although this prediction was confirmed at a high level of statistical confidence, this experiment has the same weakness as Fransella and Bannister's (1967) study of voting behaviour discussed in the last section, that is, it relies entirely on the subjects' reports concerning their own behaviour. In order to eliminate this problem Bender (1976) conducted a second experiment in which another person—the subject's spouse—was asked to report his actual behaviour towards the 'target' figures, and the spouse's report was predicted upon the basis of the subject's repertory grid performance.

Bender (1976) explicitly formulated two experimental hypotheses: (1) 'if the subject is presented with a triad of persons and asked which two persons he behaves most similarly towards, he will name the two with the highest matching score'; and (2) 'if the spouse of a subject is presented with a triad of persons known to both and asked which two persons the subject behaves most similarly towards, they will name the two with the highest matching score' (p. 93). We saw in Chapter 2 that the number of matches between any two figure profiles indicates the distance between them in the 'construct space'. Fifteen couples participated in this experiment, and all but three subjects scored better than chance expectations in their predictions and none scored below it. Both hypotheses were supported at the .00006 level of significance across all subjects (2-tailed test). Bender concludes on the basis of these results, and those of his previous study, that the way in which an individual behaves towards other persons can be predicted from knowledge about how he judges them in terms of his personal constructs.

On the other hand, Mischel (1964) distinguishes between the type of prediction which is based on the content of an individual's constructions (i.e. 'idiographic' data) and those predictions which are derived from a theoretical generalization (i.e. 'nomothetic' principles). He acknowledges that Kelly's 'clinical approach' yields predictions of the first kind, but questions whether it can be used to generate hypotheses of the second kind. Nonetheless, a recent study by Hayden (1977; Hayden et al. 1977) provides an excellent example of the 'statistical prediction' of behaviour on the basis of hypotheses derived from personal construct theory.

This work followed-up an earlier study by Reker (1974) in which a sample of 'disturbed' boys (mean age $10\frac{1}{2}$ years) attending special adjustment classes in Canadian schools were compared with normal controls in terms of their performance on a repertory grid test. Twelve personal acquaintances and twelve familiar objects were rated on 5-point scales based on a set of twelve supplied constructs. In addition, they were asked to sort people and objects into a number of personally meaningful groupings. It was found that the 'emotionally disturbed' boys showed less 'cognitive complexity' (Bieri's index, 1955; see Chapter 3) in characterizing people on constructs and discriminated between them less (Scott's H statistic; see Bonarius, 1965) than did the normal controls. On the other hand, no significant differences were observed between the two groups in construing inanimate objects. Reker interprets his results as indicating that emotionally disturbed boys are handicapped in interpersonal situations because they have relatively limited conceptual structures for interpreting and anticipating their social environment.

Hayden et al. (1977) subsequently carried out 'the first investigation of interpersonal conceptual systems to use severely emotionally disturbed children who were currently in long-term residential treatment' (p. 316). The purpose of their research was to relate measures of individual differences in cognitive structure to these children's level of effective social adaptation and ability to anticipate another person's thoughts and feelings. It is one of the few studies which have succeeded in demonstrating a direct relationship between formal characteristics of an individual's construction processes and his 'real-life' behaviour.

A repertory grid test was administered individually to thirty emotionally disturbed boys, ranging in age from 10 to 16, in a resident treatment programme in an American hospital. Their diagnoses included behaviour disorder, personality disorder, and psychosis. The elements used to elicit constructs (the same constructs were supplied to all subjects in Reker's study) were ten close-up photographs of the same eight-year-old boy taken while he was working on a difficult Block Design puzzle. The children were not told what the boy in the photograph was doing. These photographs were presented to each child in randomly selected triads and he was asked 'which two of the photographs, in your opinion, look as though the boy feels or thinks the same thing or almost the same thing?' (p. 317). The child was then asked to describe the feelings and thoughts expressed in the two similar photographs and explain how the third one was different. This procedure was used to elicit ten bi-polar constructs from each child. Finally, the children rated all ten photographs from 1 to 7 on every construct. These ratings were repeated one month later to assess their reliability.

Following this repertory grid test, each child performed a 'prediction' task in which the ten photographs were placed before him in random order and he attempted to rearrange them in the sequence in which they had originally been taken. A Spearman rank-order correlation was calculated between each child's arrangement of the photographs and the actual sequence in which they were taken in order to assess 'predictive accuracy'. Although this task is formally similar to the Picture Arrangement subtest of the WISC, predictive accuracy scores did not correlate significantly with either full scale WISC scores ($r = 0.02$) or Picture Arrangement subscores ($r = -0.01$).

Three staff members who knew each child well rated him independently on a questionnaire designed to measure 'the relative social adaptiveness of each boy's responses to various interpersonal situations' (p. 316). This scale consisted of eighteen items selected for their high discriminatory power from the taxonomy of behaviours developed by Berenson (1975) to distinguish between emotionally disturbed and normal children. Estimates of interjudge reliability for these ratings ranged from 0.78 to 0.96. Average scores on this index of 'social adjustment' were found to correlate negatively ($r = -0.36$; $p < .05$) with 'intensity' scores derived from the grid test. As we saw in Chapter 4, the latter is an index of the overall degree of intercorrelation between constructs developed by Bannister (1960), which Hayden *et al.* (1977) interpret as a measure of construct differentiation or 'cognitive complexity' (cf. Radley, 1974).

This result seems consistent with Olson and Partington's (1977) recent finding that the overall degree of intercorrelation between constructs in Kelly's (1955) 'standard' binary grid test correlates negatively ($r = -0.52$; $p < .005$) with 'an individual's ability to reconcile simultaneous different perspectives in an interaction' (p. 14), as measured by Feffer's (1959) *Role Taking Task* (discussed in Chapter 3). It also seems consistent with Adams-Webber's (1969) related finding that the lower the level of overall correlation between constructs in an individual's repertory grid the more accurate he is in inferring the personal constructs of others in a social situation. Hayden *et al.* argue on the basis of their own results that 'the more differentiated the constructs are within a sample of an emotionally disturbed boy's interpersonal conceptual system, the more appropriate that boy's behaviour is in social interchanges' (p. 319). The findings of Olson and Partington (1977) and Adams-Webber (1969) suggest that boys with more differentiated constructs are more effective in social interactions because they can infer the differing points of view of others and reconcile their own perpectives with those of others more effectively. On the other hand, we have seen that the interpretation of the overall level of intercorrelation between constructs in terms of either differentiation or integration is still highly problematic and has varied widely from one study to another (see Chapter 3).

Hayden *et al*. also report that their measure of social adjustment related positively to accuracy in arranging the photographs into their correct sequence ($r = 0.65$; $p < .01$). Thus, 'both differentiation among constructs to interpret the environment and predictive accuracy in anticipating the sequence of human behaviour are associated with an individual's interpersonal adaptiveness' (p. 318). Although predictive accuracy did not correlate significantly with intensity scores derived from the repertory grid ('differentiation'), it did relate positively to the total amount of variation in the grid ($r = 0.43$; $p < .02$) and negatively to 'bias' ($r = -0.55$; $p < .02$), that is, 'gravitation of ratings toward one pole' ('lopsidedness'). This outcome seems consistent with previous findings that construct lopsidedness not only correlates with the degree of relationship between constructs in the grid (Bavelas *et al*., 1976); but it also tends to decrease as children mature and acquire more social experience (Applebee, 1975; Barratt, 1977a); is more prevalent in the grids of primary psychopaths (Widom, 1976) and chronic schizophrenics (Radley, 1974) than in those of normals; and relates negatively to stability over time in one's interpersonal judgements (Adams-Webber and Benjafield, 1974; Benjafield and Adams-Webber, 1975; Clyne, 1975; Cochran, 1976a). Reker (1974) also reports that his sample of emotionally disturbed boys exhibited less consistency than normals in construing people from one situation to the next. He suggests that this may be a factor in the unstable patterns of friendship characteristic of emotionally disturbed children (cf. Davids and Parenti, 1958).

Hayden *et al*. also found that, with age partialled-out, differentiation and lopsidedness were negatively correlated ($r = -0.64$; $p < .01$), which is consistent with Bavelas *et al*. (1976). Surprisingly, differentiation increased significantly with age and lopsidedness did not decrease. In previous studies with normal children exactly the opposite results have been obtained; that is, lopsidedness has tended to decrease with age while differentiation showed no significant increase (Applebee, 1975, 1976; Barratt, 1977a). This discrepancy might reflect differences between normal and disturbed children (e.g. different rates of social development at comparable ages) and/or measurement procedures. Hopefully, it will be clarified by further research.

Hayden *et al*. (p. 319) offer the following concise summary of the observed pattern of correlations among their measures of social adjustment, predictive accuracy, and the structural characteristics of individual personal construct systems:

The more accurate an emotionally disturbed boy is in predicting the sequence of another person's behaviour, the more appropriate his behaviour is in social situations in general. Furthermore, the discriminatory capacity of discrete constructs within one's interpersonal conceptual system is related to one's relative accuracy in anticipating the sequence of another person's behaviour. Thus, when the child's person preceptions lack discriminability, then those social predictions facilitating effective social interactions similarly suffer.

Thus their research establishes a direct link between the structural characteristics of an individual's personal construct system and independent observations of his behaviour. Although comparisons between groups, for example, emotionally disturbed children and normal ones (Reker, 1974) in terms of repertory grid indices alone are useful in evaluating the construct validity of this instrument, and can provide helpful diagnostic cues and even hints concerning aetiology; studies which correlate measures of conceptual organization directly with specific behaviours are essential for planning and assessing the outcomes of treatment programmes. This kind of work also has greater theoretical importance. As Hayden *et al.* point out, 'if behaviour is related to the way in which the environment is perceived and interpreted, there should be a relation between the nature of conceptual structures of individuals and their behaviour in the environment' (p. 315). It is clear that more of this kind of work is much needed at this stage in the development of personal construct theory.

THE DEVELOPMENT OF SOCIALITY

There is now considerable evidence that, as children gain experience in interpreting their social environment, systematic changes occur in the content as well as the structure of their personal construct systems. As Crockett and Meisel (1974) point out, Kelly assumed that interpersonal constructs 'develop out of the perceiver's experience with other people and with socially shared interpretations of people's behaviour' (p. 290). One important question is how early do children begin to establish their own personal contexts of meaning which they can identify as their own as distinct from those of others. A recent experiment by Bannister and Agnew (1977) has thrown some light on this issue.

They randomly selected thirty-six children from the register of an English primary school in six different age and sex groups so as to comprise six boys at each of three different ages—5, 7, and 9—and three groups of six girls at equivalent ages. Each group met for an initial session during which every child answered ten questions, for example, 'What do you do at school?', 'What is your teacher like?', etc. All of their answers were tape-recorded and transcribed, removing all cues as to the identities of the children. They were then rerecorded in random order by a single adult. Approximately one month following the group session, the children were interviewed individually. After listening to all six answers to each question twice, they were asked to identify their own contribution. They were also asked why they thought the answer which they had selected was their own, and to indicate which one of the remaining five answers they were most certain was not theirs and why they were sure of this.

Bannister and Agnew found that the children's accuracy in identifying their own statements increased significantly with age. Subsequently, three judges independently considered each answer in terms of whether it was a 'somewhat unusual response differing from the common run of responses of the children in some way'. The judges exhibited 80 per cent agreement in classifying the children's responses as either 'individual' or 'less individual'. Those statements which were designated as 'individual' by at least two judges were labelled as such,

Of the fifty-nine 'individual' statements, thirty-four (58 per cent) were identified correctly by the children who made them; whereas of 301 statements classified as 'less individual', 116 (39 per cent) were correctly identified. Thus, the children were significantly ($p < .001$) more accurate in identifying their own idiosyncratic constructions than they were in recognizing their common constructions. Unfortunately, it is not reported whether older children made more 'individual' statements than younger ones. It is possible that the older children were more successful in identifying their own statements because they were more 'individualistic' in their comments in the first place.

Bannister and Agnew also report that the type of reasons given by children for recognizing or rejecting particular statements varied across age groups:

Examination of the contents of the table [see Table 13] suggests that children make progressively less use of simple memory, whether they see good or bad features in the elements of the statement, or whether they see the activities indicated in the statement as ones which they undertake or not. In complementary fashion, older children made more use of like-dislike aspects of elements in the statement, its general psychological appropriateness to them, and the impossibility or certainty of the assertion as far as they are concerned. (p. 112)

These preliminary findings lend support to the general hypothesis that as children mature socially they develop a 'reflexive' capacity to identify idiosyncratic aspects of their own construction processes. At this time, however, there is very little evidence to go on in speculating how children learn to recognize features of their own personal constructions as unique. Bannister and Agnew's research attempts to come to grips with what is a central problem in personal construct theory, which has been avoided by most investigators, possibly because of the difficulties encountered in eliciting constructions from very young children

Table 13. Frequency of use of different strategies for identifying 'me' and 'not me' statements

Strategy used	5-year-olds	7-year-olds	9-year-olds
1. Activity undertaken or not	48	15	18
2. Good or bad feature of the element	15	13	5
3. Remembered	82	29	22
4. Like-dislike some aspect	33	67	64
5. Simple repetition of statement	11	13	13
6. 'Psychologically' appropriate or inappropriate	8	49	54
7. Impossibility of certainty of an aspect	40	54	63
8. Unclassifiable	3	0	1

(Reproduced by permission of The University of Nebraska Press from Bannister, D., and Agnew, J., 'The child's construing of self', in Cole, J. K., and Landfield, A. W., *Nebraska Symposium on Motivation, 1976: Personal Construct Psychology*.)

and reliably measuring individual differences in conceptual processes at early stages in their development (cf. Salmon, 1976). The highly innovative approach employed by Bannister and Agnew may provide a basis for the rapid expansion of work in this area.

Several other developmental studies, which more or less pick up at the same age as Bannister and Agnew stop, suggest that 'psychological constructs' are relatively late in emerging. Little (1968) classified the constructs elicited from British children in terms of three categories: (1) *psychological*—concerned with character, personality, or psychological attributes; (2) *physicalistic*—describing outward appearance; and (3) *role*—dealing with habitual roles, acts, or behaviour. He found that children aged about 11 use predominantly physicalistic constructs to describe people. In mid-adolescence, psychological constructs are more prevalent. He also reports that girls use more psychological constructs than boys of the same age.

Brierley (1967) expanded Little's system of classification to six categories: (1) *kinship* (e.g. 'They are not in our family.'); (2) *social role* (e.g. 'They are my best friends.'); (3) *appearance* (e.g. 'She looked untidy this morning.'); (4) *behaviour* (e.g. 'He plays football after school.'); (5) *personality* (e.g. 'Mary has a lot of will power.'); and (6) *literal* (e.g. 'They have the same last name.'). She used this system to classify the personal constructs of ninety British school children aged 7, 10, and 13. The relative frequency of social role, appearance, and literal constructs was found to decrease significantly across these three age groups, while that of behaviour and personality constructs significantly increased. The percentage of kinship constructs decreased with age, but not significantly. The seven-year-old children used predominantly social role and appearance constructs; ten-year-olds used mostly appearance and behaviour constructs; and thirteen-year-olds employed almost entirely behaviour and personality constructs. Both Little and Brierley agree that girls use more personality (psychological) constructs than boys, and that adolescent boys place more emphasis than girls on role and behaviour constructs.

In a recent study in the US, Barratt (1977b) classified the personal constructs elicited from sixty-four elementary school children selected in four different age groups: 8, 10, 12, and 14—with eight girls and eight boys in each group. A list of seventeen role titles, including *self, ideal self,* seven same-sex peers, and eight opposite-sex peers, was used to elicit a list of figures from each child. Kelly's method of triads was employed to elicit ten constructs from every child individually. These constructs were classified on the basis of a slightly condensed version of Brierley's set of categories: (1) *appearance or physique*; (2) *social role*; (3) *behaviour*; and (4) *personality*. He reports an interrater reliability of 0.91 for this system.

As in Brierley's study, the combined frequency of usage of appearance and social role constructs declined with increasing age, and there was a corresponding increase in the relative frequency of behaviour and personality constructs. Barratt's data indicate, however, that the use of behaviour constructs declined in the two older age groups, whereas in Brierley's sample it was still increasing from

10 to 13. In all three studies, the percentage of personality constructs increased steadily with age, and girls tended to use more personality constructs than boys. In Brierley's survey girls were using more personality constructs than any other kind by thirteen, while boys of the same age were still using predominantly behaviour constructs. Barratt's results suggest essentially the same pattern of development: by age 12, girls were using significantly more personality than behaviour constructs, while this shift did not occur for boys until age 14.

For both British and American samples there is evidence of a progressive decrease in the relative importance of appearance and social role constructs from approximately 7–8 years of age to about 13–14 years, accompanied by a steady increase in the use of personality constructs. In the very youngest age groups, 7 and younger, appearance and social role constructs were used more frequently than behaviour constructs; at intermediate ages, 8–10, behaviour constructs were used most frequently, and during puberty and early adolescence, from 12–14, the use of personality constructs increased dramatically, especially for girls. Barratt hypothesizes on the basis of this evidence that there may be two major transition points: the first from about 6–8 years, when appearance and social role constructs are superseded by behaviour constructs, and the second between 11–13, in which there is a marked increase in the use of personality constructs that is more pronounced for girls than for boys.

Barratt also classified constructs on the basis of their *descriptiveness, personal involvement,* and *depth*, using the *Personal Concept Code* devised by Peevers and Secord (1973). *Discriptiveness* refers to the quality of the information which a construct provides. It consists of four categories: (1) *undifferentiating* (e.g. 'He lives around here.'); (2) *simple differentiating* (e.g. 'They are nice.'); (3) *differentiating* (e.g. 'She is great at maths.'); and (4) *dispositional* (e.g. 'They are real egotists.'). He reports an interrater reliability of 0.82 for this classification.

The results indicated 'a developmental progression from the predominant use of undifferentiating and simple differentiating items toward the use of differentiating and dispositional constructs . . . girls are more advanced than boys at 12 and 14, but not at 8 and 10 when boys seem to be marginally more advanced'. Thus, the observed increases in terms of 'descriptiveness' are closely parallel to the increases in the use of behaviour and personality constructs and decreases in the use of appearance and social role constructs from 8–14. Barratt notes that his results are consistent with previous evidence that there is an increase in the use of 'inferential concepts' in peer perception throughout late childhood and early adolescence (Gollin, 1958; Yarrow and Campbell, 1963).

Personal involvement refers to whether the *self* is part of the construct's frame of reference. Each construct was categorized as either 'egocentric' (e.g. 'I can run faster than he can.') or 'other-oriented' (e.g. 'She is very athletic.'). Barratt reports an interrater reliability of 0.98 for this index. He observed an increase with age in the relative preponderance of 'other-oriented' consructs, which he points out is consistent with the results of Scarlett, Press, and Crockett (1971, discussed below).

Depth refers to the extent to which a construct 'exemplifies sophistication of insight and attribution'. Each construct was assigned to one of three levels: (1) e.g. 'She is mean.'; (2) e.g. 'They are usually mean but sometimes they can be pretty generous.'; (3) e.g. 'He is mean, but that is because everyone used to bully him a lot'. Level 3 is assumed to indicate that there is some degree of 'elaboration of a personal theory of human personality and behaviour'. Barratt found an interrater reliability of 0.87 for this code. He reports that, despite explicit probing for 'attributional explanations', no level 3 constructs were elicited from children under 12. Also, no level 3 constructs were obtained from any boy under 14. He did observe, however, a significant increase with age in 'mean depth level'; and again, girls scored higher than boys across all ages.

Barratt argues that 'the results for the depth dimension clearly suggest that it is only when children enter puberty or early adolescence that they acquire, in any meaningful sense, the ability to generate hypothetical explanations for the characteristics which they attribute to peers'. During adolescence there seem to be simultaneous increases in the use of personality constructs, the level of descriptiveness of constructs and the ability to give reasons for attributing specific traits to oneself and others. Also girls appear to develop more quickly than do boys with respect to all three aspects of sociality, presumably because of a greater interest in interpersonal relations.

Duck (1975) employed yet another system for categorizing the constructs elicited from adolescents, which he derived partly from the systems of Little and Brierley and partly from a more recent one developed by Landfield (1971). Duck's system includes one category not employed at all by Little, Brierley, or Barratt, but used extensively by Landfield: *fact constructs* are ones 'concerned with descriptions of others in terms of characteristics objectively assessable, but not solely related to physical appearance (e.g. married-unmarried)'. Duck retained Little's *physical, role,* and *psychological* categories, and added his own *interaction* category for constructs which 'focus on behaviour in face-to-face ongoing social interaction' (e.g. *shy with people-talkative in company*).

He used this system to classify the constructs elicited from ninety-seven British school children (fifty-one girls and forty-six boys). There were three groups: (1) *early adolescence* (mean age 12 years, 3 months); (2) *mid-adolescence* (mean age 14 years, 2 months); (3) *later adolescence* (mean age 15 years, 2 months). A modification of Kelly's method of triads in which each triad was presented three times was used to elicit fifteen constructs individually from each child. Every child's list of constructs was classified in terms of the five categories listed above. The interrater reliability for three independent judges was highly significant (binomial test; $z = 9.176$).

As in all previous studies, there was a progressive increase across age groups in the percentage of psychological (personality) constructs elicited. At 12, physical constructs were still being used more frequently than psychological, role, and interaction constructs combined. By 14, psychological constructs had surpassed role, physical, and interaction constructs. Fact constructs were used more frequently than any other kind at every age level; however, the percentage of fact constructs declined steadily with increasing age. Duck interprets these findings as indicating that the 'pattern of personality development observed by other investigators (Little, 1968; Brierley, 1967) is implicitly confirmed in this study' (p. 361). His results do differ, however, from those of previous studies in one respect. Girls did not employ more psychological constructs than boys. On the other hand, Duck's findings agree with Little's in providing evidence that adolescent boys tend to use a greater percentage of role constructs than girls.

The major new finding produced by Duck's research in this area is that different types of constructs relate to friendship choices at various ages. After eliciting constructs from his subjects, he employed standard sociometric technique to make up lists of 'friends in this class' for every boy and girl. For this purpose each age group was treated as a separate population. Also, since there were only two cross-sex choices overall, and these were not reciprocated, the data for each sex were analysed independently. All cases in which a particular subject both chose and was chosen as a friend by another member of the same population were recorded as 'friendship pairs' for that subject, as distinct from 'nominal pairs', which included all other possible pairings for that subject with other members of the same population. Next, all constructs elicited from each subject were compared in terms of their similarity to the constructs elicited from all other children in the same population. Two constructs were judged to be similar if they both expressed the same concept in the same or different words: thus, 'not only would *male-female* be counted as similar to *female-male*, but also *reserved in company-unreserved* would be counted as similar to *shy in company-not shy*' (p. 357). The interrater reliability for these judgements was high (Kendall's $W = 0.78$). These data provided the basis for determining whether higher levels of construct similarity occurred in the friendship or nominal pairs of which each subject was a member (see Chapter 5).

Duck computed separately for each subject a single score representing the mean number of similarities between himself and his 'friends' and a second score representing the mean number of similarities between himself and those members of the same population who were not his friends. In all three age groups, and for both boys and girls, there was a significantly higher level of construct similarity (commonality) in the friendship pairs than in the nominal pairs. This is consistent with the results of previous research—discussed in Chapter 5—which has demonstrated that construct similarity relates to friendship choice with adults (Duck and Spencer, 1972; Duck 1973).

Duck also determined whether the relationship between construct similarity and friendship choice at each age level was different for different categories of personal constructs. His results indicated that 'in the case of the boys the basis is shifted from fact to interaction to physical constructs and in the case of girls from fact and physical to psychological and physical' (p. 359). Thus, for both girls and boys friendship choice was found to relate to similarity in terms of fact constructs in early adolescence. Later on, the trends diverge with 'girls' friendships typified by concensus on psychological constructs when boys' friendships are not' (p. 359). Duck points out that these findings do not reflect merely increases with age in the relative frequency of particular kinds of constructs because this is comparable for boys and girls. He concludes that 'it is *similarities* between constructs of particular types (rather than absolute numbers) which are associated with friendship choices of adolescents at different ages' (pp. 359–360).

As we saw in Chapter 5, Duck and Spencer (1972) showed that construct similarities predated friendship formation in a sample of British adults of both sexes, with the friends becoming more similar to each other as their relationship progressed over time. They observed also that, although similarity in terms of the whole set of constructs elicited from individuals predicted who would eventually become friends in a previously unacquainted population, it was similarity of those constructs which related to the psychological description of others that ultimately differentiated established friendship pairs from affectively neutral pairs. Duck (1975) hypothesizes that an individual generally seeks to validate his constructions of events by comparing them with the constructions of others and, therefore, the discovery of similarity between one's own constructs and those of another person is perceived as validation through consensus. Such recognition depends, of course, on the degree of psychological similarity (commonality) between individuals.

Duck further suggests that in late adolescence a relative lessening of reliance on 'fact' constructs and an increased emphasis on 'psychological' constructs in interpreting behaviour leads to greater uncertainty. He argues that 'adolescents inevitably experience the invalidation of these new (psychological) constructs to a greater extent than they have known previously with their more mundane and familiar fact, physical and role constructs' (p. 362). Therefore, they begin, according to Duck, to seek as friends people whom they perceive as using constructs which are similar to their own so as to increase their opportunities of obtaining validational support for their social construing. This hypothesis clearly implies that each individual in the course of his social development becomes increasingly aware of differences between people with respect to the personal constructs which they customarily use to structure their interpersonal relations. This is consistent with Kelly's (1970) definition of sociality, which asserts that 'to the extent that one person construes the construction processes of another he may play a role in a social process involving the other (sociality corollary)'. It follows that an individual's social development involves the acquisition of increasing skill in discriminating between persons on the basis of their personal constructs (Adams-Webber *et al.*, 1972).

An earlier study of developmental changes in the content of the 'interpersonal constructs' which children use to describe their peers was carried out by Scarlett, Press, and Crockett (1971). They hypothesized that with increasing age, differences in the way that children structure their impressions of others would follow Werner's 'orthogenetic principle' (discussed in Chapter 1) which states that 'whenever development occurs, it proceeds from a state of relative globality and lack of differentiation to a state of increasing differentiation, articulation, and hierarchic integration' (Werner, 1956, p. 126). Scarlett *et al.* submit

Applied to impression formation, this principle suggests that increasingly detailed and hierarchically organized impressions will characterize more mature individuals, whereas young children will form impressions reflecting the more global, undifferentiated and unintegrated organizations of their cognitive systems. Adopting Kelly's position (1955) that an individual's interpersonal constructs are the psychological elements with which his impressions of others are structured, it becomes necessary to consider the types of changes these constructs should undergo with increasing development. (p. 439)

They hypothesized specifically that (1) there will be an increase with age in the absolute number of interpersonal constructs that an individual uses to describe his peers (Crockett's (1965) operational definition of 'cognitive complexity' discussed in Chapter 3); (2) complex hierarchical patterns of relationship will develop among these constructs which will require qualitative changes in the nature of the constructs themselves, including a shift from a relatively egocentric mode of description to a non-egocentric mode, and from a concrete to an abstract mode; and (3) these indices of 'higher level impressions' will appear first, and will continue more pronounced in descriptions of others with whom the individual interacts most frequently.

One hundred and eight American boys in grades 1, 3, and 5 of three catholic elementary schools were interviewed individually. Each boy was asked to describe four persons in turn: a boy whom he liked, a boy he disliked, a girl he liked, and a girl he disliked. These characterizations were scored on the basis of the following set of categories: (a) *concrete-we constructs*—the subject did not distinguish between himself and the other, but described what they do together (e.g. 'We play together.'); (b) *egocentric concrete constructs*—the subject was both concrete in describing what the other person does in particular contexts, and egocentric, in that the object of the sentence was the describer himself (e.g. 'He hits me.'); (c) *non-egocentric concrete constructs*—the subject referred to concrete behaviours, but did not include himself in the sentence (e.g. 'He plays baseball.'); (d) *abstract constructs*—the subject referred to abstract attributes of the other person, i.e. qualities that were not limited to a specific context (e.g. 'He is kind.'). They report an interrater agreement of 80 per cent for this classification between two independent judges.

As hypothesized, there was a highly significant increase with age in the average number of constructs used to describe peers. They report that 'the linear component of this sum of squares accounted for virtually all the variance among the means; thus, there was no indication that the degree of differentiation of interpersonal constructs was approaching a limit for the age groups represented in this study' (p. 450). Also, as hypothesized, the modal kind of construct used by subjects to describe peers varied with age. First-grade boys used predominantly egocentric-concrete constructs, with non-egocentric-concrete constructs the next most common. Third graders also used egocentric-concrete constructs most frequently, followed by non-egocentric concrete constructs; however, they used proportionately more non-egocentric constructs—both concrete and abstract—than the first-graders. Abstract constructs were used most often by the fifth-graders, followed by non-egocentric-concrete ones. 'Thus, the expected developmental trend occurred: third-grade boys, compared to first-graders, showed proportionately more non-egocentric constructs of both types, while fifth-grade boys had shifted from egocentric to a non-egocentric and from a concrete to a relatively abstract mode of representation' (p. 451). The operational definitions of 'abstract' and 'concrete' constructs used in this study parallel closely those of 'psychological' (personality) and 'behaviour' constructs employed in the investigations of Brierley (1967), Little (1968), and Barratt (1977b), and the observed developmental trend is quite similar except that the shift from 'concrete' (behaviour) constructs to 'abstract' (psychological) constructs seems to have begun at a slightly earlier age for the subjects in Scarlett *et al.*'s sample (approximately 9–11) than for Brierley's subjects (about 13) and Barratt's subjects (about 14).

Both Barratt and Scarlett *et al.* tested elementary-school children in Massachusetts, whereas Brierley tested British children. It is possible that the observed differences reflect cultural or socio-economic background factors; however, it seems more likely that they could have arisen from the use of different methods of eliciting constructs. Scarlett *et al.* used Crockett's 'free description' method (see Chapter 3) and Barratt employed Kelly's method of triads. The latter limits the number of constructs elicited to the number of triads presented. Scarlett *et al.* found that, among their fifth-graders, those who employed many constructs to describe their peers employed more abstract (psychological) constructs than subjects who tended to use relatively few constructs. Thus, Scarlett *et al.*'s procedures may have resulted in more constructs having been elicited from fifth-graders in general, and especially from 'differentiated' (cognitively complex) fifth-graders who tend to use more constructs (Crockett, 1965), and also more abstract constructs to interpret behaviour. Barratt's finding that there is an increase with age in the relative preponderance of 'other oriented' constructs is parallel to Scarlett *et al.*'s finding that the proportion of non-egocentric constructs increases with age.

Finally, their third hypothesis was not confirmed: 'instead of higher level constructs being used at all ages to describe those whom the subjects knew best and saw most often, it appears that subjects described those whom they knew best with a disproportionate number of constructs that were *typical of their own level of development*'. For example, fifth-graders tend to use abstract constructs to describe those peers with whom they interact most frequently. This seems consistent with Duck's (1975) finding that the constructs which are most important in friendship formation among adolescents are those which are typical of their developmental level.

The variety of research topics discussed in the previous sections of this chapter indicates the rapid extension of the range of convenience of personal construct theory. The sequence of studies reviewed in this final section suggests that the focus of convenience of this theory, that is, the sector in which it provides the most efficient predictive coverage, may become the investigation of individual social development in terms of both the structure and content of personal construct systems. This is consistent with Kelly's original emphasis upon the importance of interpersonal relations in the development of individual conceptual structures, which has been the central theme of this volume.

Afterword

We have seen that the main focus of research in the psychology of personal constructs has been the formal analysis of changes in individual conceptual structures. Most of this work has been based on some form of repertory grid measurement, and has emphasized the role of interpersonal relations in both the development and collapse of cognitive organization. Recently, several major strands of investigation have begun to converge upon a single set of theoretical principles, which can be seen as governing all progressive variations within personal construct systems.

The normal course of development of an individual's interpersonal construct system, or 'implicit personality theory', can be viewed from the standpoint of this model as an evolutionary process involving the progressive differentiation of structure in terms of independently organized subsystems and the hierarchical integration of the functions of these subsystems at increasingly higher levels of abstraction. This model contains explicit parallels with the developmental theories of Piaget and Werner. Kelly, Piaget, and Werner all imply that the differentiation of substructures serves gradually to increase the deployability and scope of a cognitive system with respect to the *variety* of events which can be meaningfully discriminated within its framework. They also regard the hierarchical integration of the functions of different substructures, which can operate independently at lower levels of abstraction, within the context of superordinate structures as allowing the person to maintain a thread of consistency throughout his experience as a whole. However, according to Kelly, overall *unity* can only be sustained within the context of permeable superordinate constructs, that is, constructs to whose ranges of convenience new subordinate elements can be added discriminately.

When superordinate structures are too impermeable to subsume newly emerging substructures and thereby maintain coherence at the highest levels of abstraction, the structure of the system can become increasingly fragmented under the pressure of events until it no longer functions as an operational whole. Eventually, organized thought and action may be no longer possible, that is, the

212

individual can become clinically thought-disordered. Thus, within the framework of Kelly's model, the disintegration of conceptual processes can be accounted for in terms of the same principles that are used to explain normal cognitive development.

Although the original context of personal construct theory was psychotherapy, relatively little formal research has been done in this area. Several studies have focused upon the relationship between client and therapist in individual therapy and relations among clients in group therapy. Repertory grid techniques have been used to evaluate the therapist's skill in subsuming the constructions of the client and his ability to understand what the client's own language means to him. This problem has proved to be especially significant in attempts to restructure the thinking of psychotic clients. There is some evidence that similarities and differences between therapist and client in terms of both the structure and content of their personal construct systems may influence the outcome of therapy. This is hardly surprising in the light of the fact that similarity with respect to personal constructs plays a major role in friendship formation.

The range of convenience of personal construct theory has been extended in several directions during the last decade, including research in city planning, urban geography, architectural design, experimental aesthetics, dramatic criticism, and political debate. Perhaps the most promising new area of investigation is the systematic assessment of developmental changes in the kinds of personal constructs which are used to structure one's social environment and the implications of such changes in the field of interpersonal relations. This work is rapidly emerging as a focus of convenience of Kelly's unique model of social cognition.

In general, attempts to find behavioural correlates for various indices of individual differences in conceptual structure have produced only modest results. The most successful studies of this type have involved the evaluation of specialized treatment programmes based on principles of personal construct theory and dealing with specific problems, e.g. stuttering. Perhaps the main obstacle to progress in this area has been the indiscriminant use of grid techniques.

Considerable confusion has arisen because of a general disregard for basic issues of reliability and validity in developing operational definitions for specific constructs, such as *differentiation*, within the context of personal construct theory. This problem has been exacerbated by the widespread use of grid tests to assess a range of variables which have no logical relation at all to personal construct theory. It seems unlikely that any 'breakthroughs' will occur before these measurement problems are resolved. Until then, conceptual confusion will continue, and we shall frequently encounter a lack of 'fit' between problem and method.

Nevertheless, research activity in personal construct theory has increased at a steady rate during the last three decades in spite of these methodological problems. Perhaps interest in this theory has continued to grow because Kelly's constructive alternativism offers a viable approach to psychologists who are interested in making sense of human experience as well as anticipating behaviour. Skinner has developed the assumptions of 'American Behaviourism', both technically and philosophically, to the point where its logical possibilities should be clear to anyone who takes the trouble to study it carefully. Many psychologists, especially those concerned with 'perception' and 'thinking', have turned away from this paradigm, not because they think that it does not 'work', but rather because they are interested in those aspects of human experience which cannot in principle be reduced to the record of inputs to the organism and its past history of reinforcement.

Kelly has offered us an even more radical form of 'behaviourism', that is, a psychology in which our own behaviour is the independent rather than the dependent variable. This notion is so appealing to psychologists that, as Kelly noted, the introductory chapters of many textbooks in the field include an elaborate account of the scientific activities of psychologists themselves. Thus, it is perhaps not so surprising that an increasing number of psychologists are beginning to explore the broader range of convenience of Kelly's model of 'scientist-like' behaviour.

'The whole of science is nothing more than a refinement of everyday thinking'—Einstein, *Physics and Reality*.

References

Adams-Webber, J. (1968). Construct and figure interactions within a personal construct system: an extension of repertory grid technique. Unpublished Ph.D. thesis, Brandeis University.

Adams-Webber, J. (1969). Cognitive complexity and sociality. *Br. J. soc. clin. Psychol.*, **8**, 211–216.

Adams-Webber, J. (1970a). Actual structure and potential chaos. In D. Bannister (Ed.), *Perspectives in Personal Construct Theory*. London: Academic Press.

Adams-Webber, J. (1970b). Elicited versus provided constructs in repertory grid technique: a review. *Br. J. med. Psychol.*, **43**, 349–354.

Adams-Webber, J. (1970c). An analysis of the discriminant validity of several repertory grid indices. *Br. J. Psychol.*, **61**, 83–90.

Adams-Webber, J. (1973). The complexity of the target as a factor in interpersonal judgment. *Soc. Behav. Pers.*, **1**, 35–38.

Adams-Webber, J. (1976). Unpublished data, Brock University.

Adams-Webber, J. (1977a). The organization of judgments based on positive and negative adjectives in the Bannister–Fransella Grid Test. *Br. J. med. Psychol.*, **50**, 173–176.

Adams-Webber, J. (1977b). The golden section and the structure of self concepts. *Prcptl. Mtr. Skls.*, **45**, 703–706.

Adams-Webber, J. (1977c). Assimilation and contrast in dichotomous construction processes. Presented at the Second International Congress on Personal Construct Psychology, Oxford University.

Adams-Webber, J. (in press). A further test of the golden section hypothesis. *Br. J. Psychol.*

Adams-Webber, J. and Benjafield, J. (1972). Linguistic properties of personal constructs. Presented at the Annual Conference of the Canadian Chapter of the International Association of Cross-Cultural Psychology, Brock University.

Adams-Webber, J. and Benjafield, J. (1973). The relation between lexical marking and rating extremity in interpersonal judgment. *Can. J. behav. Sci.*, **5**, 234–241.

Adams-Webber, J. and Benjafield, J. (1974). Pollyanna's private self. Presented at the Annual Meeting of the Canadian Psychological Association, Windsor.

Adams-Webber, J. and Benjafield, J. (1976). The relationship between cognitive complexity and assimilative projection in terms of personal constructs. Presented at the Annual Conference of the British Psychological Society, University of York.

Adams-Webber, J., Benjafield, J., Doan, B., and Giesbrecht, L. (1975). Construct maldistribution, memory for adjectives and concept utilization. Unpublished manuscript, Brock University.

215

Adams-Webber, J. and Davidson, D. (1978). Unpublished data. Brock University.

Adams-Webber, J. and Mirc, E. (1976a). Assessing the development of student teachers' role conceptions. *Br. J. ed. Psychol.*, **46**, 338–340.

Adams-Webber, J. and Mirc, E. (1976b). Student teachers' conceptions of their future professional roles. Annual Meeting of the American Psychological Association, Washington, D.C.

Adams-Webber, J. and Mirc, E. (1976c). The development of student teachers' role concept subsystems. Annual Conference of the British Psychological Society, University of York.

Adams-Webber, J., Schwenker, B., and Barbeau, D. (1972). Personal constructs and the perception of individual differences. *Can. J. behav. Sci.*, **4**, 218–224.

Agnew, J. and Bannister, D. (1973). Psychiatric diagnosis as a pseudo-specialist language. *Br. J. med. Psychol.*, **46**, 69–73.

Allport, G. (1958). What units shall we employ? In G. Lindzey (Ed.), *The Assessment of Human Motives*. New York: Rinehart.

Allport, G. (1965) *Letters from Jenny*. New York: Harcourt, Brace & World.

Applebee, A. N. (1975). Developmental changes in consensus in construing within a specified domain. *Br. J. Psychol.*, **66**, 473–480.

Applebee, A. N. (1976). The development of children's responses to repertory grids. *Br. J. soc. clin. Psychol.*, **15**, 101–102.

Ashby, R. W. (1968). The contribution of information theory to pathological mechanisms in psychiatry. *Br. J. Psychiat.*, **114**, 1485–1498.

Attneave, F. (1959). *Applications of Information Theory to Psychology*. New York: Holt, Rinehart & Winston.

Baldwin, B. (1972). Change in interpersonal cognitive complexity as a function of a training group experience. *Psychol. Repts.*, **30**, 935–940.

Bandura, A. (1969). *Principles of Behavior Modification*. New York: Holt, Rinehart & Winston.

Bannister, D. (1959). An application of personal construct theory (Kelly) to schizoid thinking. Unpublished Ph.D. thesis, University of London.

Bannister, D. (1960). Conceptual structure in thought disordered schizophrenics. *J. ment. Sci.*, **106**, 1230–1249.

Bannister, D. (1962a). Personal construct theory: a summary and experimental paradigm. *Acta. Psychologica*, **20**, 104–120.

Bannister, D. (1962b). The nature and measurement of schizophrenic thought disorder. *J. ment. Sci.*, **108**, 825–842.

Bannister, D. (1963). The genesis of schizophrenic thought disorder: a serial invalidation hypothesis. *Br. J. Psychiat.*, **109**, 680–686.

Bannister, D. (1965a). The genesis of schizophrenic thought disorder: a retest of the serial invalidation hypothesis. *Br. J. Psychiat.*, **111**, 377–382.

Bannister, D. (1965b). The rationale and clinical relevance of repertory grid technique. *Br. J. Psychiat.*, **479**, 977–982.

Bannister, D. (1966). A new theory of personality. In B. M. Foss (Ed.), *New Horizons in Psychology*. Harmondsworth, Middlesex: Penguin.

Bannister, D. (1969). The myth of physiological psychology. *Bull. Br. psychol. Soc.*, **21**, 229–231.

Bannister, D. (1972). Critiques of the concept of 'loose construing': a reply. *Br. J. soc. clin. Psychol.*, **11**, 412–414.

Bannister, D. (1976). Grid test of thought disorder. *Br. J. Psychiat.*, **129**, 93.

Bannister, D., Adams-Webber, J., Penn, W., and Radley, A. (1975). Reversing the process of thought disorder: a serial validation experiment. *Br. J. soc. clin. Psychol.*, **14**, 169–180.

Bannister, D. and Agnew, J. (1977). The child's construing of self. In J. K. Cole and

A. W. Landfield (Eds.), *1976 Nebraska Symposium on Motivation*. Lincoln: University of Nebraska Press.

Bannister, D. and Bott, M. (1973). Evaluating the person. In P. Klein (Ed.), *New Approaches in Psychological Measurement*. London: Wiley.

Bannister, D. and Fransella, F. (1966). A grid test of schizophrenic thought disorder. *Br. J. soc. clin. Psychol.*, **5**, 95–102.

Bannister, D. and Fransella, F. (1967). *Grid Test of Schizophrenic Thought Disorder: Manual*. Barnstaple, Devon: Psychological Test Publications.

Bannister, D. and Fransella, F. (1971). *Inquiring Man: The Theory of Personal Constructs*. Harmondsworth, Middlesex: Penguin.

Bannister, D., Fransella, F., and Agnew, J. (1971). Characteristics and validity of the grid test of thought disorder. *Br. J. soc. clin. Psychol.*, **10**, 144–151.

Bannister, D. and Mair, J. M. M. (1968). *The Evaluation of Personal Constructs*. London: Academic press.

Bannister, D. and Salmon, P. (1966). Schizophrenic thought disorder: specific or diffuse? *Br. J. med. Psychol.*, **39**, 215–219.

Bannister, D., Salmon, P., and Lieberman, D. (1964). Diagnosis-treatment relationships in psychiatry: a statistical analysis. *Br. J. Psychiat.*, **110**, 726–732.

Barratt, B. (1977a). The development of organizational complexity and structure in peer perception. Unpublished manuscript, Harvard University.

Barratt. (1977b). The development of peer perception: a content analysis with children from 8 to 14 years. Unpublished manuscript, Harvard University.

Bartlett, F. C. (1932). *Remembering: a Study in Experimental and Social Psychology*. London: Cambridge University Press.

Bartlett, F. C. (1958). *Thinking: An Experimental and Social Study*. London: Unwin University Books.

Bateson, G., Jackson, D., Haley, J., and Weakland, J. (1956). Towards a theory of schizophrenia. *Behav. Sci.*, **1**, 251–264.

Bavelas, J. B., Chan, A. S., and Guthrie, J. A. (1976). Reliability and validity of traits measured by Kelly's repertory grid. *Can. J. behav. Sci.*, **8**, 23–38.

Bender, M.P. (1968a). Friendship formation, stability and communication amongst students. Unpublished M.A. thesis, University of Edinburgh.

Bender, M.P. (1968b). Does construing people as similar involve similar behaviour towards them? *Br. J. soc. clin. Psychol.*, **7**, 303–304.

Bender, M. P. (1974). Provided versus elicited constructs: an explanation of Warr and Coffman's (1970) anomalous finding. *Br. J. soc. clin. Psychol.*, **13**, 329–330.

Bender, M. P. (1976). Does construing people as similar involve similar behaviour towards them? A subjective and objective replication. *Br. J. soc. clin. Psychol.*, **15**, 93–96.

Benjafield, J. (1976). The golden rectangle: some new data. *Amer. J. Psychol.*, **89**, 737–743.

Benjafield, J. and Adams-Webber, J. (1972). Construct preference and social reasoning. Presented at the Annual Conference of the Canadian Chapter of the International Association of Cross-Cultural Psychology, Brock University.

Benjafield, J. and Adams-Webber, J. (1975). Assimilative projection and construct balance. *Br. J. Psychol.*, **66**, 169–173.

Benjafield, J. and Adams-Webber, J. (1976). The golden section hypothesis. *Br. J. Psychol.*, **67**, 11–15.

Benjafield, J. and Doan, B. (1971) Similarities between memory for visually perceived relations and comparative sentences. *Psychonom. Sci.*, **24**, 255–256.

Benjafield, J. and Giesbrecht, L. (1973). Context effects and the recall of comparative sentences. *Mem. Cogn.*, **1**, 133–136.

Benjafield, J. and Green, T. R. G. (1978). Golden section relations in interpersonal judgment. *Br. J. Psychol.*, **69**, 25–35.

Benjafield, J., Jordan, D., and Pomeroy, E. (1976). Encounter groups: a return to the fundamental. *Psychotherapy: Theory, Research and Practice*, **13**, 387–389.

Berenson, J. (1975). Behavior and attitude change in emotionally disturbed children through the combined use of modelling, role-playing and reinforcement. Unpublished Ph.D. thesis, University of Massachusetts.

Berlyne, D. E. (1971). *Aesthetics and Psychobiology*. New York: Appleton-Century-Crofts.

Betak, J. (1977). Personal construct theory and multioperationism in studies of environmental cognition and spatial choice. Presented at the Second International Congress on Personal Construct Theory, Oxford University.

Bieri, J. (1955). Cognitive complexity-simplicity and predictive behavior. *J. abnorm. soc. Psychol.*, **51**, 263–268.

Bieri, J. (1966). Cognitive complexity and personality development. In O. J. Harvey (Ed.), *Experience, Structure and Adaptability*. New York: Springer.

Bieri, J., Atkins, A. L., Briar, S., Leaman, R. L., Miller, H., and Tripodi, T. (1966). *Clinical and Social Judgment*. New York: Wiley.

Bieri, J. and Blacker, E. (1956). The generality of cognitive complexity in the perception of people and inkblots. *J. abnorm. soc. Psychol.*, **53**, 112–117.

Bierwisch, L. (1967). Some semantic universals of German adjectivals. *Foundations of Language*, **3**, 1–36.

Biggs, J. B. (1969). Coding and cognitive behaviour. *Br. J. Psychol.*, **60**, 287–305.

Bodden, J. and James, L. E. (1976). Influence of occupational information giving on cognitive complexity. *J. Counsel. Psychol.*, **23**, 280–282.

Bonarius, J. C. J. (1965). Research in the personal construct theory of George A. Kelly. In B. A. Maher (Ed.), *Progress in Experimental Personality Research*, Vol. 2. New York: Academic Press.

Bonarius, J. C. J. (1966). Persoonlijke constructen als zinvolle beoordelingscategorieën. *Hypothese*, **10**, 70–80.

Bonarius, J. C. J. (1967a). Extreme beoordelingen en persoonlijke constructen: een vergelijking van verschillende indices van extremeit. *Hypothese*, **12**, 46–57.

Bonarius, J. C. J. (1967b). De Fixed Role Therapy van George A. Kelly. *Ned. Tijdschr. Psychol.*, **22**, 482–520.

Bonarius, J. C. J. (1968). Personal constructs and extremity of ratings. In: *Proceedings XVIth International Congress of Applied Psychology*. Amsterdam: Swets and Zeitinger, 595–599.

Bonarius, J. C. J. (1970a). Personal construct psychology and extreme response style: an interaction model of meaningfulness and communication. Doctoral dissertation, University of Groningen, Netherlands.

Bonarius, J. C. J. (1970b). Fixed Role Therapy: a double paradox. *Br. J. med. psychol.*, **43**, 213–219.

Bonarius, J. C. J. (1977). The interaction model of communication: through experimental research towards existential relevance. In J. K. Cole and A. W. Landfield (Eds.), *1976 Nebraska Symposium on Motivation*. Lincoln: University Press.

Bonarius, M. (1968). Henkilökohtaiset konstruktiot ja äärimmäis-luokittelun käyttö. Unpublished data. University of Groningen, Netherlands.

Boucher, J. and Osgood, C. E. (1969). The Pollyanna hypothesis. *J. verb. Lrng. verb. Behav.*, **8**, 1–8.

Brierley, D. W. (1967). The use of personality constructs by children of three different ages. Unpublished Ph.D. thesis, London University.

Brody, J. (1971). Information theory, motivation and personality. In H. Schroder and P. Suedfeld (Eds.), *Personality Theory and Information Processing*. New York: Ronald.

Burdock, E. L. and Hardesty, A. S. (1969). *The Structured Clinical Interview*. New York: Springer.

Caine, T. M. and Smail, D. J. (1969a). *The Treatment of Mental Illness: Science, Faith, and the Therapeutic Personality*. London: University of London Press.

Caine, T. M. and Smail, D. J. (1969b). The effects of personality and training on attitudes to treatment: preliminary investigations. *Br. J. med. Psychol.*, **42**, 277–282.

Cameron, N. (1947). *The Psychology of the Behaviour Disorders*. Boston: Houghton Mifflin.

Cartwright, R. D. and Lerner, B. (1963). Empathy, need to change, and improvement with psychotherapy. *J. consult. Psychol.*, **27**, 138–144.

Clark, H. H. (1969). Linguistic processes in deductive reasoning. *Psychol. Rev.*, **76**, 387–404.

Clark, H. H. and Card, S. K. (1969). Role of semantics in remembering comparative sentences. *J. exper. Psychol.*, **82**, 545–553.

Clyne, S. (1975). The effect of cognitive complexity and assimilative projection on preference for the definitive or extensive role in an elaborative choice situation. Unpublished M.A. thesis, University of Windsor.

Cochran, L. (1976a). Categorization and change in conceptual relatedness. *Can. J. behav. Sci.*, **8**, 275–286.

Cochran, L. (1976b). The effect of inconsistency on the categorization of people. *Soc. Behav. Pers.*, **4**, 33–39.

Cochran, L. (1978). Differences between supplied and elicited considerations in career evaluation. *Soc. Behav. Pers.* (in press).

Craig, G. and Duck, S. W. (1977). Similarity, interpersonal attitudes and attraction: the evaluative descriptive distinction. *Br. J. soc. clin. Psychol.*, **16**, 15–21.

Crockett, W. H. (1965). Cognitive complexity and impression formation. In B. A. Maher (Ed.), *Progress in Experimental Personality Research*, Vol. 2. New York: Academic Press.

Crockett, W. H. and Meisel, P. (1974). Construct connectedness, strength of disconfirmation and impression change. *J. Pers.*, **42**, 290–299.

Cromwell, R. L. and Caldwell, D. F. (1962). A comparison of ratings based on personal constructs of self and others. *J. clin. Psychol.*, **18**, 43–46.

Cronbach, L. J. (1956). Assessment of individual differences. *Ann. Rev. Psychol.*, **7**, 173–176.

Crown, S. and Crisp, A. H. (1966). A short clinical diagnostic self-rating scale for psychoneurotic patients. *Br. J. Psychiat.*, **112**, 917.

Davids, A. and Parenti, A. (1958). Time orientation and interpersonal relations of emotionally disturbed and normal children. *J. abnorm. soc. Psychol.*, **57**, 299–305.

Davidson, T. (1977). The relation between repertory grid maldistribution and TAT hero-other congruence. Unpublished manuscript, Brock University.

Deese, J. (1969). Behavior and fact. *Amer. Psychol.*, **24**, 515–522.

Deese, J. (1973). Cognitive structure and affect in language. In L. Pliner, P. Krames, and T. Alloway (Eds.), *Communication and Affect*. London: Academic Press.

Delia, J. G. and Crockett, W. H. (1973). Social schemas, cognitive complexity and the learning of social structures. *J. Pers.*, **41**, 413–429.

Delia, J. G., Gonyea, A. H., and Crockett, W. H. (1970). The effects of subject-generated and normative constructs upon the formation of impressions. *Br. J. soc. clin. Psychol.*, **10**, 301–305.

Dewey, J. (1896). The reflex arc concept in psychology. *Psychol. Rev.*, **3**, 357–370.

Downs, R. M. (1970). The cognitive structure of an urban shopping centre. *Environment and Behaviour*, **2**, 13–39.

Downs, R. M. (1976). Personal constructions of personal construct theory. In G. T. Moore and R. G. Golledge (Eds.), *Environmental Knowing: Theories, Research and Methods*. Stroudsberg, Pa.: Dowden, Huchinson & Ross.

Duck, S. W. (1973). *Personal Relationships and Personal Constructs: A Study of Friendship Formation*. London: Wiley.

220

Duck (1975). Personality similarity and friendship choices by adolescents. *Eur. J. soc. Psychol.*, **5**, 351–365.

Duck, S. W. (1977). Inquiry, hypothesis and the quest for validation: personal construct systems in the development of acquaintance. In S. W. Duck (Ed.), *Theory and Practice in Interpersonal Attraction*. London: Academic Press.

Duck, S. W. and Spencer, C. (1972). Personal constructs and friendship formation. *J. Pers. soc. Psychol.*, **23**, 40–45.

Du Preez, P. D. (1972). The construction of alternatives in parliamentary debate. *South African J. Psychol.*, **2**, 23–40.

Du Preez, P. D. (1975). The application of Kelly's personal construct theory to the analysis of political debates. *J. soc. Psychol.*, **95**, 267–270.

Du Preez, P. D. (1977). Kelly's 'Matrix of Decision' and the politics of identity. Presented at the Second International Congress on Personal Construct Psychology, Oxford University.

Eiser, J. R. and Mower White, C. J. (1973). Affirmation and denial in evaluative descriptions. *Br. J. Psychol.*, **64**, 399–403.

Eiser, J. R. and Stroebe, W. (1972). *Categorization and Social Judgment*. London: Academic Press.

Ellis, A. (1958). Rational psychotherapy. *J. gen. Psychol.*, **59**, 35–49.

Epting, F., Suchman, D. I., and Nickeson, K. J. (1971). An evaluation of elicitation procedures for personal constructs. *Br. J. Psychol.*, **62**, 513–517.

Epting, F. and Wilkins, G. (1974). Comparison of cognitive structural measures for predicting person perception. *Percptl. Mtr. Skls.*, **38**, 727–730.

Erickson, C. W. and Wechsler, H. (1955). Some effects of experimentally induced anxiety upon discrimination. *J. abnorm. soc. Psychol.*, **51**, 458–463.

Fager, R. E. (1954). Communication in personal construct theory. Unpublished Ph.D. thesis, Ohio State University.

Fechner, G. T. (1876). *Vorschule der Ästhetik*. Leipzig: Breitkopt & Härtel.

Feffer, M. (1959). The cognitive implications of role-taking behavior. *J. Pers.*, **27**, 152–168.

Feffer, M. (1970). Developmental analysis of interpersonal behaviour. *Psychol. Rev.*, **77**, 197–214.

Feffer, M. and Suchotliff, L. (1966). Decentering implications of social interaction. *J. Pers. soc. Psychol.*, **4**, 415–422.

Ferguson, J. T., Mc Reynolds, P., and Bellachy, F. (1951). *The Hospital Adjustment Scale*. Palo Alto, Calif.: Consulting Psychologists Press.

Fjeld, S. P. and Landfield, A. E. (1961). Personal construct consistency. *Psychol. Rep.*, **8**, 127–129.

Frank, H. (1959). *Grundlagenprobleme der Informationästhetik und erste Anwendung auf die mime pure*. Quickborn: Schnelle.

Frank, H. (1964). *Kybernetische Analysen subjektiver Sachverhalte*. Quickborn: Schnelle.

Fransella, F. (1968). Self concepts and the stutterer. *Br. J. Psychiat.*, **114**, 1531–1535.

Fransella, F. (1969). The stutterer as subject or object? In B. B. Gray and G. England (Eds.), *Stuttering and the Conditioning Therapies*. Monterey, Calif.: Institute of Speech and Hearing.

Fransella, F. (1970). . . . And then there was one. In D. Bannister (Ed.), *Perspectives in Personal Construct Theory*. London: Academic Press.

Fransella, F. (1972). *Personal Change and Reconstruction*. London: Academic Press.

Fransella, F. and Adams, B. (1966). An illustration of the use of repertory grid technique in a clinical setting. *Br. J. soc. clin. Psychol.*, **5**, 51–62.

Fransella, F. and Bannister, D. (1967). A validation of repertory grid technique as a measure of political construing. *Acta Psychologica*, **26**, 97–106.

Fransella, F. and Bannister, D. (1977). *A Manual for Repertory Grid Technique*. London: Academic Press.

Fransella, F. and Joyston-Bechal, M. P. (1971). An investigation of conceptual process and pattern change in a psychotherapy group. *Br. J. Psychiat.*, **119**, 199–206.

Friendly, M. L. and Glucksberg, S. (1970). On the descriptions of subcultural lexicons: a multidimensional approach. *J. Pers. soc. Psychol*, **14**, 55–65.

Frith, C. E. and Lillie, F. J. (1972). Why does the repertory grid indicate thought disorder? *Br. J. soc. clin. Psychol.*, **11**, 73–78.

Garner, W. R. (1962). *Uncertainty and Structure as Psychological Concepts.* New York: Wiley.

Garside, R. F. and Van der Spuy, H. I. J. (1968). Unpublished data, cited in Slater, P. (1972). The measurement of consistency in repertory grids. *Br. J. Psychiat.*, **121**, 45–51.

Gathercole, C. E., Bromley, E., and Ashcroft, J. B. (1970). The reliability of repertory grids. *J. clin Psychol.*, **26**, 513–516.

Gollin, E. S. (1958). Organizational characteristics of social judgment: a developmental investigation. *J. Pers.*, **26**, 139–154.

Greenberg, J. H. (1966). *Language Universals.* The Hague: Mouton.

Halpern, H. M. and Lesser, L. N. (1960). Empathy in infants, adults, and psychotherapist. *Psychoanalysis and the Psychoanalytic Review*, **47**, 32–42.

Hamilton, D. L. (1968). Personality attributes associated with extreme response style. *Psychol Bull.*, **69**, 192–203.

Hamilton, D. L. and Gifford, R. K. (1976). Illusory correlation in interpersonal perception: a cognitive basis of stereotypic judgments. *J. exper. soc. Psychol.*, **12**, 392–407.

Hamilton, H. W. and Deese, J. (1971). Does linguistic marking have a psychological correlate? *J. verb. Lrng. verb. Behav.*, **10**, 707–714.

Harrison, J. (1973). Retailers' mental images of the environment. Unpublished Ph.D. thesis, Bristol University.

Harrison, J. and Sarre, P. (1971). Personal construct theory in the measurement of environmental images: problems and methods. *Environ. & Behav.*, **3**, 351–374.

Harvey, O. J. (1966). *Experience, Structure and Adaptability.* New York: Springer.

Harvey, O. J., Hunt, D. E., and Schroder, H. M. (1961). *Conceptual Systems and Personality Organization.* New York: Wiley.

Hayden, B. (1977). Interpersonal conceptual structures, predictive accuracy and social adjustment of emotionally disturbed boys. Presented at the Second International Congress on Personal Construct Psychology, Oxford University.

Hayden, B., Nashby, W., and Davids, A. (1977). Interpersonal conceptual structures, predictive accuracy and social adjustment of emotionally disturbed boys. *J. abnorm. Psychol.*, **86**, 315–320.

Haynes, E. T. and Phillips, J. P. N. (1973). Inconsistency, loose construing and schizophrenic thought disorder. *Br. J. Psychiat.*, **123**, 209–217.

Heather, N. (1976). The specificity of schizophrenic thought disorder: a replication and extension of previous findings. *Br. J. soc. clin. Psychol.*, **15**, 131–137.

Heidbrieder, E. (1933). *Seven Psychologies.* New York: Appleton-Century-Crofts.

Heim, A. W. and Watts, K. P. (1958). A preliminary note on the Word-in-Context test. *Psychol. Rep.*, **4**, 214.

Higgins, K. and Schwarz, J. C. (1976). Use of reinforcement to produce loose construing: differential effects for schizotypic and non-schizotypic normals. *Psychol. Rep.*, **38**, 799–806.

Hill, A. B. (1976). Validity and clinical utility of the grid test of thought disorder. *Br. J. Psychiat.*, **128**, 251–254.

Hinkle, D. N. (1965). The change of personal constructs from the viewpoint of a theory of implications. Unpublished Ph.D. thesis, Ohio State University.

Honess, T. (1976). Cognitive complexity and social prediction. *Br. J. soc. clin. Psychol.*, **15**, 23–32.

Honikman, B. (1976a). Construct theory as an approach to architectural and en-

222

vironmental design. In P. Slater (Ed.), *Explorations of Intrapersonal Space*, Vol. 1. London: Wiley.

Honikman, B. (1976b). Personal Construct theory and environmental meaning: applications to urban design. In G. T. Moore and R. G. Golledge (Eds.), *Environmental Knowing: Theories, Research and Methods*. Stroudsburg: Pa.: Dowden, Hutchinson & Ross.

Hope, K. (1966). Cos and cosmos. *Br. J. Psychiat.*, **112**, 1155–1163.

Hope, K. (1969). The complete analysis of a data matrix. *Br. J. Psychiat.*, **115**, 1069–1079.

Hovland, C. I. and Sherif, M. (1952). Judgmental phenomena and scales of attitude measurement. *J. abnorm. soc. Psychol.*, **47**, 822–832.

Hoy, R. M. (1973). The meaning of alcoholism for alcoholics: a repertory grid study. *Br. J. soc. clin. Psychol.*, **12**, 98–99.

Hudson, R. (1974). Images of the retailing environment: an example of the use of the repertory grid methodology. *Environ. & Behav.*, **6**, 470–495.

Hunt, D. E. (1951). Studies in role construct repertory: conceptual consistency. Unpublished M.A. thesis, Ohio State University.

Irwin, M., Tripodi, T., and Bieri, J. (1967). Affective stimulus value and cognitive complexity. *J. Pers. soc. Psychol.*, **5**, 444–448.

Isaacson, G. I. (1966). A comparative study of meaningfulness of personal and common constructs. Unpublished Ph.D. thesis, University of Missouri.

Isaacson, G. I. and Landfield, A. W. (1965). The meaningfulness of personal and common constructs. *J. indiv. Psychol.*, **21**, 160–166.

Jakobson, R., Fant, G., and Halle, M. (1952). Preliminaries to speech analysis. *MIT Acoust. Lab. Rept.*, **13**, Cambridge, Mass.: MIT Press.

Jaspars, J. M. F. (1963). Individual cognitive structures. *Proceedings of the 17th International Congress of Psychology*. Amsterdam: North-Holland.

Jaspars, J. M. F., Feldbreigger, R., and Bongaerts, L. (1968). Het leren van sociale structuren. *Hypothese*, **13**, 2–10.

Johnson, S. (1967). Hierarchical clustering schemes. *Psychometrika*, **32**, 241–254.

Johnson, W., Dailey, F. L., and Spriestersbach, D. C. (1963). *Diagnostic Methods in Speech Pathology*. New York: Harper & Row.

Jones, R. E. (1954). Identification in terms of personal constructs. Unpublished Ph.D. thesis, Ohio State University.

Jones, R. E. (1961). Identification in terms of personal constructs: reconciling a paradox in theory. *J. consult. Psychol.*, **25**, 276.

Kanouse, D. E. and Hanson, L. R. (1972). *Negativity in Evaluations*. Morristown, N.J.: General Learning Press.

Kant, I. (1902). *The Critique of Pure Reason*, 2nd ed. New York: Macmillan (original edition 1787).

Kapp, R. A. (1970). Convergent and discriminant validation of cognitive complexity and self-regard by the multitrait-multimethod matrix method. Unpublished Ph.D. thesis, Ohio State University.

Karst, T. O. and Trexler, L. D. (1970). Initial study using fixed role and rational-emotive therapy in treating public speaking anxiety. *J. consult. clin. Psychol.*, **34**, 360–366.

Kelly, G. A. (1955). *The Psychology of Personal Constructs*. New York: Norton.

Kelly, G. A. (1961). The abstraction of human processes. *Proceeding of the 14th International Congress of Applied Psychology*, Munksgaard, Copenhagen.

Kelly, G. A. (1965). The strategy of psychological research. *Bull. Br. psychol. Soc.*, **18**, 1–15.

Kelly, G. A. (1969). *Clinical Psychology and Personality: The Selected Papers of George Kelly* (Ed. B. A. Maher). New York: Wiley.

Kelly, G. A. (1970). A brief introduction to personal construct theory. In D. Bannister (Ed.), *Perspectives in Personal Construct Theory*. London: Academic Press.

Kelly, J. V. (1964). Instruction Manual for IBM 1620 Program to Process George Kelly's Rep Grid, Version II. Unpublished Manual, Ohio State University.

Kirby, D. M. and Gardner, R. C. (1972). Ethnic stereotypes: norms on 208 words typically used in their assessment. *Can. J. Psychol.*, **26**, 140–154.

Koestler, A. (1954). *The Invisible Writing*. New York: Macmillan.

Koffka, K. (1935). *Principles of Gestalt Psychology*. London: Routledge & Kegan Paul.

Kogan, N. and Wallach, A. M. (1964). *Risk-taking: A Study in Cognition and Personality*. New York: Holt, Rinehart and Winston.

Kretschmer, E. (1936). *Physique and Character*. New York: Cooper Square Publ.

Laing, R. D. and Esterson, A. (1964). *Sanity, Madness and the Family*. London: Tavistock Publications.

Landfield, A. W. (1965). Meaningfulness of self, ideal and other as related to own versus therapist's personal construct dimensions. *Psychol. Rep.*, **16**, 605–608.

Landfield, A. W. (1968). The extremity rating revisited within the context of personal construct theory. *Br. J. soc. clin. Psychol.*, **7**, 135–139.

Landfield, A. W. (1970). High priests, reflexivity and congruency of client-therapists' personal construct systems. *Br. J. med. Psychol.*, **43**, 207–212.

Landfield, A. W. (1971). *Personal Construct Systems in Psychotherapy*. Chicago: Rand McNally.

Landfield, A. W., Stern, M., and Fjeld, S. P. (1961). Social conceptual processes and change in students undergoing psychotherapy. *Psychol. Rep.*, **8**, 63–68.

Langley, C. W. (1971). Differentiation and integration of systems of personal constructs. *J. Pers.*, **39**, 10–25.

Leary, T. (1957). *The Interpersonal Diagnosis of Personality*. New York: Ronald.

Leitner, L. M., Landfield, A. W., and Barr, M. A. (1976). Cognitive complexity: a review and elaboration within personal construct theory. Unpublished manuscript, University of Nebraska-Lincoln.

Lemon, N. (1975). Linguistic development and conceptualization. *J. cross-cultural Psychol.*, **6**, 173–188.

Lemon, N. and Warren, N. (1974). Salience, centrality and self-relevance of traits in construing others. *Br. J. soc. clin. Psychol.*, **13**, 119–124.

Leventhal, H. (1957). Cognitive processes and interpersonal predictions. *J. abnorm. soc. Psychol.*, **55**, 176–180.

Levy, L. H. (1956). Personal constructs and predictive behavior. *J. abnorm. soc. Psychol.*, **53**, 54–58.

Lidz, T. (1964). *The Family and Human Adaptation*. London: Hogarth.

Lidz, T. (1968). The family and the transmission of schizophrenia. In D. Rosenthal and S. S. Kety (Eds.), The transmission of schizophrenia. *J. Psychiat. Res. Supp.*, **1**, 175–184.

Lidz, T., Wild, C., Shafer, S., Rosman, B., and Fleck, S. (1962). Thought-disorder in the parents of schizophrenic patients: a study utilizing the object sorting test. *J. Psychiat. Res.*, **1**, 193–200.

Liftshitz, M. (1974). Quality professionals: does training make a difference? A personal construct theory study of the issue. *Br. J. soc. clin. Psychol.*, **13**, 183–189.

Little, B. R., (1968). Factors affecting the use of psychological versus non-psychological constructs on the rep test. *Bull. Br. psychol. Soc.*, **21**, 34.

Locke, H. J. and Wallace, K. M. (1959). Short marital-adjustment and prediction tests: their reliability and validity. *Marriage and Family Living*, **21**, 251–255.

McCloskey, J. (1974). Differential change in interpersonal judgment. Unpublished B.A. thesis, Brock University.

McFayden, M. and Foulds, G. A. (1972). Comparisons of provided and elicited grid content in the grid test of schizophrenic thought disorder. *Br. J. Psychiat.*, **121**, 53–57.

McGahan, P. (1972). The neighbour role and neighbouring in a highly urban area. *Sociological Quarterly*, **13**, 397–408.

McPherson, F. M., Armstrong, J., and Heather, B. B. (1975). Psychological construing, 'difficulty' and thought disorder. *Br. J. med. Psychol.*, **48**, 303–315.

McPherson, F. M., Blackburn, I. M., Draffan, J. W., and McFayden, M. (1973). A further study of the grid test of thought disorder. *Br. J. soc. clin. Psychol.*, **12**, 420–427.

McPherson, F. M. and Buckley, F. (1970). Thought-process disorder and personal construct subsystems. *Br. J. soc. clin. Psychol.*, **9**, 380–381.

Maher, B. A. (1966). *The Principles of Psychopathology: An Experimental Approach.* New York: McGraw-Hill.

Mair, J. M. M. (1964). The derivation, reliability and validity of grid measures: some problems and suggestions. *Bull. Br. psychol. Soc.*, **17**, 55.

Mair, J. M. M. (1966). Prediction of grid scores. *Br. J. Psychol.*, **57**, 187–192.

Mair, J. M. M. (1967). Some problems in repertory grid measurement: 1. The use of bipolar constructs. *Br. J. Psychol.*, **58**, 261–270.

Mair, J. M. M. (1970a). Psychologists are human too. In D. Bannister (Ed.), *Perspectives in Personal Construct Theory.* London: Academic Press.

Mair, J. M. M. (1970b). Experimenting with individuals. *Br. J. med. Psychol.*, **43**, 245–256.

Mair, J. M. M. (1977). The community of self. In D. Bannister (Ed.), *New Perspectives in Personal Construct Theory.* London: Academic Press.

Makhlouf-Norris, F., Jones, H. G., and Norris, H. (1970). Articulation of the conceptual structure in the obsessional neurosis. *Br. J. soc. clin. Psychol.*, **9**, 264–274.

Maslow, A. H. (1953). Love in healthy people. In A. Montague (Ed.), *The Meaning of Love.* New York: Julian Press.

Mayer-Gross, W. Slater, E., and Roth, M. (1954). *Clinical Psychiatry.* London: Cassell.

Mayo, C. W. and Crockett, W. H. (1964). Cognitive complexity and primacy recency effects in impression formation. *J. abnorm. soc. Psychol.*, **68**, 335–338.

Meaders, W. W. (1957). Real similarity and interpersonal perception. Unpublished Ph.D. thesis, University of North Carolina.

Meehl, P. E. and Rosen, A. (1955). Antecedent probability and the efficiency of psychometric signs, patterns, or cutting scores. *Psychol. Bull.*, **52**, 194–216.

Meertens, R. W. (1967). Zinvolheid van beoordelingscategorieën. Unpublished thesis, University of Groningen.

Metcalfe, R. J. A. (1974). Own versus provided constructs in a reptest to measure cognitive complexity. *Psychol. Rep.*, **35**, 1305–1306.

Miller, A. D. (1969). Amount of information and stimulus valence as determinants of cognitive complexity. *J. Pers.*, **37**, 141–157.

Miller, A. D. and Bieri, J. (1965). Cognitive complexity as a function of the stimulus objects being judged. *Psychol. Rep.*, **16**, 1203–1204.

Mischel, T. (1964). Personal constructs, rules, and the logic of clinical activity. *Psychol. Rev.*, **71**, 180–192.

Mischel, T. (1974). Motivation, emotion and the conceptual schemes of common sense. In R. S. Peters (Ed.), *Psychology and Ethical Development.* London: Allen & Unwin.

Mischel, W. (1968). *Personality and Assessment.* New York: Wiley.

Mitsos, S. B. (1961). Personal constructs and the semantic differential. *J. abnorm. soc. Psychol.*, **62**, 433–434.

Morris, J. B. (1977). The prediction and measurement of change in a psychotherapy group using the repertory grid. In Fransella, F. and Bannister, D. *A Manual for Repertory Grid Technique.* London: Academic Press (Appendix 1).

Morse, E. (1965). An exploratory study of personal identity based on the psychology of personal constructs. Unpublished Ph.D. thesis, Ohio State University.

Moss, A. E. St. G. (1974a). Hamlet and role-construct theory. *Br. J. med. Psychol.*, **47**, 253–264.

Moss, A. E. St. G. (1974b). Shakespeare and role-construct therapy. *Br. J. med. Psychol.*, **47**, 235–252.

Muntz, H. J. and Power, R. (1970). Thought disorder in the parents of thought-disordered schizophrenics. *Br. J. Psychiat.*, **117**, 707–708.

Neisser, U. (1967). *Cognitive Psychology*. New York: Appleton-Century-Crofts.

Neisser, U. (1976). *Cognition and Reality*. San Francisco: W. H. Freeman & Co.

Nidorff, L. J. and Crockett, W. H. (1965). Cognitive complexity and the integration of conflicting information in written impressions. *J. soc. Psychol.*, **66**, 165–169.

Noble, C. E. (1961). Measurements of association value (a), rated associations (a'), and scaled meaningfulness (m') for the 2100 CVC combinations of the English alphabet. *Psychol. Rep.*, **8**, 487–521.

O'Hare, D. P. A. and Gordon, I. E. (1976). An application of repertory grid technique to aesthetic measurement. *Percpt. Mtr. Skls.*, **42**, 1183–1192.

Olson, J. M. and Partington, J. T. (1977). An integrative analysis of two cognitive models of interpersonal effectiveness. *Br. J. soc. clin. Psychol.*, **16**, 13–14.

Osgood, C. E. and Richards, M. M. (1973). From Yang and Yin to *and* and *but*. *Language*, **49**, 380–412.

Osgood, C. E., Suci, G. J., and Tannenbaum, P. H. (1957). *The Measurement of Meaning*. Urbana: University of Illinois Press.

Oswalt, R. M. (1974). Person perception: subject-determined and investigator-determined concepts. *J. soc. Psychol.*, **94**, 281–285.

Paul, G. L. (1966). *Insight Versus Desensitization in Psychotherapy: An Experiment in Anxiety Reduction*. Stanford, Calif.: Stanford University Press.

Payne, D. E. (1956). Role constructs *versus* part constructs and interpersonal understanding. Unpublished Ph.D. thesis, Ohio State University.

Pedersen, F. A. (1958). Consistency data on the role construct repertory test. Unpublished manuscript, Ohio State University.

Peeters, G. (1971). The positive-negative asymmetry: on cognitive consistency and positive bias. *Eur. J. soc. Psychol.*, **1**, 455–474.

Peevers, B. H. and Secord, P. F. (1973). Developmental changes in attribution of descriptive concepts to persons. *J. Pers. soc. Psychol.*, **27**, 120–128.

Pervin, L. A. (1975). *Personality: Theory, Assessment and Research*. New York: Wiley.

Piaget, J. (1960). *The Psychology of Intelligence*. New York: Harcourt-Brace.

Piaget, J. (1969). The problem of common mechanisms in the human sciences. *The Human Context*, **1**, 163–185.

Poch, S. M. (1952). A study of changes in personal constructs as related to interpersonal prediction and its outcomes. Unpublished Ph.D. thesis, Ohio State University.

Poole, A. D. (1976). A further attempt to cross-validate the Grid Test of Schizophrenic Thought Disorder. *Br. J. soc. clin. Psychol.*, **15**, 179–188.

Press, A. N., Crockett, W. H., and Rosenkrantz, P. S. (1969). Cognitive complexity and the learning of balanced and unbalanced social structures. *J. Pers.*, **37**, 541–553.

Radley, A. R. (1974). Schizophrenic thought disorder and the nature of personal constructs. *Br. J. soc. clin. Psychol.*, **13**, 315–327.

Rawson, K. (1973). Residential mobility and housing preferences. Unpublished thesis, School of Architecture, University of Kansas.

Rehm, L. P. (1971). Effects of validation on the relationship between personal constructs. *J. Pers. soc. Psychol.*, **20**, 267–270.

Reid, F. (1975). A note on measures of similarity and scaling metrics for users of the repertory grid. *Technical Report No. 45*, Centre for the Study of Human Learning, Brunel University.

Reid, W. A. and Holley, B. J. (1972). An application of repertory grid techniques to the study of choice of university. *Br. J. educ. Psychol.*, **42**, 52–59.

Reker, G. I. (1974). Interpersonal conceptual structures of emotionally disturbed and normal boys. *J. abnorm. Psychol.*, **83**, 380–386.

Reynolds, D. J. (1967). The Temple Fear Survey Inventory. Unpublished manuscript, Temple University.

226

Richardson, F. C. and Weigel, R. G. (1971). Personal construct theory applied to the marriage relationship. *Experimental Publication System*, **10**, ms No. 371–5.
Riley, S. and Palmer, J. (1976). Of attitudes and latitudes: a repertory grid study of perceptions of seaside resorts. In P. Slater (Ed.), *Explorations of Intrapersonal Space*, Vol. 1. London: Wiley.
Romney, D. (1969). Psychometrically assessed thought disorder in schizophrenic and control patients and in their parents and siblings. *Br. J. Psychiat.*, **115**, 999–1002.
Rosenberg, S. (1977). New approaches to the analysis of personal constructs in person perception. In J. K. Cole and A. W. Landfield (Ed.), *1976 Nebraska Symposium on Motivation*. Lincoln: University of Nebraska Press.
Rosenberg, S. and Jones, R. A. (1972). A method for investigating and representing a person's implicit theory of personality: Theodore Dreiser's view of people. *J. Pers. soc. Psychol.*, **22**, 372–386.
Rosenthal, D. (1955). Changes in some moral values following psychotherapy. *J. consult. Psychol.*, **19**, 431–436.
Rotter, J. B. (1954). *Social Learning and Clinical Psychology*. Englewood Cliffs, N.J.: Prentice-Hall.
Rotter, J. B., Chance, J. and Phares, J. (1972). *Applications of a Social Learning Theory of Personality*. New York: Holt, Rinehart & Winston.
Rowe, D. (1971). An examination of a psychiatrist's predictions of a patient's constructs. *Br. J. Psychiat.*, **118**, 231–234.
Rowe, D. (1976). Grid technique in the conversation between patient and therapist. In P. Slater (Ed.), *Explorations in Intrapersonal Space*, Vol. 1. London: Wiley.
Rowe, D. and Slater, P. (1976). Studies of the psychiatrist's insight into the patient's inner world. In P. Slater (Ed.), *Explorations of Intrapersonal Space*, Vol. 1. London: Wiley.
Rowles, G. D. (1972). Choice in geographic space: exploring a phenomenological approach to location decision making. Unpublished M.Sc. thesis, University of Bristol.
Ryle, A. (1975). *Frames and Cages: The Repertory Grid Approach to Human Understanding*. London: University of Sussex Press.
Ryle, A. (1976). Some clinical applications of grid technique. In P. Slater (Ed.), *Explorations in Intrapersonal Space*, Vol. 1. London: Wiley.
Ryle, A. and Breen, D. (1972a). A comparison of adjusted and maladjusted couples using the double dyad grid. *Br. J. Med. Psychol.*, **45**, 375–382.
Ryle, A. and Breen, D. (1972b). Some differences in the personal constructs of neurotic and normal subjects. *Br. J. Psychiat.*, **120**, 483–489.
Ryle, A. and Breen, D. (1972c). The use of the double dyad grid in the clinical setting. *Br. J. med. Psychol.*, **45**, 383–389.
Ryle, A. and Breen, D. (1974a). Change in the course of social work training: a repertory grid study. *Br. J. med. Psychol.*, **47**, 139–147.
Ryle, A. and Breen, D. (1974b). Social-work tutors' judgment of their students. *Br. J. med. Psychol.*, **47**, 149–152.
Ryle, A. and Lunghi, M. W. (1970). The dyad grid: a modification of repertory grid technique. *Br. J. Psychiat.*, **117**, 323–327.
Ryle, A. and Lunghi, M. W. (1971). A therapist's prediction of a patient's grid. *Br. J. Psychiat.*, **118**, 555–560.
Salmon, P. (1970). A psychology of personal growth. In D. Bannister (Ed.), *Perspectives in Personal Construct Theory*. London: Academic Press.
Salmon, P. (1976). Grid measures with child subjects. In P. Slater (Ed.), *Explorations in Intrapersonal Space*, Vol. 1. London: Wiley.
Salmon, P., Bromley, J., and Presley, A. S. (1967). The word-in-context test as a measure of conceptualization in schizophrenics with and without thought disorder. *Br. J. med. Psychol.*, **40**, 253–259.
Sander, E. K. (1961). Reliability of the Iowa Speech Disfluency Test. *J. Speech. Hear. Disorders, Monogr. Suppl.*, **7**, 21–30.

Sarre, P. V. (1973). Personal construct theory in the measurement of the perceived environment. Unpublished Ph.D. thesis, University of Bristol.

Scarlett, H. H., Press, A. N., and Crockett, W. H. (1971). Children's descriptions of their peers. *Child Devlop.*, **42**, 439–453.

Schroder, H. M., Driver, M. J., and Streufert, S. (1967). *Human Information Processing.* New York: Holt, Rinehart & Winston.

Seaman, J. M. and Koenig, F. (1974). A comparison of measures of cognitive complexity. *Sociometry*, **37**, 375–390.

Sechrest, L. B. (1962). Stimulus equivalents of the psychotherapist. *J. indiv. Psychol.*, **18**, 172–176.

Sechrest, L. B. (1963). Incremental validity. *Educ. psychol. Measurement*, **23**, 33–53.

Sechrest, L. B. and Jackson, D. N. (1961). Social intelligence and accuracy of interpersonal predictions. *J. Pers.*, **29**, 167–181.

Shoemaker, D. J. (1952). The relation between personal constructs and observed behavior. Unpublished M.A. thesis, Ohio State University.

Shoemaker, D. J. (1955). Personal constructs and interpersonal predictions. Unpublished Ph.D. thesis, Ohio State University.

Shotter, J. (1970). Men, the man-makers: George Kelly and the psychology of personal constructs. In D. Bannister (Ed.), *Perspectives in Personal Construct Theory.* London: Academic Press.

Skene, R. A. (1973). Construct shift in the treatment of a case of homosexuality. *Br. J. med. Psychol.*, **46**, 287–292.

Skinner, B. F. (1957). *Verbal Behavior.* New York: Appleton-Century-Crofts.

Slane, S. and Barrows, D. (1974). Unpublished data, cited in Leitner *et al.* (1976).

Slater, P. (1964). *The Principal Components of a Repertory Grid.* London: Andrews & Co.

Slater, P. (1965). The use of the repertory grid in the individual case. *Br. J. Psychiat.*, **111**, 965–975.

Slater, P. (1967). Notes on Ingrid 67. Unpublished manual, Institute of Psychiatry, University of London.

Slater, P. (1969). Theory and technique of the repertory grid. *Br. J. Psychiat.*, **121**, 45–51.

Slater, P. (1972). The measurement of consistency in repertory grids. *Br. J. Psychiat.*, **121**, 45–51.

Slater, P. (1976). Monitoring changes in the mental state of a patient undergoing psychiatric treatment. In P. Slater (Ed.), *Explorations in Intrapersonal Space*, Vol. 1. London: Wiley.

Slater, P. (1977). *Dimensions of Intrapersonal Space.* London: Wiley.

Smail, D. J. (1970). Neurotic symptoms, personality and personal constructs. *Br. J. Psychiat.*, **117**, 645–648.

Smail, D. J. (1972). A grid measure of empathy in a therapeutic group. *Br. J. med. Psychol.*, **45**, 165–169.

Smith, S. and Leach, C. (1972). A hierarchical measure of cognitive complexity. *Br. J. Psychol.*, **63**, 561–568.

Sperlinger, D. (1976). Aspects of stability in the repertory grid. *Br. J. med. Psychol.*, **49**, 341–347.

Stefan, C. F. (1973). The effect of a role enactment on high school students' performance and self-image. Unpublished Ph.D. thesis, Ohio University.

Stringer, P. (1974). A use of repertory grid measures for evaluating map formats. *Br. J. Psychol.*, **65**, 23–24.

Stringer, P. (1976a). Repertory grids in the study of environmental perception. In P. Slater (Ed.), *Explorations in Intrapersonal Space*, Vol. 1. London:Wiley.

Stringer, P. (1976b). The demands of personal construct theory: a commentary. In G. T. Moore and R. G. Colledge (Eds.), *Environmental Knowing: Theories, Research and Methods.* Stroudsburg, Pa: Dowden, Hutchinson & Ross.

Thomas, L. F. (1977). Psycho grid analysis: the development of psychic mirroring devices. Presented at the Second International Congress on Personal Construct Psychology, Oxford University.

Tripodi, T. and Bieri, J. (1963). Cognitive complexity as a function of own and provided constructs. *Psychol. Rep.*, **13**, 26.

Van Os, H. (1968). De mate van extremiteit in beoordelingen van pubers en volwassenen. Unpublished thesis, University of Groningen.

Vygotsky, L. S. (1962). *Language and Thought*. Cambridge, Mass.: MIT Press.

Walk, R. D. (1956). Self-ratings of fear in a fear-involving situation. *J. abnorm. soc. Psychol.*, **52**, 171–178.

Warr, P. B. (1971). Pollyanna's personal judgments. *Eur. J. soc. Psychol.*, **1**, 327–338.

Warr, P. B. (1974). Inference magnitude, range and evaluative direction as factors affecting relative importance of cues in impression formation. *J. Pers. soc. Psychol.*, **30**, 191–197.

Warr, P. B. and Coffman, T. L. (1970). Personality, involvement and extremity of judgment. *Br. J. soc. clin. Psychol.*, **9**, 108–121.

Warren, N. (1964). Constructs, rules and the explanation of behaviour. Presented at the Symposium on Construct Theory and Repertory Grid Methodology, Brunel University.

Warren, N. (1966). Social class and construct systems: a examination of the cognitive structure of two social class groups. *Br. J. soc. clin. Psychol.*, **5**, 254–263.

Watson, J. B. (1919). *Psychology from the Standpoint of a Behaviorist*. Philadelphia: J. B. Lippincott & Co.

Watson, J. P. (1970). A measure of patient-therapist understanding. *Br. J. Psychiat.* **117**, 319–321.

Weigel, R. G., Weigel, V. M., and Richardson, F. C. (1973). Congruence of spouses' personal constructs and reported marital success: pitfalls in instrumentation. *Psychol. Rep.*, **33**, 212–214.

Werner, H. (1957). *Comparative Psychology of Mental Development*. New York: International Universities Press.

Werner, H. and Kaplan, B. (1963). *Symbol Formation: An Organismic Developmental Approach to Language and Expression of Thought*. New York: Wiley.

Wheelwright, P. (1966). *The Presocratics*. New York: Odyssey Press.

Widom, C. (1976). Interpersonal and personal construct systems in psychopaths. *J. consult. clin. Psychol.*, **44**, 614–623.

Wijesinghe, O. B. A. and Wood, R. R. (1976). A repertory grid study of interpersonal perception within a married couples psychotherapy group. *Br. J. med. Psychol.*, **49**, 287–293.

Williams, D. (1970). *Primary & Secondary Structures in Cognitive Organization*. Swansea: University College.

Williams, E. (1971). The effect of varying the elements in the Bannister–Fransella Grid Test of Thought Disorder. *Br. J. Psychiat.*, **119**, 207–212.

Winter, D. A. (1975). Some characteristics of schizophrenics and their parents. *Br. J. soc. clin. Psychol.*, **14**, 279–290.

Wissema, A. (1968). Zinvolheid en onverenigbaarheid. Unpublished data, University of Groningen.

Yarrow, M. R. and Campbell, J. D. (1963). Person perception in children. *Merrill-Palmer Quarterly*, **9**, 57–72.

Zajonc, R. B. (1968). Attitudinal effects of mere exposure. *J. Pers. soc. Psychol.*, **9**, 1–27.

Zalot, G. and Adams-Webber, J. (1977). Cognitive complexity in the perception of neighbours. *Soc. Behav. Pers*, **5**, 281–283.

Zimring, F. M. (1971). Cognitive simplicity-complexity: evidence from disparate processes. *J. Pers.*, **39**, 1–9.

Author Index

Numbers in italic indicate pages on which authors appear in the References section.

229

232

Wood, R. R., 110, *228*

Yarrow, M. R., 206, *228*

Zajonc, R. B., 161, *228*
Zalot, G., 48, 183, *228*
Zimring, F. M., *53, 228*

Subject Index